Jewish Renaissance and Revival in America

D1279893

JEWISH RENAISSANCE AND REVIVAL IN AMERICA

Essays in Memory of Leah Levitz Fishbane, ז"ל

Eitan P. Fishbane &
Jonathan D. Sarna, editors

BRANDEIS UNIVERSITY PRESS
Waltham, Massachusetts

BRANDEIS UNIVERSITY PRESS
An imprint of University Press of New England
www.upne.com
© 2011 Brandeis University
All rights reserved
Manufactured in the United States of America
Designed by Doug Tifft
Typeset in Bulmer MT by Integrated Publishing Solutions

This book was published with the generous support of the
Lucius N. Littauer Foundation.

University Press of New England is a member of the Green
Press Initiative. The paper used in this book meets their minimum requirement for recycled paper.

For permission to reproduce any of the material in this book,
contact Permissions, University Press of New England, One
Court Street, Suite 250, Lebanon NH 03766; or visit www
.upne.com

Library of Congress Cataloging-in-Publication Data
Jewish renaissance and revival in America : essays in memory of
Leah Levitz Fishbane / Eitan P. Fishbane & Jonathan D. Sarna,
editors.
    p. cm. — (Brandeis series in American Jewish history, cul-
ture, and life)
    Includes bibliographical references and index.
    ISBN 978-1-61168-192-5 (pbk. : alk. paper) — ISBN
978-1-61168-193-2 (e-book)
    1. Jews—United States—History—19th century.
2. Jews—United States—History—20th century. 3. Jews—
United States—Intellectual life—19th century. 4. Jews—
United States—Intellectual life—20th century. 5. Jews—
United States—Social conditions—19th century. 6. Jews—United
States—Social conditions—20th century. 7. Jews—United
States—Societies, etc.—History—19th century. 8. Jews—
United States—Social life and customs. I. Fishbane, Leah
Levitz. II. Fishbane, Eitan P., 1975– III. Sarna, Jonathan D.
    IV. Series.
E184.353.J49 2011
973$'$.04924—dc23   2011030021

5   4   3   2   1

Contents

Preface

Eitan P. Fishbane

If memory leads us into the mysterious border between past and present, it also awakens the desire to see the future through its magical lens. How do we offer tribute to the work and humanity that was accomplished in a lifetime? How do we give expression to the creativity that was only just begun, whose vitality carried so much promise? And that is surely one of the reasons we mourn—we cry out for what now will never be, for what would have been done had she but the time.

This project has been a labor of love, beginning with the conference I organized at The Jewish Theological Seminary in 2008 in memory of my late wife, Leah Levitz Fishbane. At the time of her death, Leah was completing the third chapter of a Ph.D. dissertation in American Jewish History under the guidance of Professor Jonathan Sarna at Brandeis University. Her dissertation research and writing represented the devoted work of many years, all the while giving herself wholeheartedly to her family and to the raising of our daughter, Aderet. But tragedy intervened before the work could be completed. Leah was struck down suddenly by a previously undiagnosed brain tumor at the age of thirty-two.

As a talented and committed historian, Leah entered into the reimagined world of nineteenth-century Philadelphia and New York, often feeling the excitement and passion of the young Jewish leaders and thinkers she studied—as they sought to revive Jewish religious and social life in their time, writing and speaking on behalf of a renewal of the Jewish religious home, observance of Shabbat, the creation of new frameworks for the growth of American Jewish community, and the cultivation of cultural and spiritual renaissance.

This volume seeks to further the research to which Leah was so devoted—to explore the subjects of religious and social revival in American Judaism: urgent now just as they were in the nineteenth century. Leah was deeply shaped by the work of her mentor, Jonathan Sarna, both in his now classic essay on the great awakening in American Judaism and in his landmark study of the Jewish Publication Society. Leah was intrigued by the circle of personalities that Sarna studied in *JPS: The Americanization of Jewish Culture*, and she sought to understand how such a remarkable collection of individuals (men who went on to found The Jewish Theological Seminary, the Jewish Publication Society, along with other major cultural initiatives) came to be. She became particularly fascinated with their early formation as ambitious and precocious youth—an interest that led to Leah's inquiry into the Young Men's Hebrew Association and its attendant literary and social achievements.

In constructing the original conference, and then in coediting this volume with Jonathan Sarna, I have sought to bring Leah's unpublished work to light while also advancing new research into the broader question of renaissance and revival in American Jewish culture. The result is a series of essays by leading scholars of American Jewish history, and of modern Judaism more broadly, which work together to form a portrait of the ways in which American Jews have approached the project of spiritual and cultural renewal. The work presented in these pages reflects a diverse set of concerns—ranging from the culture of reading in Victorian Philadelphia (Arthur Kiron), to the German-American nexus in the pursuit of religious humanism (Paul Mendes Flohr), to the spiritual roots and renaissance of late-twentieth-century Ḥavurah and Renewal Judaism (Arthur Green). And yet this diversity is held together as we observe the historical development of Jewish attitudes toward cultural revival and spiritual rebirth from nineteenth-century America to our own day.

As I prepare to transfer this book to the publisher, I am filled with gratitude to the numerous people and institutions that helped make this volume a reality. First, let me thank all those who enabled the original memorial conference to come to fruition: The Jewish Theological Seminary, my intellectual and professional home, for serving as the host of the conference—and most especially Tom Kagedan and Beth Lutzker (then) in the JTS Department of Public Events; the other generous sponsors of the conference—the Department of Near Eastern and Judaic Studies at Brandeis University; the University of Pennsylvania Libraries, where, under the auspices of Dr. Arthur Kiron, Leah was working on the American Geniza Project; the Deanne & Arnold Kaplan Foundation, generous supporters of the American Geniza Project and the University of Pennsylvania Libraries; and, finally, the Leah Levitz Fishbane Memorial Fund at JTS, which exists because of the generosity of caring friends and family. It perhaps goes without saying, but the conference and resulting volume would not have been possible without the great efforts of the speakers and contributors, and it is my honor to thank them here: To Prof. Jonathan Sarna, Prof. Arthur Kiron, Prof. Lance Sussman, Prof. Shuly Rubin Schwartz, Prof. Eugene Sheppard, Rabbi Sharon Brous, Prof. Arthur Green, Prof. David Kaufman, Prof. Arnold Eisen, and Prof. Paul Mendes-Flohr—my deep gratitude and appreciation.

The publication of this book was also made possible through the financial support of a number of generous individuals. I wish to recognize and thank them for their very meaningful support:

> The many donors to the Leah Levitz Fishbane Memorial Fund at JTS
> Mr. Neal Castleman
> Mrs. Barbara Levitz and Mr. Jack Levitz
> Mrs. Lee Gibbs
> Mr. Mitchell Levitz
> Mrs. Stephanie Levitz Englander
> Dr. Mona Fishbane and Prof. Michael Fishbane
> Prof. Jonathan Sarna and Prof. Ruth Langer

Let me also express my sincere appreciation to Dr. Phyllis Deutsch, editor-in-chief of University Press of New England, for her enthusiastic support of this project, as well as for the professionalism of her guidance. Many thanks as well to Mr. Peter Fong and Mr. Will Hively for their devoted and careful editorial work at the production stage; Prof. Pamela Nadell for her detailed and helpful review of the book for the press; Jeffrey K. Weiss for indexing; Ms. Claire Pingel, associate curator at the National Museum of American Jewish History, and Mr. Steve Siegel, archivist at the 92nd Street Y, for their efforts on behalf of this project. Thanks in particular to Mr. Siegel for locating the "Grand Revival" handbill in the archives of the Y; we are thrilled to include this image in our volume. Special gratitude goes to my coeditor, Jonathan Sarna, both for his dedication to this project and for the generous support and mentorship that he gave to Leah during her graduate studies at Brandeis.

My warm appreciation to Leah's parents, Barbara and Jack Levitz—I am grateful for their kindness and I admire their strength of character amid this darkest of times. Special thanks as well to Barbara for her help with meticulous proofreading. My deep gratitude to my parents, Mona and Michael Fishbane, for their unbounded love and support. Finally, it is a great pleasure to thank my wife, Rabbi Julia Andelman, and my daughter, Aderet Fishbane, for creating a home of blessing and love. I am grateful to Julia for her under-standing and support on this difficult road, and it is my hope that Aderet will enter these pages as she grows, seeing in them one window into the mind and heart of her mother.

EITAN FISHBANE

Adar II 5771 / March 2011

Jewish Renaissance and Revival in America

Introduction

Leah Levitz Fishbane and "The Road to Renaissance"

On the "fateful night" of October 5, 1879, a group of earnest young Jews from Philadelphia and New York met at an undisclosed Philadelphia location and bound themselves together in a solemn covenant "for God and Judaism." They called themselves Keyam Dishmaya, an Aramaic term signifying their goal to uphold the dictates of heaven, and they pledged to do all in their power to bring Jews back "to the ancient faith."[1]

With this quotation, Leah Levitz Fishbane opened the first chapter of her unfinished dissertation, now published in this volume, titled "The Road to Renaissance: Young American Jews and the Emergence of New Communal Leadership in Post–Civil War America."[2] Leah had begun her graduate work at Brandeis intending to focus on the young Jews who promoted a twentieth-century Jewish renaissance in Germany: the famous circle of teachers and students surrounding Franz Rosenzweig. But at some point, influenced in part by my *A Great Awakening: The Transformation That Shaped Twentieth Century American Judaism and Its Implications for Today* (1995), she switched to American Jewish history and decided to focus in-depth on a remarkable group of young people who created "intellectual projects and communal institutions with the shared aim of revitalizing American Jewish life." She paid particular attention to the best-known figures in this group: men such as Solomon Solis-Cohen, Max Cohen, Mayer Sulzberger, Cyrus Sulzberger, and Cyrus Adler; women such as Mary Cohen, Nina Morais Cohen, and Henrietta Szold.

Leah was particularly interested in this group's genesis. "What brought these devoted young Jews to such an inspired moment of purpose and kinship on that October night during the Jewish holiday of Sukkot in 1879?" she asked. "How did it come to pass that a group of friends, not much past the age of majority, and from two different cities, felt compelled to come together to sanctify a holy pact between them to transform American Jewry?" "In what ways," she wondered, "did their formative years—a coalescence of familial, communal, religious and educational values—inform their obvious love for Judaism, its legacy of riches, and their belief in its continued relevance for their generation?"

Leah's training in German Jewish history held her in good stead as her research proceeded. At one point, for example, she suggested provocatively that Shulamit Volkov's discussion of "dissimilation" in reference to early-twentieth-century German-Jewry might profitably be applied to American Jewry of the 1870s and '80s.[3] Elsewhere, she concluded that "just as in Germany, where it took a generation of young Jews born after the emancipation to create a confident and far-reaching Jewish renaissance," so "likewise in America, it took an American-born generation, confident in their ability to be both Americans and Jews, to formulate an assertive and confident agenda for an American Jewish awakening of cultural and religious vitality in the late nineteenth century."

The first chapter of Leah's dissertation, titled "Common Bonds: A Collective Portrait," describes the "shared world of events and experiences" that shaped the men and women whose careers she had set out to explore. "As children and adolescents," she finds, "they watched together the American crisis of Civil War and Reconstruction, the changing tide of emancipation and nationalism in Europe, and the rise of anti-Semitism in their own country and abroad. They also saw the challenges that world and American Jewish leaders faced in confronting these events." The majority of this group had at least one parent who was not American born and came to America in the mid-nineteenth century from either Germany (including Posen) or England. They enjoyed a comfortable economic footing. Even the families of immigrants quickly rose to become middle to upper class. Coinciding with their upward economic mobility, these immigrant families embraced social and civic participation in their local and national communities: voluntary associations, charities, and political causes. Parents passed on to their children a strong sense of civil responsibility and social belonging in America, as well as a sense of Jewish communal responsibility. Their American-born children, in turn, made those values their own. "As they matured from children into adults," Leah concludes, "this group of young Jews . . . became publishers, doctors, lawyers, businessmen, scholars, educators, or writers who were determined to serve and transform the American Jewish community as lay leaders."

Many of Leah's subjects, such as Cyrus Sulzberger, Mayer Sulzberger, and

Cyrus Adler, turned out to have been related to one another. Others were close neighbors in either Philadelphia or New York. In the case of Philadelphia, a great many of them belonged to the same synagogue, Congregation Mikveh Israel. As a group, they all studied in similar kinds of institutions (public school and, for the most part, college), and they acquired Jewish learning at home, in supplementary settings, and in many cases, especially in Philadelphia, as pupils of local rabbis.

Religiously, however, they diverged—even as teenagers. Leah found a marvelous letter from Max Cohen to Solomon Solis-Cohen expressing astonishment that "you at times shaved yourself on the Sabbath without any scruples." Philip Cowen, she found, worked as a young teenager on the Sabbath, and even cashed checks on the day of rest. Other members of the group, by contrast, were much more punctilious. The aforementioned Max Cohen was especially observant in his early days, and in one of his letters he divided his associates at the *American Hebrew* into two columns: one labeled "Jewish traditionalists" and the other, "namby-pamby reformers." Fascinatingly, Cohen placed Rabbi Frederic de Sola Mendes in both columns, which—as Leah perceptively noticed—was precisely correct. In 1879, Mendes was just in the midst of a journey that would transform him from a moderate traditionalist into a moderate reformer.

Leah properly wondered why more of these young people, given their interest in strengthening Judaism, did not themselves become rabbis (the rabbis among them, like Mendes, were immigrants). Several of them, she shows, actually considered such a career, especially Solomon Solis Cohen, who eventually became a doctor. Her conclusion, essentially, is that given the kind of Judaism that her subjects wanted to promote, they had nowhere to train as rabbis. They rejected the Judaism and Reform rabbinical training being offered by the Hebrew Union College in Cincinnati, yet as patriotic American-born youngsters, whose parents had left Europe to find a better life, they had no interest in studying for the rabbinate at one of the prestigious European rabbinical seminaries. "They concluded," she suggests, "that their best choice was to serve the community as what Cyrus Adler called a 'lay-rabbi.' As doctors, businessmen, lawyers, and civic leaders, they could continue to serve the Jewish community through the creation and support of new institutions, journalistic enterprises, Jewish education, and Jewish scholarship—reflecting the compatibility of American Jewish and civic life." Of course, later in the 1880s, many among them helped to establish The Jewish Theological Seminary of America. It was designed to be precisely the kind of modern traditional seminary (reflecting what Sabato Morais liked to call "enlightened Orthodoxy") that they themselves might have attended, had it existed earlier.

Leah planned to devote the second major chapter of her dissertation to the role played by the Young Men's Hebrew Association (YMHA) in sparking the late-nineteenth-century Jewish renaissance. David Kaufman, in his *Shul with a Pool* (1999), has already alerted us to some of the significance of the YMHA, particularly insofar as it was a forerunner of the Jewish community center. Leah, however, concentrated more narrowly on a brief period in the history of the organization, beginning in 1877, when young Jews, some of them the same people who would later establish the *American Hebrew*, took active roles in the New York and especially the Philadelphia branches of the Y, and refocused it around education and culture. During their short tenure (five or six years), they created, in Leah's words, "an intensified program of Jewish education and experience, geared toward revitalizing young Jews faced with the challenges of indifference, assimilation, anti-Semitism and faithlessness." To her delight, she found an obscure 1887 retrospect in the monthly journal of the YMHA in New York that confirmed her thesis. "A dozen years go [in 1875]," it recalled, "there were probably not a dozen Jews in the United States (ministers excepted) who were competent enough to deliver an English lecture on any subject connected with Jewish history or literature. The establishment of the YMHAs has brought about something of a *renaissance*—so much that in this city [New York], as in Philadelphia, whole courses of lectures on such subjects have been successfully given, the lecturers being entirely young laymen." By the mid-1880s, the "young laymen" had moved on to bigger and better organizations, and the Ys had become more involved in immigrant absorption. But for a brief moment, as Leah persuasively showed, the Y served as a training ground for ambitious young men who sought to transform Jewish life.

What of Jewish women? Leah's files bulged with significant primary material on this subject, much of it dealing with Mary Cohen, and at one time she was planning to produce a whole chapter on how women in this period were "promoted to the role of Jewish teacher, ritual caretaker, spiritual sustainer, and role model for the young generation." Sadly, that chapter remained unwritten.

Leah also planned chapters on the emergence of the *American Hebrew* and on the agenda that its young, exuberant editors put forth: the centrality of the Sabbath, Jewish unity, the influence of women and the home, Jewish education, and Jewish peoplehood. Within a decade, by 1889 or 1890, these young Jews had transformed themselves from "youthful challengers to established leaders." Leah hoped, in her concluding chapter, to explain how this happened. "How," she asked, "did these young leaders, acutely aware of their inexperience and lack of stature in 1879 when they founded the *American Hebrew*, evolve to become the established leadership of the American Jewish community within the span of only a decade? At what point, and under what circumstances, did they (themselves only first-generation Americans!) come to be perceived no longer as the youthful and exuberant challengers, but rather as the conservative "German-Jewish establishment"? Her goal, in other words, was to understand the full trajectory of the renaissance she had hoped to study: the background of the people who made it happen, the institutions that they created, their larger cultural and educational agenda, and finally the institutionalization of the renaissance; how it moved from the margins to the mainstream, and became established.

Others will need to complete the work that Leah's death left tragically unfinished. Some of the essays in this book begin that work. Here, in Leah's memory, let me sketch out several broad factors that help to explain why the late-nineteenth-century awakening took place and why it succeeded in achieving so many of the goals that those who embarked on the "road to renaissance" set for themselves.

Young people in the late nineteenth century first became engaged in the work of "saving Judaism" in response to what would be described today as a major cultural crisis. In the late 1870s, a period of "rapid change and unexpected intrusions" affected the American Jewish community.[4] It disrupted lives and called into question some of the major assumptions upon which young Jews had been raised. These young Jews grew up, following the Civil War, during a period of confident optimism in American Jewish life. The American Jewish community's wealth and power greatly expanded during their childhood and young adult years. More Jews entered government service than ever before. Magnificent synagogues and temples rose up on the main thoroughfares of major American cities. Liberal Jews and Protestants spoke warmly of universalism. And many Jews dreamed optimistically of a "new era," ushering in a "golden age of a true universal brotherhood."[5]

An era of enormous social and economic change nurtured these dreams. Historians speak of the period from 1870 to 1914 as the "second industrial revolution." During these years, successive waves of foreign immigration, as well as internal migration from farms to cities, changed the face of the United States. Railroads and steamships tied distant regions together, and rapid transit systems such as the subway and the trolley did the same for ever-expanding urban neighborhoods. The telegraph and then the telephone revolutionized business and personal communications. Electrification soon transformed many additional aspects of American life. Young people were thus continually embracing technological innovations that radically reshaped their lives. For young Jews, these momentous changes may have inspired them to believe that big changes in the Jewish sphere were likewise possible.[6]

Yet, as early as the 1870s, the hopes that had inspired so many Jews began to give way to grave disappointment. Just as the situation for African Americans worsened during the last quarter of the nineteenth century, with a renewal of segregation and anti-Black violence following an all-too-brief flirtation with freedom and equality during Reconstruction, so Jews experienced a sharp and unexpected drop in their confidence, status, and social acceptance at approximately the same time.[7]

Jews were shaken first of all by an internal crisis: the defection of Felix Adler, one of the young men upon whom American Jews had pinned great hopes. The son of Temple Emanu-El of New York's rabbi, Adler had been sent to study in Germany to prepare to follow in his father's footsteps. In 1876–77, however, he publicly abandoned Judaism in favor of what he called Ethical Culture. Renouncing belief in a theistic God and in the particularities of the Jewish religion, he advocated in their place a universalistic faith focused on ethics and the teachings of world religions. His critiques of Reform Judaism, and his growing Jewish following, especially among women and young people, unnerved many Jewish leaders—especially when he announced that "Judaism is dying." On the heels of this, some well-publicized cases of intermarriage, including that of Helen, the daughter of Isaac Mayer Wise, who eloped in 1878 with the Presbyterian attorney James Molony and was married by a Unitarian minister, deepened Jewish nervousness. Was Reform Judaism really the answer, some wondered? Had the effort to modernize Judaism gone too far? Would assimilation triumph?[8]

Developments within American Protestantism added yet another dimension to the mood of uneasiness that developed within the American Jewish community. The spiritual crisis and internal divisions that plagued Protestant America during this era—one that confronted all American religious groups with the staggering implications of Darwinism and biblical criticism—drove Evangelicals and liberals alike to renew their particularistic calls for a "Christian America." Some in Congress advocated a Constitutional amendment to "more fully recognize the obligations of the Christian religion." Visions of a liberal religious alliance and of close cooperation between Jews and Unitarians evaporated in the face of these challenges. Although interfaith exchanges continued, Jews came to realize that many of their Christian friends continued to harbor hopes that one day Jews would "see the light." Much to the embarrassment of Jewish leaders, some Christian liberals looked to the Ethical Culture movement as a harbinger of Judaism's future course.[9]

Finally and most importantly, "antisemitism"—a word coined in Germany at the end of the 1870s to describe and justify ("scientifically") anti-Jewish propaganda and discrimination—unnerved American Jews. The rise of racially based anti-Jewish hatred in Germany, a land to which many American Jews had close ties and that they had previously revered for its liberal spirit and cultural advancement, came as a shock. Here German Jews had assumed that emancipation, enlightenment, and human progress would diminish residual prejudice directed toward them, but suddenly they saw it espoused in the highest intellectual circles, and by people in whom they had placed great faith. What made this situation even worse was that antisemitism and particularly social discrimination soon spread to America's own shores. Anti-Jewish hatred was certainly not new to America, but Jews had previously considered it something of an anachronism, alien both to the modern temper and to American democracy. Like Jews in Germany, they optimistically assumed that prejudice against them would in time wither away. The two well-publicized incidents of the late 1870s—Judge Hilton's exclusion of banker Joseph Seligman from the Grand Union Hotel (1877) and Austin Corbin's public announcement that "Jews as a class" would be unwelcome at Coney Island (1879)—proved so shocking precisely because they challenged this assumption. "The highest social element . . . ," Corbin explained, "won't associate with Jews, and that's all there is about it." Antisemitic manifestations of every sort, from social discrimination to anti-Jewish propaganda to efforts to stem the tide of Jewish immigration, rose to new heights during the years that followed, and Jews experienced a substantial decline in their social status.[10]

All these developments—burgeoning antisemitism, calls for a "Christian America," the challenge to Judaism posed by Felix Adler's de-Judaized Ethical Culture movement, and growing alarm over indifference, ignorance, and intermarriage in Jewish life—ran counter to the starry-eyed optimism of an earlier generation of Jewish leaders. Even as changing technology transformed their lives, the clash between glowing expectations and grim realities posed a cultural crisis of the highest order for American Jews. As is so often the case, young people—alive to the possibilities of change—were the first to discern that crisis. They understood before their parents did that old assumptions needed to be replaced and outdated paradigms forsaken. That is why they formed organizations like Keyam Dishmaya. Their goal was to "save" Judaism, to engage in activities that would "redeem" Jews "to the ancient faith."[11]

If factors such as a cultural crisis, fear for Jewish survival, and technological change underlay the late-nineteenth-century awakening, other factors, as Leah too recognized, proved essential to its success. First, the late-nineteenth-century Jewish awakening was fortunate to find leaders who provided meaning and direction to those looking to transform Jewish life. These people, who were to be the prime focus of Leah's work, not only inspired masses of followers and created dozens of organizations to further their work, they also, in the case of people such as Cyrus Adler and Henrietta Szold, continued to lead the Jewish community well into the twentieth century. Absent a coterie of purpose-driven leaders like these, the movement of young people that Leah studied never would have gotten off the ground or achieved what it did. A truism when it comes to movements of change bears repeating here: *leadership matters.*

In addition to developing leaders, young Jews in the late nineteenth century also established organizations. Indeed, something of an organizational frenzy took hold in American Jewish life at the end of the nineteenth century. Fully thirteen of the nineteen national Jewish organizations listed in the first volume of the *American Jewish Year Book* (1899) were founded in the century's last two decades, and so were a great many local organizations. These organizations, analogous to the "benevolent empire" founded by Protestants in the beginning of the nineteenth century, sought to provide "meaning and direction" to Jews suffering from the social and cultural strains of a transitional era.[12] Taken as a group, they reflected the nineteenth-century Jewish awakening's most important goals and values: cultural and religious renewal and the promotion of Jewish education. A list of only a few of the activities and organizations undertaken by the men and women traveling on what Leah called "the road to renaissance" illustrates the point:

- educational programs for Jewish singles at the Young Men's Hebrew Associations (1870s)
- The Jewish Theological Seminary (1886)
- the Jewish Publication Society (1888)
- the Baltimore Night School for Russian immigrants organized and headed by Henrietta Szold (1889)

- the American Jewish Historical Society (1892)
- the Jewish Chautauqua Society (1893)
- the National Council of Jewish Women (1893)
- Gratz College (1893)
- the *Jewish Encyclopedia* (1901–1906)
- Hadassah (1912)
- Jewish library collections across the United States for native Jews and immigrants alike (1898–1914)[13]

All these developments—and this list is by no means complete—reflect an extraordinary moment, perhaps unmatched until our own time, when a group of Jewish leaders seeking to promote cultural transformation placed adult Jewish education, for women as well as for men, at the top of their Jewish agenda and created a whole series of communal institutions to promote it. These institutions mobilized underserved populations (notably women), took advantage of the era's technological innovations, and promoted the goals of Jewish cultural and religious renewal. They were the instruments through which a generation of idealistic Jews, from a very young age, pursued their mission.

Finally, in addition to leaders and new organizations, the movement that began in the 1870s sought to advance its goals through the written word. Its leaders first gave expression to their ideas in YMHA publications such as the *Association Review* (which Leah was the first to discover and study). Soon thereafter, they established a much more important communal organ, *The American Hebrew*, a highbrow weekly whose premier issue appeared in New York on November 21, 1879, edited by nine leaders of the movement, aged twenty-one to twenty-nine. "Our work shall consist of untiring endeavors to stir up our brethren to pride in our time-honored faith," the new periodical announced in its opening number. The newspaper's publisher, Philip Cowen, recalled half a century later that "we were fully convinced that not only New York Judaism, but American Judaism, awaited its journalistic redeemers."[14]

The *American Hebrew* served as a prime vehicle of expression for the young Jews who were attempting to transform American Jewry. It provided them with a platform from which to advance their cause. No movement of change can advance without such a platform and mouthpiece. For in the end, it is not enough just to have able leaders and innovative organizations; to succeed, a movement of young people must also vigorously promote its program in the marketplace of ideas.

The "road to renaissance" that Leah Levitz Fishbane was researching serves in many respects as a paradigm for thinking about American Jewish youth movements as a whole. It reflected the necessary preconditions for a movement's development: cultural crisis, religious challenge, and an era of social and economic change. It also displayed all the necessary ingredients for success: effective leadership, organizational energy, and a journalistic platform from which to advance the cause. Perhaps for this reason, the young people of the time enjoyed extraordinary success. Within a few decades, they and their ideas moved from the periphery of American Jewish life to its center, redefining American Judaism and the priorities of American Jewish life.

Leah, like at least one of the young men who took part in the movement she was analyzing, did not live long enough to see the success of the project she began. "What a sad loss," gasped one of the trove of letters from the Solomon Solis-Cohen papers that she was studying. It spoke of the death of the much-beloved Marcus Noodle, a founder and leader of the YMHA of New York, who died, far too young, in 1879. According to the contemporary letter, Noodle "filled a place in his home, in his business connections, and in Society, which will long be vacant and yet longer be inadequately filled." Max Cohen, shaken to the core by Noodle's death, concluded that "there was hope for the rising generation if it honored such a man as Marcus Noodle was. For 'twas . . . a life of beauty, bereft of its lost promise, yet a life flowing with the best elements of humanity, refined by culture."

So it was with Leah. Hers too was a life of beauty; a life filled with the love of family and friends; a life flowing with the best elements of humanity, refined by culture; a life rich with scholarly promise. "The Road to Renaissance" that Leah was constructing lies tragically unfinished. Her great hope—that her dissertation would "broaden our understanding of the important cultural crises and imperatives of the post–Civil War period which paved the way for new developments in American Jewish communal, cultural and religious life at the turn of the twentieth century"—is itself part of Leah's unforgettable legacy. A portion of that hope, at least, is realized through the publication of this volume.

NOTES

1. Jonathan D. Sarna, *American Judaism: A History* (New Haven: Yale University Press, 2004), p. 135.

2. This and subsequent quotations from Leah Levitz Fishbane's unpublished work draws upon her dissertation prospectus, notes, and chapter drafts in my possession. Two of these chapters are published for the first time in this volume.

3. See Shulamit Volkov, "The Dynamics of Dissimilation: Ostjuden and German Jews," in *The Jewish Response to German Culture: From the Enlightenment to the Second World War*, ed. J. Reinharz and W. Schatzberg (Hanover, NH: University Press of New England, 1985), pp. 192–211.

4. William G. McLoughlin employs this phrase in his "Timepieces and Butterflies: A Note on the Great Awakening Construct and Its Critics," *Sociological Analysis* 44 (1983), p. 108.

5. Sarna, *American Judaism*, p. 124.

6. Alfred D. Chandler, *The Visible Hand: The Management Revolution in American Business* (Cambridge, MA: Harvard University Press, 1977); idem, "Industrial Revolution," *The Reader's Companion to American History*, ed. Eric Foner and John A. Garraty (New York: Houghton Mifflin, 1991), pp. 559–63.

7. Eric Foner, *Reconstruction: America's Unfinished Revolution* (New York: Harper, 2002).

8. Benny Kraut, *From Reform Judaism to Ethical Culture: The Religious Evolution of Felix Adler* (Cincinnati: Hebrew Union College, 1979). On the intermarriage of Helen Wise, see Anne C. Rose, *Beloved Strangers: Interfaith Families in Nineteenth-Century America* (Cambridge, MA: Harvard University Press, 2001), pp. 77–78, 115–18.

9. Paul A. Carter, *The Spiritual Crisis of the Gilded Age* (Dekalb: Northern Illinois University Press, 1971); Naomi W. Cohen, "Challenges of Darwinism and Biblical Criticism to American Judaism," *Modern Judaism* 4 (May 1984), pp. 121–57; Geoffrey Cantor and Marc Swetlitz, eds., *Jewish Tradition and the Challenge of Darwinism* (Chicago: University of Chicago Press, 2006); Marc Swetlitz, "American Jewish Responses to Darwin and Evolutionary Theory," in *Disseminating Darwinism: The Role of Place, Race, Religion, and Gender*, ed. Ronald L. Numbers and John Stenhouse (New York: Cambridge University Press, 1999), pp. 209–45; Benny Kraut, "Judaism Triumphant: Isaac Mayer Wise on Unitarianism and Liberal Christianity," *AJS Review* 7–8 (1982–83), pp. 202–25; Benny Kraut, "The Ambivalent Relations of American Reform Judaism with Unitarianism in the Last Third of the Nineteenth Century," *Journal of Ecumenical Studies* 23 (Winter 1986), pp. 58–68.

10. Naomi W. Cohen, "American Jewish Reactions to Anti-Semitism in Western Europe, 1875–1900," *Proceedings of the American Academy of Jewish Research* 45 (1978), pp. 29–65, esp. 31; Michael A. Meyer, *Judaism within Modernity: Essays on Jewish History and Religion* (Detroit: Wayne State University Press, 2001), pp. 323–44; Leonard Dinnerstein, *Antisemitism in America* (New York: Oxford University Press, 1994), pp. 39–41; Stephen Birmingham, *Our Crowd* (New York: Dell, 1967), pp. 169–80; *Coney Island and the Jews* (New York: G. W. Carleton & Co., 1879); Michael Selzer, ed., *Kike! A Documentary History of Anti-Semitism in America* (New York: Meridian, 1972), p. 56.

11. Jonathan D. Sarna, *A Great Awakening: The Transformation That Shaped Twentieth Century American Judaism and Its Implications for Today* (New York: CIJE, 1995), pp. 13–14.

12. Donald G. Matthews, "The Second Great Awakening as an Organizing Process," *American Quarterly* 21 (1969), pp. 23–43.

13. Robert Singerman, "Books Weeping for Someone to Visit and Admire Them: Jewish Library Culture in the United States, 1850–1910," *Studies in Bibliography and Booklore* 20 (1998), pp. 99–144.

14. *American Hebrew*, November 21, 1879, p. 3, reprinted in Philip Cowen, *Memories of an American Jew* (New York: International Press, 1932), p. 55, see also 49; Sarna, *A Great Awakening*, pp. 15–16.

1 Common Bonds

A Collective Portrait

On the "fateful night" of October 5, 1879, a group of earnest
young Jews from Philadelphia and New York met at an undisclosed Philadelphia location and bound themselves together
in a solemn covenant "for God and Judaism." They called
themselves Keyam Dishmaya, an Aramaic term signifying their
goal to uphold the dictates of heaven, and they pledged to do
all in their power to bring Jews back "to the ancient faith."[1]

With this story, Jonathan Sarna describes an extraordinary moment
of dedication. An intimate circle of young friends pledged their
shared commitment to embark upon a comprehensive and seri-
ous program of Jewish revitalization in America. This meeting, while not one
of the well-known critical moments in American Jewish history, is nevertheless deeply significant, for it encapsulates the emergence of a new phase of
intellectual, institutional, and religious growth in American Jewish life—the
beginning of a "great awakening," as Sarna has termed it. In many ways, it
was a symbolic moment as well as a practical one, and the young Jews who
made this oath to strengthen Judaism in America believed it to be a turning
point in their own lives and in the life of American Judaism. The lens of history and hindsight seems to affirm their belief that this was, indeed, a moment of transformation in American Jewish life, and recent scholarship has
shown that the last quarter of the nineteenth century marked the beginning
of a renewed effort among these young Jews and their friends, colleagues,
and mentors to create and encourage new institutions, new approaches, and
new contexts for the improved commitment of American Jewry to honor its
past and its potential.[2]

What brought these devoted young Jews to such an inspired moment of
purpose and kinship on that October night during the Jewish holiday of Sukkot in 1879?[3] How did it come to pass that a group of friends, not much past

the age of majority, and from two different cities, felt compelled to come together to sanctify a holy pact between them to transform American Jewry? In what ways did their formative years—a coalescence of familial, communal, religious, and educational values—inform their obvious love for Judaism, its legacy of riches, and their belief in its continued relevance for their generation? Our exploration into the evolution of this fascinating group of young Jews from Philadelphia and New York—individuals who would come to lead American Jewry with energy and effectiveness well into the twentieth century— will begin with these very questions.

We do not know the names of all the persons present that night in Philadelphia, but we might venture to guess that it was many of the same young Jews who, in the following months, went on to found the weekly *American Hebrew* newspaper. At the same time, they simultaneously participated in creating revived Hanukkah celebrations in their respective cities through the auspices of the Young Men's Hebrew Association.[4] At the center of the circle were Solomon Solis-Cohen of Philadelphia (1857–1948), Max Cohen of New York (1853–1943), and Cyrus L. Sulzberger of New York (1858–1932), who had moved there only two years earlier from Philadelphia. Cyrus Sulzberger and Solomon Solis-Cohen were very close friends in Philadelphia, and when Sulzberger moved to New York in 1877 at the age of nineteen, he moved next door to Max Cohen.[5] In doing so, he became a neighbor of Philip Cowen (1853–1943) and Daniel P. Hays (1854–1923), both of whom lived in the same neighborhood as Max Cohen in New York, thus widening their circle of like-minded peers.[6] Cowen, prior to founding the *American Hebrew*, had already worked with Cyrus Sulzberger and Solomon Solis-Cohen on their joint publishing venture of the *Association Review*. This intellectually substantial (if amateur) journal was published under the auspices of the junior "Associate" cohort of the Young Men's Hebrew Association (YMHA) of Philadelphia for the short period of 1877–1878.[7] Cowen's participation in the *Association Review*, and his initial interactions with Sulzberger and Solis-Cohen, which began in 1876, formed the basis for their future friendship.[8] Daniel P. Hays, like Cowen, was an active member of the YMHA of New York, as was another close member of this circle, Samuel Greenbaum of New York (1854–1930).[9] Greenbaum had been close friends with Cowen since 1867, and their fathers (as well as Daniel Hays' father) also enjoyed a close relationship.[10] All of these young friends came together in 1879 to found the *American Hebrew*, along with Frederic de Sola Mendes (1850–1927), the young rabbi who succeeded Rev. Samuel Myer Isaacs at Congregation Shaaray Tefila in New York, and his brother Henry Pereira (H. P.) Mendes, who similarly came as a young rabbi to America to succeed Rev. J. J. Lyons as the hazan of New York's Congregation Shearith Israel. Another member of the original editorial board was Jacob Fonseca da Silva Solis (1853–1894), who was a cousin of both Solomon Solis-Cohen and Daniel P. Hays. Cyrus Adler (1863–1940) was another member of this circle, and although he was a bit younger than the rest, he would play a key role in most, if not all of their collaborations.[11] These young men were also joined in their efforts by a number of young Jewish women who were close acquaintances and colleagues. Mary M. Cohen (1854–1911) and Nina Morais Cohen (1855–1918), both of Philadelphia, and later Henrietta Szold (1860–1945) of Baltimore, were among the women who were instrumental in lending literary and spiritual voice to a number of projects.[12] Together, and with the encouragement and advice of their peers, mentors, teachers, and families, these young Jewish men and women, beginning in their late teens and early twenties, would work both as individuals and in cooperation for many decades in creating intellectual projects and communal institutions with the shared aim of revitalizing American Jewish life.

What were the common bonds that held this group so tightly together? It is clear that although this group of young Jews hailed from somewhat different backgrounds, they shared a great deal of formative cultural, familial, religious, social, and economic commonalities. Most were born in America within a decade of one another, from roughly the early 1850s to the early 1860s. They seem to have viewed one another as part of the same generation, growing up in a shared world of events and experiences. As children and adolescents, they watched together the American crisis of Civil War and Reconstruction, the changing tide of emancipation and nationalism in Europe, and the rise of antisemitism in their own country and abroad. They also saw the challenges that world and American Jewish leaders faced in confronting these events.[13] The majority of this group had at least one parent who was not American born and came to America in the mid-nineteenth century from either Germany (including Posen) or England.[14] They enjoyed a comfortable economic footing, and even the families of immigrants quickly rose to become middle to upper class.[15] Coinciding with their upward economic mobility, their families all embraced social and civic participation in their local and national communities. Through voluntary associations, charities, and political causes, their parents passed on to these youths a strong sense of civic responsibility and social belonging in America, as well as a sense of Jewish communal responsibility, a tradition that would be embraced even further by their American-born children. As they matured from children into adults, this group of young Jews, despite their continued passion for serving the Jewish community, overwhelmingly rejected the path to the rabbinate, and instead became publishers, doctors, lawyers, businessmen, scholars, educators, or writers who were determined to serve and transform the American Jewish community as lay leaders.[16] Solomon Solis-Cohen became a prominent physician. Max Cohen, Samuel Greenbaum, and Daniel P. Hays all went on to successful careers in law. Philip Cowen was a printer and editor, Cyrus L. Sulzberger was a businessman, and Cyrus Adler was a well-known Orientalist. Their decision to pursue these various careers did not keep them from devoting themselves to the advancement and welfare of American Jewry throughout the course of their lives. When we consider their strong sense of civic, as well as communal and religious duty, it is not surprising that they would choose paths that would enable them to serve both general society as well as the Jewish community. Indeed, their decision seems to embody the conviction that their commitment to the religious and practical welfare of their fellow Jews was in no way contradictory to their full participation in American civic and cultural life.

Individual Journeys

Before we continue our exploration of these Jews as a collective peer circle, it may be useful to begin with brief biographical sketches of some of the key members of the group during their formative years.

Solomon Solis-Cohen, who stood at the heart of this group, was born in Philadelphia in 1857. His mother, Judith Simhah Solis, was herself American born, and traced her lineage to a prominent and patriotic American Jewish family. Solomon's father, Myer David Cohen, an immigrant to America, was born in Bromberg, Germany. The family belonged to Philadelphia's Congregation Mikveh Israel, absorbed its Portuguese rites and the religious ideology of first Rev. Isaac Leeser and then Rev. Sabato Morais. Nevertheless, it is likely that Myer Cohen's German background made a strong imprint on the family. Indeed the Solis-Cohen family seems to reflect both the progressive spirit of mid-nineteenth-century German-Jewish *Bildung* and respectability, as well as a steadfast Americanized and modern religious traditionalism and conservatism, embodied by both Leeser and Morais.[17] It is therefore not surprising that Solomon Solis-Cohen held strongly to his belief that science and traditional Judaism were not at odds with one another, and his efforts to uphold this ideal were consistent with his belief in both progress *and* traditionalism.[18] These two values may reflect both his father's German-Jewish background as well as the modern "enlightened" traditionalism of his Sephardic maternal line, and in particular, the teachings of Solomon Solis-Cohen's greatest teacher, Sabato Morais.[19] Solomon Solis-Cohen was a devoted student of Judaism and had a particular love of medieval Hebrew literature. He was a poet, a translator, and a writer of essays and editorials. He was an early leader in the Young Men's Hebrew Association of Philadelphia. He edited the Philadelphia YMHA's *Association Review* (with Cyrus L. Sulzberger) and later worked to establish a national union of YMHAs. He also played a central role in the success of the *American Hebrew* as one of the founding editors. While in college, he enjoyed intensive tutorials from his primary teacher and intellectual-religious advisor, Sabato Morais, and although he decided to pursue a career in medicine, Solis-Cohen continued to study Hebrew literature intensively with Morais until 1885. He went on to become a prominent physician in Philadelphia, even as he upheld his commitment to serving the Jewish community as a writer, educator, and translator. He was a founder of the Jewish Publication Society and The Jewish Theological Seminary, and worked for the welfare of Jewish immigrants from Eastern Europe in the late nineteenth and early twentieth centuries.

Max Cohen, whose concern for the spiritual life of American Jewry is best illustrated in his writings on Jewish issues for the Young Men's Hebrew Association and the *American Hebrew*, as well as in his early correspondence with Solomon Solis-Cohen, Cyrus L. Sulzberger, and Philip Cowen, was born in New York City in 1853 to Julius Cohen and Bertha Fernbach.[20] Cohen attended New York City public schools, and grew up in the same upper-middle class "uptown" neighborhood as Philip Cowen and Samuel Greenbaum. Like his friends, Max Cohen and his family were part of the Adereth-El synagogue, which was traditional and followed the Ashkenazic-German rite.[21] Of all the members of the group, we know the least about Cohen, who, although a successful lawyer and known communal activist, did not develop the same degree of public persona as some of the other members of the group. Nevertheless, Cohen's devoted commitment to the group and their aspirations is evidenced in his published writings as well as in his correspondence. In particular, Cohen's letters to Solomon Solis-Cohen reveal the deep attachment between the two, both as friends and intellectual confidants.[22] In addition to his involvement in the Young Men's Hebrew Association and the *American Hebrew*, Cohen was instrumental in the founding of The Jewish Theological Seminary, and later contributed to the *Jewish Encyclopedia*.[23]

Cyrus L. Sulzberger was born in Philadelphia in 1858. His father, Leopold Sulzberger, immigrated to the United States from Bavaria in 1838. Cyrus Sulzberger's mother, Sophie Lindauer, seems to have also been of German origin.[24] During his youth in Philadelphia, Cyrus L. Sulzberger studied at the Hebrew Education Society, as well as Philadelphia public schools.[25] The Sulzbergers were members of Philadelphia's Mikveh Israel Congregation, and his father, Leopold, who was "known in the Philadelphia Jewish community for his piety," was Mikveh Israel's *shohet*.[26] As he grew to maturity, Cyrus adopted his father's devotion to Judaism. Reflecting on Sulzberger's life and commitment to Judaism, David de Sola Pool offered the following remarks:

> Cyrus L. Sulzberger was a man of superlative integrity. His heart beat true. His was a heart of wisdom, and he loved the wisdom of his ancient people. He was an intensely religious man, a man in whom religion was neither a cult nor an occasional profession of faith. It was the very fibre of his being.[27]

At the age of nineteen, Sulzberger left Philadelphia for New York, and took a job as a bookkeeper at the firm of Nathan Erlanger, where he grew into a successful businessman. He became neighbors and close friends with Philip Cowen, Max Cohen, Daniel P. Hays, and Samuel Greenbaum, and was involved in the Adereth-El community, eventually becoming president of the synagogue's school.[28] He also became a member of the Portuguese synagogue, Shearith Israel—hardly surprising considering Shearith Israel's long-standing relationship with Sulzberger's former synagogue, Philadelphia's Mikveh Israel.[29]

Solidifying his role as a young lay leader, Sulzberger continued to show a deep interest in Jewish education and Jewish affairs, and devoted much of his time to the spiritual, political, and economic welfare of the Jewish community.[30] Through his leadership in the Young Men's Hebrew Association, first as an associate member in Philadelphia (including his editorship of the Philadelphia YMHA's *Association Review* with Solomon Solis-Cohen in 1877–1878), and later as a full member of the New York association, Sulzberger worked to strengthen the educational and communal aims of the young movement. His primary work in this regard was his call (along with Solis-Cohen and others) for a national union of YMHAs. He believed that in pooling the resources of the various YMHAs and speaking out boldly as a unified body, the movement—and with it its young leaders—would have a greater impact on the direction of American Jewry. As part of this effort, Sulzberger and Solis-Cohen came together to edit the YMHA's *Association Bulletin* (1881–1883), a monthly journal, which published YMHA lectures, offered new articles, and shared news among the various YMHAs across the country.[31] His work in the YMHA and the *Association Bulletin* complemented his simultaneous efforts as one of the founding editors of the *American Hebrew*. Sulzberger continued his work in the Jewish community throughout the remainder of his life, and served the community as a leader in the Jewish Publication Society, the American Jewish Committee, United Hebrew Charities, the Industrial Removal Office, the Jewish Agricultural and Industrial Aid Society, and the New York *Kehilla* movement.

Philip Cowen, who is best known for his role as the publisher and one of the founding editors of the *American Hebrew*, was born in New York City in 1853.[32] His father, Raphael Keil, was from Prussia, and his mother, Julia Manasseh, was from Posen. They were married in Germany in 1846, and lived for a short time in England where, following his wealthier brother's example, they changed their family name to Cowen before immigrating to America. As a young boy, Cowen attended the New York City public schools, and he also attended the religious school attached to Congregation Shearith Israel.[33] He also learned from private tutors and cantors. Once the family had settled "uptown" they were part of the Adereth-El synagogue. Cowen was a neighbor and close friend of Max Cohen, Daniel P. Hays, and especially Samuel Greenbaum, all of whom were also involved, like Cowen, in the new Young Men's Hebrew Association (the New York YMHA was founded in 1874). This group formed the core of their New York circle, which later welcomed Cyrus L. Sulzberger after he moved next door to Cowen and the others in 1877. Unlike the other members of the group, who had (in many cases) both a strong Jewish and secular education, Cowen dropped out of college, and cycled through a few jobs until he settled into a career as a printer, first opening a printing office with Samuel Greenbaum (who went on to become a successful lawyer and judge).[34] His role as a printer, and his earnest interest in Jewish affairs and Jewish journalism, led him first to his participation with Solomon Solis-Cohen and Cyrus Sulzberger in the Philadelphia YMHA's *Association Review*, and then to his central role in the founding, editing, and printing of the *American Hebrew*. Cowen's direction of the *American Hebrew* reflects a Jewish leader whose primary interest was the unity and welfare of the Jewish community, and who believed in the value of constructive and earnest debates over Jewish issues by scholars and community leaders of differing perspectives.[35] Cowen continued to devote his energies to American Jewish journalistic and literary enterprises, and his editorial voice was greatly influential on American Jewry. His role in the United States Immigration Service also enabled him to advocate for the welfare of Jewish immigrants to America.

Daniel P. Hays was born in Pleasantville, New York, in 1854. His parents, David Hays and Judith S. Peixotto, were both native to America, and traced their ancestry to the time of the American Revolution. In this way, Hays is unique among his peers of the group, most of whom had at least one parent who was an immigrant.[36] Hays attended public schools, and he went on to study at the City College of New York and Columbia University Law School. His religious education seems to have been at least partially provided under the auspices of Shearith Israel. Hays became a prominent lawyer, and in 1884 founded the firm of Hays & Greenbaum with Samuel Greenbaum. In addition to his career as a lawyer and communal worker, Hays was also a poet, and was known for the intersection of his religious devotion and poetic ability.[37] Although Hays was among the more religiously liberal of the group—and his life's trajectory eventually brought him to align with moderate Reform Judaism, his commitment to Judaism and its practice in America was steadfast. In a speech delivered toward the end of his life at the Golden Jubilee celebration of the Union of American Hebrew Congregations (UAHC), Hays offered the following remark:

> Judaism is a religion, the mother of all religions. . . . It is the spiritual legacy of the Jew and has enriched the civilization of the world by a knowledge of God and all that makes for righteousness. We need no excuse for the observance of our religion in a land where freedom of conscience is a part of the fundamental law. . . . Judaism in America is not merely a privilege. It is an obligation we owe to ourselves and to the State. By its observance we purchase the privilege and discharge the obligation. Let us, the delegates to this Golden Jubilee Convention, reaffirm our devotion and consecration to Judaism as a religion and pledge ourselves to so maintain and preserve it, fearlessly, sincerely, and conscientiously.[38]

He was, like most of his peers, keenly aware of his civic duties as an American, as well as his responsibilities to the Jewish community, and he believed that these two elements of his person were deeply connected and in perfect harmony. Upon his death, Adolph Ochs wrote of him: "An American in every angle of his thought . . . he was the type of Jew that has and demands the respect of all intelligent people whatsoever their religious affiliations; one who made the word Jew as it should be—a badge of honor and pride. He was a Jew by religion, an American by birth, and his faith and nationality were consistent and suffered no evasion or equivocations; and so, with one God and one country, he was regarded as indigenous to the soil."[39] His commitment to American Jewry and Judaism was manifest as a young man in his leadership role in New York's Young Men's Hebrew Association and the *American Hebrew*, and (as he matured) through his involvement in The Jewish Theological Seminary (prior to its 1902 reorganization),[40] the *Jewish Encyclopedia*, and the Union of American Hebrew Congregations.

Samuel Greenbaum was born in London in 1854, and came to America with his parents, Louis Greenbaum and Rachel Deborah Schlesinger, at the age of three. He is one of the few members of this group who was not born in America. Nevertheless, because he was so young when he arrived, he shared many of the features of the others' upbringing. He was educated in the New York City public schools, and continued on to the City College of New York and Columbia University Law School.[41] Greenbaum was a close childhood friend of Philip Cowen (whose father shared a strong friendship with Greenbaum's father), and along with Max Cohen and Daniel Hays, Greenbaum was part of the Adereth-El synagogue.[42] Along with the others, Greenbaum participated in the Young Men's Hebrew Association, serving as president of the New York association, and he devoted himself to the *American Hebrew* as one of the original founding editors. Samuel Greenbaum became a successful lawyer in the firm he founded with Daniel P. Hays, and Greenbaum was appointed to the New York State Supreme Court in 1900, all the while continuing to serve the Jewish community as a lay leader. He was involved in The Jewish Theological Seminary, the Educational Alliance, as well as the Baron de Hirsch Fund and Jewish Welfare Board.[43]

Cyrus Adler, the youngest member of the group, but also one of the most well known, was born in Van Buren, Arkansas, in 1863. His parents, Samuel Adler and Sarah Sulzberger, were from Germany, and immigrated to America in the mid-nineteenth century. When Cyrus was an infant, his father became ill, and the family moved between Philadelphia and New York, where he spent time with his maternal grandfather, Leopold Sulzberger (the father of Cyrus L. Sulzberger), whom Adler would later describe as "a man rigidly devoted to

Judaism and all of its observances."[44] With Samuel Adler's death in 1867, when Cyrus was only three and one-half years old, Cyrus Adler and his mother settled in Philadelphia to live with her brother, David Sulzberger. Adler's formative years were therefore spent in Philadelphia, and much of his upbringing and cultural-religious education were provided by the leaders of the Philadelphia Jewish community—most notably, his uncle, David Sulzberger, who headed the Hebrew Education Society; Sabato Morais, the beloved hazan of Mikveh Israel synagogue; and Mayer Sulzberger, Adler's significantly older cousin and mentor.[45] Adler attended the Hebrew Education Society, as well as Central High School and the University of Pennsylvania. During college he, like Solomon Solis-Cohen, studied intensively with Sabato Morais, and he enjoyed other tutorials with Samuel Hirsch, George Jacobs, and Marcus Jastrow. Upon his decision to study for a doctorate in Semitics at Johns Hopkins University in Baltimore, Adler also came under the influence and friendship of Benjamin Szold, a progressive but conservative-leaning rabbi whose daughter, Henrietta, only a few years older than Adler, became a close colleague of Adler's, particularly in their leadership of the Jewish Publication Society.[46] While Adler deeply appreciated the willingness of such a diverse group of rabbis to devote their energies to his education, his own approach to Judaism was rooted firmly in the traditionalist camp.[47] In time, Adler would become one of the most influential leaders of what was to evolve into Conservative Judaism—a role anchored in his involvement with The Jewish Theological Seminary. Adler's devotion to the development of Jewish studies in America was a consistent theme during the course of his life. During his college years, Adler catalogued the Leeser Library under the auspices of the Philadelphia YMHA. This was one of his first projects aimed at strengthening Jewish education in America.[48] Adler was also involved in the *American Hebrew* as its Philadelphia correspondent until 1894, the year in which he joined the editorial board.[49] A major figure in the growth of American Jewish scholarship, Adler was instrumental in the founding of The Jewish Theological Seminary, the Jewish Publication Society, and the American Jewish Historical Society.

Collective Journeys: Religious Life, Education, and Lay Leadership

Beyond the specific details that made up each of these young Jews' individual stories, and despite some of the differences in their geographical and cultural backgrounds, they all shared a deeply felt commitment to Jewish heritage and community that bound them together in friendship and practical work for American Jewry. Nevertheless, they also embodied a somewhat diverse spectrum of approaches to Jewish legal and ritual standards. The Philadelphians, who in general tended to be a more homogeneous group, can largely be described as traditional.[50] The families all belonged to Congregation Mikveh Israel, a community whose leadership under Rev. Isaac Leeser and later under Rev. Sabato Morais long stressed the value of ritual observance in public, in the synagogue, and in the home. The community's affirmation of Jewish tradition did not, however, see itself as antithetical to American language, style, and values. The community and families embraced the modern sermon in English, and set high standards for etiquette, membership, civic participation, and patriotism. Mikveh Israel's emphases on ritual observance, love for Jewish tradition, as well as loyalty to America and its ideals, were reinforced at home, and the families were all exemplary lay leaders in the synagogue. One of the most active families in Mikveh Israel was the family of Mary M. Cohen and her older brother Charles. In his eulogy for Henry Cohen (the father of Charles and Mary), Sabato Morais offers a portrait of religious and communal loyalty:

> For Henry Cohen did not hide his attachment to the ancestral observances, because he enjoyed the familiar intercourse of the cultured and respected among the professors of another creed. He reverenced his religion, and held tenaciously thereunto—as an inalienable birthright—in the presence of the world. Without seeking a controversy, the intelligent Hebrew keenly relished the opportunity which enabled him to explain the reason for continuing loyal to the Law and the Prophets. Nor had our chief, whose demise I deplore, been merely an occasional visitor in the Minor Sanctuary. All saw him, undeterred by distance, in his usual seat, an earnest worshipper, ready to signify his appreciation of the honors belonging to his tribe as a scion of the stock of Aaron, by generous donations.[51]

Henry Cohen's legacy of devotion to the ritual observances of Judaism and his commitment to lay leadership was carried forth into the lives of his children. Mary M. Cohen offered her assertive voice for the importance of Jewish tradition, observance, spiritual vibrancy, and education as a writer and communal worker in the Hebrew Sunday Schools and charities. Her older brother, Charles, succeeded his father's post as *Parnas* of Mikveh Israel, and followed in his father's footsteps as a strong lay leader in Philadelphia. With such leaders at its helm, it is not surprising that the youths who grew up in this community were able to draw strength and confidence from the community's commitment to Jewish tradition and its leadership in civic, communal, and religious affairs. Nevertheless, we might expect that the specific decisions of a family or an individual to uphold various laws and rituals were somewhat different. Their approaches to Sabbath observance and its boundaries, for example, offer a window into some of the subtle choices made among even the more traditional of the group. In a letter to Solomon Solis-Cohen in 1880, Max Cohen writes the following:

> In conversing[?] with Y. A. [Yizhak Aryeh (Cyrus L. Sulzberger)] he casually let fall the remark, that you at times shaved yourself on the Sabbath without any scruples. I thought at first he was joking, but he assured me of the truth of what he had said. Why Sol, I was astonished, and I am hardly a pietist.[52]

While both Max Cohen (who was from New York) and Solomon Solis-Cohen (from Philadelphia) believed that they shared a traditional approach to Sabbath observance, it is clear that they also made different choices as to its specific parameters. Considering the fact that the Philadelphians, while traditional, did not generally consider themselves "orthodox"—and in fact often criticized orthodoxy as well as reform—it is not surprising that they would approach observance with a significant degree of variation.

In New York, the pattern of religious orientation and observance among the group was even more diverse. Max Cohen, whose letter is cited above, exemplifies the more traditional of the New Yorkers, along with Cyrus L. Sulzberger (who spent most of his formative years in Philadelphia). As an example of the wide spectrum of observance among the New Yorkers, let us juxtapose Cohen's concern for the observance of the Sabbath (illustrated in his critical letter to Solis-Cohen regarding shaving on the Sabbath) with the following story recounted by Philip Cowen in his memoir:

> I had just passed my thirteenth year when I entered the City College. At school I had stood high in arithmetic and algebra; but geometry stumped me. . . . So rather than take the chance of flunking . . . I determined to leave college, much to the chagrin of my parents. I found a job at the Allerton Stock Yards. . . . When the stockmen shipped their herds, they came to town to get the money and see the sights. Checks meant nothing to them; they wanted the cash, so after they endorsed the checks I usually went to the West Side Bank . . . and had the checks cashed for them. . . . One Saturday, I went to cash a check for $3,500. On the way back the car was detained by a horse falling into a hole.[53]

In the context of Cowen's story, we inadvertently learn that he went out to work and engaged in financial transactions on a Saturday in violation of the

Jewish Sabbath. At the age of thirteen he was likely still living in his parents' home, and one wonders what response his parents had to his working on the Sabbath. Did his father also work on the Sabbath? Unfortunately, Cowen tells us little of his family's approach to Sabbath or other ritual observance, except to say that his father "was religiously-minded, and conceived it to be the duty of a *ba'al habayith*, the master of a household, to take his place in communal life."[54] His father, Raphael Cowen, was highly involved in Jewish communal life, and enjoyed active participation in his synagogue community as well as various Jewish (and non-Jewish) fraternal and charitable organizations. Cowen's synagogue, Adereth-El, was traditional and was founded in 1857 by upwardly mobile German-Jewish immigrants. In 1868, the synagogue participated with other traditional synagogues such as B'nai Jeshurun and Shaaray Tefilla in the Sabbath Convention of New York, which called for greater observance of the Sabbath among New York Jewry.[55] Although Cowen does not provide any details about Jewish observance in his parental home, and despite his youthful Sabbath-breaking tale, it is clear that by 1879, when Cowen had reached the age of twenty-six, he and the other founders of the *American Hebrew* placed the encouragement of Sabbath observance at the forefront of the paper's goals.

Once the group had solidified its partnership and friendship around the *American Hebrew* project, they continued to debate their different approaches to religious observance, even though they all shared a strong commitment to Sabbath observance (at least in general terms). A rare glimpse of the group and their breakdown according to religious observance (at least as it was seen by one of its members) is found in a letter that Max Cohen wrote to Solomon Solis-Cohen on December 25, 1879. Cohen graphs the members of the *American Hebrew* editorial board based on religious observance, and asserts the following list of "Jewish" traditionalists and "namby-pamby" reformers, thus revealing his own traditional biases:

Jewish	*Namby-Pamby*
H. P. Mendes	D. P. Hays
S. Solis-Cohen	M. Cordozo [treasurer]
Cyrus L. Sulzberger	Samuel Greenbaum
Max Cohen	Phil Cowen
F. de Sola Mendes	F. de Sola Mendes[56]

While keeping in mind Max Cohen's own antireform bias, it is nevertheless interesting to note that Sulzberger, Cohen, and Solis-Cohen all saw themselves in the same camp of traditionalists, along with H. P. Mendes, who was then the rabbi at Shearith Israel in New York (the sister congregation to Philadelphia's Mikveh Israel). Daniel P. Hays, Samuel Greenbaum, and Philip Cowen, all from New York, were clearly to the left [in terms of desire to reform; the right-hand column above]. It is interesting to note that in spite of their religious differences, New Yorkers Max Cohen and Cyrus L. Sulzberger (who were quite traditional) and Philip Cowen, Greenbaum, and Hays (who were more liberal) were all members of the tradition-oriented Adereth-El congregation (though Daniel P. Hays and Cyrus L. Sulzberger were also involved in Shearith Israel congregation). Most interesting here is the placement of Rabbi Frederic de Sola Mendes both in the traditional and reform camps. Mendes was trained at the Breslau seminary, and in 1874 came to New York as an assistant to Rabbi S. M. Isaacs at Shaaray Tefilla, a traditional congregation. Taking over from Isaacs after his death, Mendes gradually pulled the congregation from a traditional approach to ritual toward a moderate reform approach.[57] In 1879, Frederic de Sola Mendes was in the midst of his journey from moderate traditionalism to moderate reform, which explains his placement on both ends of Cohen's religious spectrum.

Perhaps one of the most remarkable similarities among the members of this group was their common pattern of general education. Almost all of the young American Jews from this group were educated in the public schools of the cities in which they lived. In Philadelphia, Solomon Solis-Cohen, Cyrus L. Sulzberger, and Cyrus Adler all graduated from Central High School, and Nina Morais graduated from the public school's female counterpart, the Girls' Normal School.[58] Many went on to study at the University of Pennsylvania.[59] In New York, Philip Cowen, Max Cohen, Samuel Greenbaum, and Daniel P. Hays all attended New York public schools, and some continued their studies at City College of New York and Columbia College.[60]

In their Jewish studies, the Philadelphia contingent—including Cyrus L. Sulzberger (during his childhood in Philadelphia), Solomon Solis-Cohen, and Cyrus Adler—studied at the all-day Hebrew Education Society. The Hebrew Education Society, as it was described by Cyrus Adler, was "a parochial school . . . which was a combination of religious school and ordinary day school, and was recognized by the then Public School System of the city as fitting its graduates for high school. It added to the customary subjects Hebrew and the elements of the Jewish religion."[61] By the early 1870s, the school, which from 1867 also included the short-lived Maimonides College, was on the decline. In the wake of the school's fledgling years, a group of former students began during their high school and college years to study in intensive group tutorials with some of Philadelphia's leading rabbis and Jewish scholars, most notably Rev. Sabato Morais of Mikveh Israel, Marcus Jastrow of Rodeph Shalom, Rev. Samuel Hirsch of Kenneseth Israel, and Rev. George Jacobs of Beth El Emeth.[62] Cyrus Adler relates that some took part in tutorials with all of these scholars, who represented distinct approaches to Judaism, while others, such as Solis-Cohen, took only tutorials with Sabato Morais. Still others "scattered about" among the teachers.[63] Adler offers the following description of the tutorials:

> Dr. Morais read the Bible, the *Code* of Maimonides and the *Guide to the Perplexed*. Dr. Jastrow, though a talmudist, read with us an ethical work, the *Menorat ha-Maor*, Dr. Hirsch, talmud; Mr. Jacobs gave us lectures in history; and Mr. Elkan taught Hebrew grammar to the younger students. . . .
>
> We boys went four evenings in the week, Monday, Tuesday, Wednesday, and Thursday, to these respective instructors from the hours of eight to ten. It is noteworthy that in spite of the theological rancor which then ran very high, these various instructors did not permit their different views to creep into their instruction.[64]

All of these scholars, regardless of their personal religious-ideological orientation, devoted their time and knowledge to young Jews who wanted to learn.[65] Those who eagerly agreed to extra hours of study for the sake of their Jewish education were given the foundation for a lifelong love of Jewish sources and learning, which would guide them in their careers as scholars, doctors, rabbis, and teachers.

We know much less about the Jewish educational experiences of the New York group. In his memoir, however, Philip Cowen offers an account of some of his educational encounters, explaining that he attended the religious school of the traditional Portuguese synagogue (Shearith Israel), and that he also studied privately with tutors in Hebrew.[66] It is likely that others in his close circle, whose families shared common friendships as well as institutional affiliations, such as Max Cohen, Samuel Greenbaum, and Daniel P. Hays, took similar paths.[67]

Another striking feature that was common among this group was their nearly unanimous decision to pursue careers outside the rabbinate, and to serve the community as lay leaders. The reasons for their widespread rejection of the rabbinate varied according to their individual circumstances, and unfortunately we have little documentary evidence to shed light on the processes that led to each person's career decisions.[68] Yet the fact that so many of them, fully devoted to the cause of Judaism in America, both spiritual and practical, would decide not to pursue rabbinical studies either at the Hebrew Union College of Cincinnati or abroad, leaves one to wonder if there were some common rationales among the group. In an article that explores the professional path of Morris Jastrow Jr., son of Rabbi Marcus Jastrow, and classmate of Cyrus Adler, Harold Wechsler seeks to uncover why Morris Jastrow, who was well on his way to succeeding his father as rabbi of Rodeph Shalom in Philadelphia, chose instead to accept a full-time position as professor of Semitics at the University of Pennsylvania. Making note of Morris Jastrow's internal struggles over the best way for him to serve the Jewish community, Wechsler also points to Marcus Jastrow's hesitation toward sending his son Morris to train in Cincinnati at Isaac M. Wise's Hebrew Union College as a contributing factor to his decision to send Morris Jastrow to study for the rabbinate in Europe.[69] Marcus Jastrow's concerns about the Cincinnati school, and about Isaac Mayer Wise more generally, were shared by Morais and his disciples in Philadelphia, such as Adler and Solis-Cohen. Their ambivalence toward Wise and the Hebrew Union College may be a key to understanding why they rejected the path to the rabbinate. In the case of Solomon Solis-Cohen, who in the course of his intensive studies with Sabato Morais gave serious consideration to entering the Jewish ministry, it seems that he did not see Hebrew Union College as a viable option for his studies. In a letter to Solis-Cohen in 1881, Abram S. Isaacs[70] writes with concern over Solis-Cohen's decision to pursue a career in medicine:

> I heard yesterday from Miss Morais that you had resolved on studying medicine, and had given up your idea of entering the ministry, or at least postponed it. I regret very much the fact and do hope you will reconsider it. There is no hope for American Judaism if young men of good social position refuse to step forward, but allow refugees of doubtful character and foreigners, who cannot understand our spirit, to take the position rightly theirs. Hence the Jewish pulpit is degraded, and there are social barriers between the rabbi and the educated refined layman. I had come to look upon you as a co-worker. . . . I meant to have written to you a few months ago as to your progress in Hebrew studies. We are not to be baffled by circumstances—the price of food and clothing and the rent of a room—but we must baffle circumstances and rise above them. $300.00 a year would support you in Breslau, though I think you would do better in England.[71]

Isaacs' letter is illuminating on many levels. His suggestion of Breslau and England for Solis-Cohen's rabbinical studies (and the obvious omission of Cincinnati's Hebrew Union College [HUC]) is surely not accidental. Both

Isaacs and Solis-Cohen upheld traditional Judaism, even as they encouraged Jewish *Wissenschaft* and an evolving Jewish history and law. These values were embodied in the Breslau Theological Seminary and its "historical school." Later, these values would be central to the creation of The Jewish Theological Seminary (with which Solis-Cohen was deeply involved), which posed the first strong American alternative to HUC. Solis-Cohen's editorials in the *American Hebrew*, and Abram S. Isaacs' editorials for his own *Jewish Messenger*, often criticized Wise and the leadership of the Cincinnati UAHC and HUC, and it is therefore not surprising that neither one would look favorably on Solis-Cohen's potential training at HUC. Isaacs also raises the possibility of financial obstacles to Solis-Cohen pursuing his rabbinical studies. While this may have been a real concern for Solis-Cohen, it is difficult to believe that this was his primary obstacle.[72] Scholarships and secondary jobs to assist with living costs were certainly available, especially considering Solis-Cohen's strong connections through his family and the Jewish community. It seems more likely that one of his primary concerns was his hesitation to leave Philadelphia, not unlike his mentors Sabato Morais and Mayer Sulzberger.[73] While there were, to be sure, multiple considerations involved in the decision not to attend a seminary,[74] one can imagine that in light of the fact that the Philadelphians of this group were so deeply attached to Philadelphia and American civic culture, and considering their deeply felt concerns about Wise's approach to Judaism in America, it would have been a difficult sacrifice of both personal and ideological ideals to train either in Cincinnati or Europe. There was, as yet, no other alternative to Cincinnati in America for Jews to train for an Americanized rabbinical position, due to the closure of Philadelphia's Maimonides College in 1873. This may also explain the passionate interest of this group in the creation of an alternative rabbinical seminary in America, The Jewish Theological Seminary, in 1886. Could the strong resistance to Isaac Mayer Wise also have played a role in the decision of their peers from New York to serve American Jewry as lay leaders instead of rabbis—especially considering the fact that a number of the New Yorkers, such as Cowen, Hays, and Greenbaum, tended to be more liberal than their Philadelphia counterparts? Even the more liberal of the New York group may not have felt confident in the direction of Wise's Union of American Hebrew Congregations, and with it, the Hebrew Union College. They also expressed a great deal of ambivalence toward Kaufman Kohler (despite their general respect for his knowledge and scholarship) who, in the early 1880s, was emerging as one of the strongest new voices in the reform movement.[75]

For both the Philadelphians and New Yorkers, their distrust of Wise and the new direction of reform seems to have grown stronger as the movement began to move toward more radical, or what they perceived as reckless approaches to Jewish ritual and ideology, culminating in the Cincinnati "Trefa Banquet" of 1883 and the Pittsburgh Platform of 1885. During the decade of 1875–1885 the UAHC asserted great influence on American Jewry through its oversight of the Hebrew Union College and the Board of Delegates. It was precisely during these years that rising leaders such as Solomon Solis-Cohen and his peers were deciding their future careers.[76] Indeed, Isaacs' letter leaves the impression that American Jewish leaders, especially those of a more moderate stance toward ritual and liturgical reform, perceived the American rabbinate and American Jewry in general to be in a state of crisis. Their concern was driven by a combination of forces: growing fears about the radicalization of Reform on the one hand, and the quickening pace of immigration from Eastern Europe on the other. Isaacs feared that the new immigrants, in filling American Jewish pulpits, would bring both a radicalization of orthodoxy, and a disintegration of American-style Judaism.[77] Isaacs believed in the potential of an Americanized conservative, or at least moderate, approach to Judaism. If Isaacs, who trained for the rabbinate abroad at the Breslau seminary, was concerned for the future of an Americanized rabbinate, we might expect that Solis-Cohen and his peers—who were so deeply entrenched in American civic life—would feel this urgency with even greater intensity. To my mind, their devotion to America may have stood at the very heart of their decision to become lay leaders. It is possible that their strong American sensibility led them to believe that a rabbinical education abroad would not produce authentically "American" rabbis. If Cincinnati could not provide the ideological framework for a conservative American Judaism, perhaps they concluded that their best choice was to serve the community as what Cyrus Adler called a "lay-rabbi." As doctors, businessmen, lawyers, and civic leaders they could continue to serve the Jewish community through the creation and support of new institutions, journalistic enterprises, Jewish education, and Jewish scholarship—reflecting the compatibility of American Jewish and civic life.[78]

Children of America: Native-Born Awareness and the Dynamics of Immigration and Generation

The fact that the majority of these young Jews were actually born in America may have played a significant role in their formative development and self-awareness as Jews and Americans. While I hesitate to generalize about the character of this group based solely on an immigrant/native-born generational dynamic, it is impossible to ignore the undeniable sense of ease and naturalness in their identity as native-born American Jews. Perhaps it was precisely the fact of being born American citizens—even eligible for their country's highest office—that endowed them with the confidence to turn inward to Jewish interests without fearing accusations of "foreign loyalties" or an unwillingness to participate fully in American society. Such concerns may have been more characteristic of their parents, many of whom were immigrants whose self-consciousness as foreign-born citizens may have led to a perceived need to overtly *prove* their patriotism.[79] There seems to have been some awareness of the different generational perspectives and experiences among the families of this group. One notable example of this awareness is found in a remarkable letter written by the mother of Mary M. Cohen, Matilda (Samuel) Cohen, who immigrated to America from England with her new husband, Henry Cohen, in 1844. Matilda's letter was written in 1864, in the midst of the American Civil War, to General Benjamin Butler, a controversial political and military figure, in response to General Butler's published account of the capture of five Jews accused of smuggling across the military blockade.[80] In her articulate protest of Butler's comment that he was "from the force of circumstances, unacquainted with any other Israelites than those engaged in contraband trade," Matilda Cohen offers the following rebuttal:

> This is a satisfactory explanation as far as it goes but when I refer you to the history of my people, your intellectual mind will readily perceive the injustice you have done to us. I am a native of England, but America is the land of my adoption, having dwelt here 20 years, my sons and daughters glory in "being natives here and to the manner born." Mr. Cohen is among the earliest members of the Union League, taking a deep interest in the success of the national cause. I have established a Hebrew Women's Aid (see circular enclosed) which cooperates with the U.S. Sanitary Commission and has added many stores for the sick and wounded soldiers. I see a great and glorious future for this country if, at the close of this war it truly proves itself to be the "Land of the free" to all races, and to all religions.[81]

Matilda Cohen rightly understood that for the American-born Jews of our study and their peers, American patriotism and civic responsibility were the primary foundations of their identity, and that this enabled them to publicly confront their minority identity as Jews unapologetically and self-assuredly.

Consider the following lines written by Max Cohen as a young man to Solomon Solis-Cohen in 1879:

> the great question for contemporary Judaism is whether it will continue to do God's work or cease to be. We see the alternative as every thinking man must. And while we have abounding faith that the d[. . . ?] will never prevail. We must realize that it is only by virtue of our own volition. Israel must ever be what its children make it. And the conditions that have hampered our fathers, and that have sent their legacy to us in the form of enfeebled powers.[82]

Indeed, as they observed their own generation and looked ahead to the next generation of American Jews, they were convinced that it was *Jewish* loyalty that had to be learned, asserted, and regained. *Americanism*, it seemed, was already unstrained and confident, even taken for granted among American Jewish youth. As these leaders observed this dynamic among their own generation, their sense of urgency grew, leading them to articulate new ideas for the re-Judaization of American Jewish youth.[83]

If we are right to assume that native identity had an important role to play in the ability of this group to speak out confidently in defense of their "minority" identity as Jews, is it reasonable to draw a connection between native-born generations and periods of Jewish revival? Let us look to similar examples of the interplay of generational dynamics and the politics of Jewish identity. The early decades of the nineteenth century in America also saw a young generation of Jews, many of them American born, at the forefront of efforts to revitalize Jewish life.[84] American Jewish leaders of the early 1800s, armed with an uncompromising American patriotism, were able to express the notion that looking inward with pride toward their Jewish heritage was not antithetical to their civic loyalty to America.[85] Hence, these years produced an explosion of Jewish communal institutions designed to strengthen American Jewish identity through education, philanthropy, communal organization, and an Americanized style of Jewish ritual and religious engagement that would appeal to younger, more acculturated American Jews.[86]

Returning to the late nineteenth century, developments abroad in Central Europe illustrate a somewhat similar generational dynamic. In the case of late nineteenth and early twentieth century Central Europe, we might compare the impact of *emancipation* in Europe with the corresponding impact of *immigration* in America during the same period. Let us turn to Germany as a case in point. Between the years of 1869 and 1871, Germany, in its process of unification, granted rights of citizenship to its Jews. The long process leading up to that point of emancipation—a journey that saw moments of hope as well as frustration over the course of the nineteenth century—inevitably caused many Jews, both as individuals and as a community, to prove themselves worthy of emancipation through both public and private expressions of German patriotism and acculturation, and often even radical assimilation.[87] As the turn of the century approached, however, we find that a new generation of young German Jews who were born *after* the granting of citizenship, and likely empowered by their born right to equality, rose to lead German Jewry in a revitalization of its own German Jewish religious and cultural life, even in the face of growing antisemitic and exclusionary German nationalism.[88] Far more secure than their parents' generation in their German identity and civic rights, the younger German Jews challenged the established German-Jewish leadership and their fellow young Jews to reexamine their approach to Jewish identity, and to embrace their Jewish heritage through education, new spiritual models, ethnic and communal pride, cultural projects, and new institutions. It is remarkable that, in both America and Germany, we see at midcentury a marked cautiousness toward outward Jewish expression of identity and communal-cultural inwardness just at the time that the larger German and American societies touted the spirit of liberalism and tolerance. By the end of the nineteenth century, even as anti-Jewish sentiment was on the rise in both Germany and America, and one would most expect caution and anxiety over minority identity, we find the opposite to be the case. It was at this very point that a younger generation asserted their Jewish identity, even as they continued to express confidence in their participation in the larger national culture. It seems plausible that just as in Germany, where it took a generation of young German Jews born after the emancipation to create a confident and far-reaching Jewish renaissance, likewise in America it took an American-born generation, confident in their ability to be both Americans and Jews, to formulate an assertive and confident agenda for American Jewish awakening of cultural and religious vitality in the late nineteenth century.[89]

NOTES

1. Jonathan Sarna, *American Judaism: A History* (New Haven: Yale University Press, 2004), p. 135.

2. See ibid., chapter 4; Sarna, "The Late Nineteenth Century American Jewish Awakening," in W. Conser and S. Twiss, eds., *Religious Diversity and American Religious His-*

tory: Studies in Traditions and Cultures (Athens: University of Georgia Press, 1997)—this also appeared as A Great Awakening: The Transformation That Shaped Twentieth Century American Judaism and Its Implications for Today (New York: Council for Initiatives in Jewish Education, 1995) and is available online at http://www.mandelfoundation.org/MandelCMS/English/VirtualLibrary/Publications/AGreatAwakening.htm/; Sarna, JPS: The Americanization of Jewish Culture (Philadelphia: JPS, 1989); Shuly Rubin Schwartz, The Emergence of Jewish Scholarship in America (Cincinnati: Hebrew Union College Press, 1991); Faith Rogow, Gone to Another Meeting: The National Council of Jewish Women, 1893–1993 (Tuscaloosa: University of Alabama Press, 1993); Jack Wertheimer, ed., Tradition Renewed: A History of the Jewish Theological Seminary, 2 vols. (New York: Jewish Theological Seminary, 1997); Murray Friedman, When Philadelphia Was the Capital of Jewish America (Philadelphia: Balch Institute Press, 1993).

3. The Hebrew Calendar shows that October 5, 1879, was during Ḥol Hamoed (the intermediate days) of Sukkot (when travel and work are permitted), only a few days before the final celebration of the fall Jewish holiday cycle culminating in Simḥat Torah. We might imagine these friends sitting in the sacred space of the sukkah, anticipating new initiatives in the spirit of their pact for the coming year. In this way it is also not surprising that one of the first opportunities that they seized upon to breathe new life into the community would be the festival of Hanukkah—the first Jewish festival after Simḥat Torah.

4. Cyrus L. Sulzberger, Solomon Solis-Cohen, and Max Cohen are the only three for whom we have evidence of their presence at the meeting. See Cyrus L. Sulzberger (signed Yizhak Aryeh) to Solomon Solis-Cohen, New York, October 5, 1880; and Max Cohen to Solomon Solis-Cohen, New York, September 28, 1880 (in reference to the first anniversary of Keyam Dishmaya), Solomon Solis-Cohen Collection, National Museum of American Jewish History (hereafter NMAJH), "Jewish Affairs 1880."

5. Philadelphia Inquirer, November 27, 1877, p. 1. The newspaper article describes the departure of young Cyrus L. Sulzberger from Philadelphia, and notes that Solomon Solis-Cohen and Hyman P. Rosenbach accompanied Sulzberger to the train station. Mayer Sulzberger Collection, Center for Advanced Judaic Studies (hereafter CAJS), MS 25, Box 10, FF 2.

6. Philip Cowen, Memories of an American Jew (New York: The International Press, 1932), p. 30. Cowen remarks in his memoir: "Next to Samuel Greenbaum, Cyrus Sulzberger was my closest friend." Ibid., p. 130. It should also be noted that Daniel P. Hays and Solomon Solis-Cohen were cousins.

7. Benjamin Rabinowitz, The Young Men's Hebrew Associations, 1854–1913 (New York: National Jewish Welfare Board, 1948), pp. 17–18. While I have not been able to locate any full copies of the original Association Review, we know from scrapbook clippings and correspondence that Sulzberger and Solis-Cohen sought out knowledgeable and sophisticated literary contributions on a regular basis from Sabato Morais, Mary M. Cohen, and others. See, for example, Charles and Mary M. Cohen collection, CAJS, MS 3, Box 5, Item 2; MS 3, Box 4, Item 1. The Association Review was published under the associate branch of the YMHA. There were two categories of membership in the YMHA during this period. "Active" members enjoyed full voting and office-holding rights and had to be

at least twenty-one years of age. "Associate" members were younger than twenty-one, and generally did not enjoy full voting or office-holding rights (though each YMHA had its own local rules of membership). Rabinowitz, *Hebrew Associations*, pp. 63–65. The role of the YMHA, as well as the significance of associate-level membership, its parameters, and the involvement of young Jews such as Sulzberger, Cohen, Greenbaum, Solis-Cohen, and others during the first decade of the New York and Philadelphia associations will be treated subsequently in chapter 2.

8. Cowen writes, "[The *Association Review*] was my first real journalistic experience, and from it arose the very strong friendship that subsists to this day among the three of us [i.e. Cowen, Sulzberger, and Solis-Cohen]." Cowen, *Memories*, p. 41. It is unclear what brought Max Cohen and Solis-Cohen into close alliance and friendship, though it is likely that the two met and quickly became friends through the common friendship of Sulzberger (who was close with Solis-Cohen in Philadelphia and also with Max Cohen, his new neighbor in New York whom he met through Philip Cowen) once he had moved from Philadelphia to New York in 1877. We have some evidence that Max Cohen did not know Cyrus Sulzberger prior to his arrival in New York, based on Philip Cowen's memorial tribute to Sulzberger, in which he remarks, "When he [Sulzberger] came to New York in 1877 I was the only person that he knew." *American Hebrew*, May 6, 1932, vol. 130, no. 25, p. 636. The correspondence between Solis-Cohen, Sulzberger, and Cohen reveals the depth of their closeness as early as 1879.

9. In his memoir, Cowen recalls that he and Greenbaum knew each other through the close friendship of their fathers, and that the Greenbaum, Cowen, and Cohen families were all members of the same synagogue, Adereth El in New York City. In addition, we learn that Cyrus Sulzberger became principal of the synagogue's religious school, and he eventually married Daniel Hays' sister Rachel Hays, who assisted Sulzberger at the school. Sulzberger and Hays were also members of Shearith Israel congregation. Cowen, *Memories*, pp. 28–30. These early relationships grew through their adulthood. For example, building on their friendship, Daniel P. Hays and Samuel Greenbaum opened the law practice of Hays & Greenbaum in 1884, a partnership that lasted until 1900, when Greenbaum was appointed to the New York State Supreme Court. See *American Hebrew*, August 29, 1930, vol. 127, no. 5, p. 396.

10. Cowen, p. 24, pp. 129–30.

11. Adler, who is considered to be the youngest of this peer group, and who was only sixteen years old at the time of the founding of the *American Hebrew*, was given the role of "Philadelphia correspondent." Adler, *I Have Considered the Days* (Philadelphia: Jewish Publication Society, 1941), p. 33. He was not a member of the editorial board until 1894, when he replaced Jacob Fonesca da Silva Solis, upon his death. Cowen, *Memories*, p. 43. It is also relevant to note Adler's familial connections to other members of this peer circle. In addition to being the younger cousin of Mayer Sulzberger, who was one of this group's primary mentors (and who will be discussed in chapter 2), Adler's uncle, David Sulzberger (with whom Adler lived after the death of his father), was a half brother of Cyrus L. Sulzberger (their father was Leopold Sulzberger). Despite the closeness in their ages, Cyrus Adler was also the nephew of Cyrus L. Sulzberger (Adler's mother, Sarah

Sulzberger, was Leopold Sulzberger's sister). See the Sulzberger family tree in the *Jewish Encyclopedia* (New York: Funk and Wagnalls, 1905), vol. 11, p. 585.

12. Mary M. Cohen, a writer, teacher, and devoted student (even if not formally so) of Sabato Morais, contributed numerous writings to the *Association Review* and *American Hebrew*. Nina Morais was the daughter of Rev. Sabato Morais of Congregation Mikveh Israel, who played a primary role in the formative religious and education development of the Philadelphia segment of this young peer group, including Solomon Solis-Cohen, Cyrus Adler, Mary M. Cohen, and Cyrus Sulzberger during his early years in Philadelphia. Nina Morais also contributed writings and essays to several Jewish publications, and was devoted to Jewish communal leadership and education. Henrietta Szold, who lent her literary, intellectual, and communal energies to many of this group's later projects, was the daughter of Rabbi Benjamin Szold of Congregation Oheb Shalom of Baltimore. Rabbi Benjamin Szold worked closely with Rabbi Marcus Jastrow of Rodeph Shalom of Philadelphia to formulate a more conservative approach to reform. Along with Morais, Jastrow was also one of this group's primary teachers.

13. Of course, the youngest members of this peer group, such as Cyrus Adler and Henrietta Szold, saw little of Civil War America, as they were born in 1863 and 1860, respectively. Solomon Solis-Cohen (b. 1857) and Cyrus Sulzberger (b. 1858) were young children during the war. The older members, born in 1853 or 1854, such as P. Cowen, D. Hays, Max Cohen, S. Greenbaum, and Mary Cohen, were already school-age children during the war, and it can be assumed that it made an impact on both their American identity and Jewish identity as they watched their country and community debate both national issues and controversies affecting American Jewry. This may have especially been true for those who had older siblings or relatives involved directly in the war. On the impact of the Civil War on American Jewry see Bertram Korn, *American Jewry and the Civil War* (Philadelphia: Jewish Publication Society, 1951), especially pp. 32–188, 217–219. The rise of antisemitism in Europe and America was a growing crisis seen by all members of the group. In particular, the infamous incidents of antisemitism in America during the 1870s, Austin Corbin's explicit exclusion of Jews from Coney Island and the Hilton-Seligman Saratoga affair, were likely formative events in their lives.

14. The exceptions to this were Samuel Greenbaum, who was born in London but was brought to America at the age of three; and brothers Frederic de Sola Mendes (born in Jamaica) and H. P. Mendes (born in England), who came to America as young rabbis (trained in Europe) to take pulpits in New York City. Another exception was Daniel P. Hays, who was born in America, but whose parents were both American-born descendants of prominent American Jewish families.

15. The Philadelphians were among the cultural and civic elite of the community, and even though they were not extraordinarily wealthy, their parents were leaders and influential members of Philadelphia's charitable associations and civic institutions. In New York, the families were also "uptowners," although they were certainly not the financial peers of the Seligmans, Warburgs, Schiffs, and the other members of New York's "Our Crowd." Regardless of geographic location, nearly all the young Jews in our study enjoyed comfortable economic standing, but were not among the highest economic elite

among Americans or even American Jews. In this way, comparisons drawn between Philadelphia and New York that have concluded that Philadelphians were the intellectual-spiritual force while New Yorkers provided the financial capital likely would not apply to this group of young Jewish New Yorkers (i.e., Cowen, Cohen, Greenbaum, Hays, et al.). See, e.g., J. Sarna, "Alternative to New York," *Commentary* 78, 4 (1984), p. 75; Sarna, *JPS*, p. 21; and David Dalin, "Patron Par Excellence: Mayer Sulzberger and the Early Seminary," in Wertheimer, ed., *Tradition Renewed*, vol. 1, pp. 660–61. These Philadelphians and New Yorkers seem to have drawn equally from their shared intellectual and financial resources in creating and promoting their Jewish communal agenda. And while it is true that many of their projects were later supported financially by such important benefactors as Jacob Schiff, it is clear that the day-to-day practical and intellectual work of creating and managing these projects was squarely in the hands of both the New York and Philadelphia contingents. Schiff, while certainly enabling many of these projects to succeed through his financial support, was not part of the group's inner circle during their early years (he did not arrive in America until 1875 at the age of twenty-eight). Naomi W. Cohen, *Jacob H. Schiff: A Study in American Jewish Leadership* (Hanover, NH: Brandeis University Press, 1999), chapter 1. Even Cyrus L. Sulzberger, who eventually became a wealthy businessman, was not yet wealthy during his early years. While recent scholarship has begun to illuminate the influential role of Philadelphia Jewry in the nineteenth and early twentieth centuries—the so-called "Philadelphia Group"—it seems that the New York segment of their peer group—including such young leaders as Daniel P. Hays, Max Cohen, Samuel Greenbaum, Philip Cowen, and Cyrus L. Sulzberger—have yet to be fully recognized for their contributions to Jewish cultural vitality during this period. In historical perspective, these New York Jewish leaders often seem to be overshadowed both by their wealthier and more politically influential counterparts from New York, such as Jacob Schiff and Louis Marshall, on the one hand, and by the rising Eastern European immigrant population of New York at the end of the nineteenth century, on the other.

16. The most notable exceptions to this rule were Frederic de Sola Mendes and his brother H. P. Mendes, who were both European-trained rabbis but who were also not born or raised in America.

17. It should not be assumed, however, that "progressive" necessarily meant religious reform in the context of either Europe or America, but rather a general affinity toward modernity. This could be embodied in a gradual approach to ritual change, openness toward science and secular knowledge, acceptance of the limited use of the vernacular, and contemporary aesthetics in the synagogue.

18. Solomon Solis-Cohen, *Judaism and Science* (Philadelphia: Private printing, 1940).

19. Philip Rosen notes that despite the family's emphasis on the maternal line, "nevertheless, an examination of his lifelong pursuit and contributions to the American Jewish community show a compatibility of ideas and philosophy with American Jews of German descent." Philip Rosen, "Dr. Solomon Solis-Cohen and the Philadelphia Group," in Friedman, ed., *When Philadelphia Was the Capital of Jewish America*, pp. 106–8. The

question of cultural influence within the so-called "Philadelphia Group" has important implications for our understanding of the intellectual and cultural legacy of late-nineteenth- and twentieth-century American Judaism. Arthur Kiron has argued that the figure of Sabato Morais—who was born and educated in Italy—may stand at the heart of this question. Kiron questions the long-held assumption of the German and Historical School's influence on Morais (and we might conclude on his disciples as well), and offers substantial proof for the influence of Italian-Sephardic humanism and other European general and Jewish ideological trends on Morais' thinking. See Arthur Kiron, "Varieties of Haskalah: Sabato Morais' Program of Sephardi Rabbinic Humanism in Victorian America," in Russ Brann and Adam Sutcliffe, eds., *Renewing the Past, Reconfiguring Jewish Culture: From al-Andalus to the Haskalah* (Philadelphia: University of Pennsylvania Press, 2004), pp. 121–45. Others have argued that many of the institutions created by Morais and his disciples were rooted in the German-Jewish ideologies of *Bildung, Wissenschaft*, and the religious-intellectual values of the Breslau Jewish Theological Seminary. Bertram Korn, for example, asserts that, "American Jewish life . . . represents a direct continuation of the effort of post-Emancipation European (primarily German) Jewry to create a new intellectual and spiritual rationale for Jewish identity. The American Jewish community is the primary heir of the intellectual achievements of German Jewry—the movements and trends in German Jewish life which resulted from the struggle to rationalize life in the two worlds of the Jewish tradition and modern society. The outlines of American Jewish cultural and intellectual life were in large measure engendered by German Jewish thinkers." See Bertram Korn, *German Jewish Intellectual Influences on American Jewish Life, 1824–1972*, B. G. Rudolph Lectures in Judaic Studies (Syracuse, NY: Syracuse University, April 1972). Similarly, Moshe Davis' study on the Historical School and Conservative Judaism in America (upon which Morais had an enormous impact) emphasizes German-Jewish intellectual influences. See Moshe Davis, *The Emergence of Conservative Judaism* (Philadelphia: Jewish Publication Society, 1963). While Kiron's argument provides an important corrective to an American Jewish historiography that has perhaps placed too much emphasis on the German-Jewish intellectual and cultural influences on nineteenth- and early-twentieth-century American Jewish life, it is likely that the intellectual currents of both schools were at play, particularly for the group of leaders in Philadelphia, where Morais' influence shared a stage with the German-oriented religious and intellectual legacies of Isaac Leeser (who was of German origin, despite his leadership of the Portuguese Mikveh Israel), as well as with Marcus Jastrow (of Poland, but who was closely associated with the Breslau intellectuals—in particular, historian Heinrich Graetz), Benjamin Szold (of Hungary, and who was himself ordained at the Breslau Theological Seminary), Alexander Kohut (after his arrival in America in the 1880s, also ordained at the Breslau Seminary), and even reformers such as Samuel Hirsch (b. Prussia), Adolph Huebsch (b. Hungary), Gustav Gottheil (b. Posen), and Kaufman Kohler (b. Bavaria). Other rabbinical influences, such as Samuel Myer Isaacs (b. Holland) and George Jacobs (b. Jamaica) straddled the Ashkenazic-Portuguese divide. Another influential figure in the lives of this group was Mayer Sulzberger, who was born in Germany, and came to Philadelphia as a child in the wake of the failed German Revolutions of 1848–1849. While not a rabbi, Mayer Sulzberger stood as an important role model and mentor, especially for the young Philadelphians who were largely at least ten years his junior. Sulzberger was the most well-known disciple of Leeser, and likely was a primary conduit for transmitting Leeser's ideas and values to his younger peers (many of whom were only young children at the time of Leeser's death). In the case of Solomon Solis-Cohen, although he himself was closely aligned with Morais, and although the family remained members of Mikveh Israel after the departure of Leeser to Beth El Emeth in 1857 (as did Mayer Sulzberger's family and the other families from this group), it is clear that the family held the figure and legacy of Leeser in the highest regard. Indeed, Solomon Solis-Cohen's youngest brother was named Isaac Leeser Solis-Cohen, in honor of this great American Jewish leader.

20. NMAJH, Solomon Solis-Cohen Collection File 1, Drawer 1, 84.44.1: "Jewish Affairs 1879" and "Jewish Affairs 1880."

21. It is interesting to note that while the Philadelphia families of the group were all members of the traditional-Portuguese Mikveh Israel synagogue, the families of the New Yorkers were members of the traditional-Ashkenazic Adereth-El. While it does seem, however, that many of the New Yorkers maintained certain connections to Shearith Israel, either through early education or eventual membership, it is clear that they did not align themselves with the German-reform Emanu-El synagogue. Regardless of the details of their formal synagogue membership, they were also influenced intellectually and religiously by the writings and sermons of such prominent New York religious leaders as Samuel Myer Isaacs (Shaaray Tefila), Rev. J. J Lyons (Shearith Israel), Rev. Gustav Gottheil (Emanu-El), and Rev. Adolph Huebsch (Ahavat Hesed). It can also be assumed that as their peers, the young rabbis Dr. Frederic de Sola Mendes and Henry (Haim) P. Mendes, arose to the religious leadership of Shaaray Tefila and Shearith Israel in the mid-1870s, respectively, Cohen and others increasingly came under their sphere of influence as well.

22. In one letter he remarks, "To revert for a moment to a thought I gleaned from reading your essay [Solomon Solis-Cohen's "Occident and Orient" (1878)]. The Occident has built a railroad connecting Phil + N.Y. with rapid communication, but alas! poor me! This needs time and money. The Orient would not let us live apart. When you can spare a few minutes, write to me and spend the time when you can." Max Cohen to Solomon Solis-Cohen, New York, October 14, 1879, NMAJH, Solomon Solis-Cohen Collection, File 1, Drawer 1, 84.44.1: "Jewish Affairs 1879." Elsewhere, he describes the effort amongst the two to maintain a high level of intellectual and spiritual discourse: "In such a stress of affairs," Cohen writes, "I would not trust myself to write you, as I wish very much to keep our correspondence from drifting into the gossipy t—pical[?], but to retain it on the plane on which we have instituted it. As an example of this exalted aspiration, I will begin to speak of myself." Cohen goes on to discuss the reception of his essay the "Restoration of the Jews." See Max Cohen to Solomon Solis-Cohen, New York, December 22, 1879, NMAJH, Solomon Solis-Cohen Collection, File 1, Drawer 1, 84.44.1: "Jewish Affairs 1879."

23. *American Jewish Year Book* (hereafter *AJYB*) 5665 (1904–5), p. 76.

24. Sophie Lindauer was Leopold Sulzberger's second wife.

25. Morris Waldman, "Cyrus L. Sulzberger," *AJYB* 5694 (1933–34), p. 145.

26. Henry Morais, *The Jews of Philadelphia* (Philadelphia: The Levytype Company, 1894), p. 58. *Jewish Encyclopedia*, vol. 11, p. 584.

27. The quotation is from David de Sola Pool's memorial address given at Sulzberger's funeral. Morris D. Waldman, "Cyrus L. Sulzberger," *AJYB* 5694 (1933–34), p. 156. Also quoted in Leon Freeman, "Cyrus L. Sulzberger Served Well," *American Hebrew*, May 6, 1932, vol. 130, no. 25, p. 635.

28. Waldman, "Cyrus L. Sulzberger," p. 152.

29. In his tribute to Sulzberger, H. P. Mendes of Shearith Israel writes: "Cyrus Sulzberger removed to New York and naturally joined the Synagogue of which his own in Philadelphia was the daughter. A further and a powerful attachment to the mother-Synagogue was formed by his choosing for a wife one of the esteemed daughters of the congregations, Rachel Hays [sister of Daniel P. Hays]." *American Hebrew*, May 6, 1932, vol. 130, no. 25, p. 636.

30. By the end of his life, Sulzberger was considered one of the "Big Four" American Jewish philanthropist-spokesmen alongside Jacob Schiff, Louis Marshall, and Nathan Bijur. *American Hebrew*, May 6, 1932, vol. 130, no. 25, pp. 636, 648.

31. We will continue our examination of this phase of the YMHA movement in a subsequent chapter.

32. We are fortunate to have a detailed autobiographical account of Cowen's life in his memoir, *Memories of an American Jew*. Philip Cowen and Cyrus Adler were the only two members of the group's inner circle to publish their memoirs, which are extraordinary sources for the study of American Jewry in the late nineteenth and early twentieth centuries. See Cowen, *Memories*, and Adler, *I Have Considered the Days*.

33. Cowen, *Memories*, p. 28.

34. Cowen, *Memories*, p. 34.

35. The editorial dynamics of the *American Hebrew* will be dealt with further in the next chapter.

36. It is also interesting to note that Daniel P. Hays' wife, Rachel Hershfield, also traced her ancestry to the time of the American Revolution. *American Hebrew*, November 30, 1923, vol. 114, no. 3, p. 48; *AJYB* 5666 (1905–6), p. 67.

37. The *American Hebrew* quotes from a funeral address offered by Dr. Maurice Harris (Temple Israel, N.Y.): "We can ill spare one in whom this religious quality so luminously shone. It is to be explained in part from his poetic nature—for he was a poet, too. The religious and the poetic merge one in the other, both discern the beautiful in the common place and give to daily life the sublimating touch." *American Hebrew*, November 30, 1923, vol. 114, no. 3, p. 49. In his memoir, Philip Cowen describes Daniel P. Hays as "the poet-laureate of our group." Cowen, *Memories*, p. 41.

38. Quoted in *American Hebrew*, November 30, 1923, vol. 114, no. 3, p. 48.

39. *American Hebrew*, November 30, 1923, vol. 114, no. 3, p. 49.

40. In a fascinating letter reacting to an upcoming 1912 commencement coinciding

with the twenty-fifth anniversary of JTS, Solomon Solis-Cohen writes to Edgar Nathan to express his concern over the neglect of the early seminary and its activists (including such figures as Max Cohen, Daniel P. Hays, Philip Cowen, and others). In the letter, Solis-Cohen alludes to the fact that it was this very neglect of the early founders (and likely the lack of consideration for their original purposes and posture toward the school) that may have led some, such as Hays and Frederic de Sola Mendes, who were among the more liberal of the original group—yet certainly moderate—to withdraw from the institution's leadership and align with competing institutions. Hence, the letter reads: "Interesting information [about the early founders] can also be gotten from the files of the *American Hebrew*, which will give the history of the beginnings. For example, F. de Sola Mendes and his congregation took part. I believe they are now on the other side of the fence, as is also D. P. Hays. Whose is the fault? This is a serious matter, because we need all the support we can get, and shutting the door and turning our back is not exactly an invitation to enter. . . . My idea is that a foundation of some kind, scholarship, fellowship, professorship, or something, should be named in honor of the founders not yet recognized . . . hence, there might be a Szold foundation or a Szold-Jastrow foundation . . . or . . . simply a Founders' scholarship. . . . Hertz should receive an honorary degree . . . by ignoring the old Seminary you simply ignore your claim to having furnished a chief rabbi to England. . . . Also, every one who was an officer or teacher of the old Seminary should be specifically invited to attend. . . . This may seem like a trivial matter, but I can assure you it is not. . . . In other words, your next commencement should be devoted to acknowledgment and recognition of the pioneers and their achievements. . . . Your committee ought to inquire into all these matters and set them straight. You can imagine all the indignation that I have bottled up these many years for the sake of the cause, for what I have told you is not one-tenth. Now is the golden—or at least silver—opportunity to make all right." Solomon Solis-Cohen to Edgar Nathan, March 29, 1912, Solomon Solis-Cohen Collection, NMAJH, File 3, Drawer 1, "Addenda."

41. *AJYB* 5665 (1904–5), pp. 105–6. *American Hebrew*, August 29, 1930, vol. 127, no. 15, p. 396.

42. Cowen, *Memories*, p. 24.

43. *American Hebrew*, August 29, 1930, vol. 127, no. 15, p. 396. *AJYB* 5665 (1904–5), pp. 105–6.

44. Adler, *I Have Considered the Days*, pp. 7–11.

45. Ira Robinson, "Cyrus Adler, the Philadelphian," in Friedman, ed., *When Philadelphia Was the Capital of Jewish America*, pp. 92–105.

46. Cyrus Adler to Sabato Morais, November 7, 1883, in Ira Robinson, *Cyrus Adler: Selected Letters*, vol. 1 (Philadelphia: Jewish Publication Society, 1985), p. 5.

47. Adler, *I Have Considered the Days*, pp. 38–40.

48. Adler, *I Have Considered the Days*, pp. 20–21.

49. Adler, *I Have Considered the Days*, p. 33; Cowen, *Memories*, p. 43.

50. Solomon Solis-Cohen, Cyrus Adler, Cyrus L. Sulzberger, Mary M. Cohen, and Nina Morais were all tradition-oriented Jews who were members of Mikveh Israel.

51. Sabato Morais, "Eulogy for Henry Cohen," June 20, 1879. Quoted in Henry Morais, *Jews of Philadelphia*, pp. 66–67.

52. Max Cohen to Solomon Solis-Cohen, New York, August 18, 1880, Solomon Solis-Cohen Collection, NMAJH, "Jewish Affairs 1880."

53. Cowen, *Memories*, pp. 34–35.

54. Cowen, *Memories*, p. 22.

55. "The Sabbath: An Appeal to the Israelites of New York," in *Jewish Messenger*, August 21, 1868, pp. 2–3. In addition to Cowen, the families of Samuel Greenbaum, Max Cohen, Daniel P. Hays, and Cyrus Sulzberger were also members of Adereth-El.

56. Max Cohen to Solomon Solis-Cohen, December 25, 1879, Solomon Solis Cohen Collection, NMAJH, File 1, Drawer 1, 84.44.1: "Jewish Affairs 1879."

57. Moshe Davis, *The Emergence of Conservative Judaism*, pp. 349–51.

58. Henry Morais, *Jews of Philadelphia*, p. 319–20; *AJYB* 5666 (1905-6), p. 49.

59. *AJYB* 5665 (1904-5), pp. 54–55, 77–78; *AJYB* 5666 (1905-6), p. 107.

60. Cowen, *Memories*, p. 25. *AJYB* 5665 (1904-5), pp. 76, 79, 105–6, 112. It is also interesting to note that many of their future spouses also attended the public schools, including Selina (Ullman) Greenbaum (married to Samuel Greenbaum), Rachel (Hershfield) Hays (married to Daniel P. Hays), and Rachel (Hays) Sulzberger (married to Cyrus L. Sulzberger), *AJYB* 5666 (1905-6), pp. 64, 67.

61. Adler, *I Have Considered the Days*, pp. 12–13. Most began their studies at the Hebrew Education Society and then transferred over to the Central High School, probably by their early teens, where they would receive their B.A. and M.A. degrees.

62. Adler, *I Have Considered the Days*, pp. 15–16, pp. 38–42. Mikveh Israel was traditional-Portuguese, Rodeph Shalom was moderate or conservative-Reform, Kenneseth Israel was radical reform, and Beth El Emeth, which was created as a pulpit for Isaac Leeser after his dismissal from Mikveh Israel, was traditional.

63. Adler, *I Have Considered the Days*, p. 39.

64. Adler, *I Have Considered the Days*, pp. 39–40.

65. Adler, *I Have Considered the Days*, p. 38.

66. Cowen, *Memories*, p. 28.

67. There is little biographical source material available about Greenbaum, Cohen, and Hays during their early years, specifically their Jewish education and religious home life. We do know, however, that the Hays family was also members of the Shearith Israel congregation, and it is likely that Daniel P. Hays, like Cowen, was also educated under its auspices.

68. It is not clear, therefore, to what extent each one seriously considered the rabbinate before choosing other careers, with the exception of Solis-Cohen, for whom we have evidence of his consideration of the rabbinate. See A. S. Isaacs to Solomon Solis-Cohen, May 10, 1882, Solomon Solis-Cohen Collection, NMAJH, "Jewish Affairs 1881."

69. See Harold S. Wechsler, "Pulpit or Professoriate: The Case of Morris Jastrow, Jr.," *American Jewish History* 74, 4 (1984), pp. 338–55.

70. Abram S. Isaacs (1852–1920), American rabbi and son of Rabbi Samuel Myer

Isaacs (Shaaray Tefila, N.Y.), trained at the conservative Breslau Theological Seminary; co-editor of New York's *Jewish Messenger*.

71. A. S. Isaacs to Solomon Solis-Cohen, May 10, 1881, Solomon Solis-Cohen Collection, NMAJH, "Jewish Affairs 1881."

72. We do have evidence of Solis-Cohen's financial concerns and his consideration of practical matters in choosing his career. See, for example, Cyrus Sulzberger to Solomon Solis-Cohen, n.d., "Tuesday Midnight" (1880?), Solomon Solis-Cohen Collection, NMAJH, "Jewish Affairs 1880."

73. In the case of Solomon Solis-Cohen, his reluctance to leave Philadelphia seems to have rested on at least three major concerns: first, the death of his father and his subsequent responsibility to care for his widowed mother; second, his desire to continue his studies; and third, his ability to observe the Sabbath. These three issues are addressed in a letter from Cyrus L. Sulzberger to Solis-Cohen, where Cyrus lays out the "pros" and "cons" of what seems to have been a job offered to Solis-Cohen in the western part of the country. Among the list of "cons" is the following remark: "You, the eldest son at home, would be compelled to leave your widowed mother. You would be compelled to give up—temporarily at least—your studies. I doubt whether after a few years you would not have to begin almost entirely anew. If you want to continue studying, it is immaterial whether you are worth a few $ more or less as brains not capital would furnish the foundation of your business. By no means least, Shabat! Can you observe it? Remember how all important this is. Whatever other inducements there may be do not lose sight of this." See Cyrus Sulzberger to Solomon Solis-Cohen, n.d., "Tuesday Midnight" (1880?), Solomon Solis-Cohen Collection, NMAJH, "Jewish Affairs 1880." While the letter is not referring to the decision of entering a seminary (either in Cincinnati or Europe), it does shed light on Solis-Cohen's education and career choices at this point in his life.

74. See n. 73.

75. Philip Cowen to Solomon Solis-Cohen, June 27, 1880, Solomon Solis-Cohen Collection, NMAJH, File 1, Drawer 1, 84.44.1: "Jewish Affairs 1880 #1."

76. Solomon Solis-Cohen, for example, received his M.A. degree in 1877, and graduated from Jefferson Medical College in 1883.

77. Isaacs' letter was written in May of 1881, in the immediate wake of the radical shift in Russian Jewry's position, triggered by the March assassination of Czar Alexander II, followed by waves of pogroms in the spring, which led to a new phase of immigration by Russian Jews to America.

78. Adler writes in his memoir: "My uncle [David Sulzberger] I think set great store for me in many ways. . . . His ideal for me was that I was to be a good Jewish scholar, a good general scholar, a lawyer—in order to support myself; I was then to give myself to the Jewish people as a sort of lay rabbi, with any additional duties that might arise." Cyrus Adler, *I Have Considered the Days*, p. 12.

79. We can be sure, however, that American Jews and their leaders, even in the most confident of generations, continued to feel that they needed to make known Jewish patriotic contributions to American civic life. Hence we see the move toward a systematic

chronicling of American Jewish participation in American politics, military, and general culture as part of the project of American Jewish awakening, most notably in the creation of the American Jewish Historical Society.

80. Butler's remarks were published in the *Jewish Messenger*, February 26, 1864. Matilda Cohen to Gen. Benjamin Butler, Philadelphia, February 28, 1864, Charles and Mary M. Cohen Collection, CAJS, MS 3, Box 3, FF 18.

81. Matilda Cohen to Gen. Benjamin Butler, Philadelphia, February 28, 1864, Charles and Mary Cohen Collection, CAJS, MS 3, Box 3, FF 18.

82. Max Cohen to Solomon Solis-Cohen, New York, October 14, 1879, NMAJH, Solomon Solis-Cohen Collection, File 1, Drawer 1, 84.44.1: "1879 Jewish Affairs."

83. This attempt to reintroduce and strengthen Jewish identity among American Jewish youth might be compared to the process of "dissimilation" discussed by Shulamit Volkov in reference to German Jewry at the turn of the twentieth century, when antisemitism, nationalism, Eastern European migration, and growing ethnic diversity in Central Europe led to a gradual rejection of the mid-nineteenth-century assimilationist ethic in Germany. See Shulamit Volkov, "The Dynamics of Dissimilation" in Jehuda Reinharz and Walter Schatzberg, eds., *The Jewish Response to German Culture* (Hanover, NH: University Press of New England, 1985), pp. 195–211.

84. The emergence of Hebrew Sunday Schools, Jewish day schools, Jewish periodicals, published translations of Jewish literature and foundational religious sources, the Charleston Reform movement, new congregations geared toward American Jewish youth and young families, Jewish charities and voluntary associations, all attest to a revitalization of American Jewry during the early nineteenth century. For a description of American Jewry in the early decades of the nineteenth century, see Ira Rosenwaike, *On the Edge of Greatness: A Portrait of American Jewry in the Early National Period* (Cincinnati: American Jewish Archives, 1985); Malcolm Stern, "The 1820s: American Jewry Comes of Age," in Jonathan D. Sarna, ed., *The American Jewish Experience* (New York: Holmes and Meier Publishers, 1986); Jonathan D. Sarna, *Jacksonian Jew* (New York: Holmes and Meier Publishers, 1981); Sarna, *American Judaism*; Dianne Ashton, *Rebecca Gratz: Women and Judaism in Antebellum America* (Detroit: Wayne State University Press, 1997); Lance Sussman, *Isaac Leeser and the Making of American Judaism* (Detroit: Wayne State University Press, 1995); Sarna, "Cult of Synthesis in American Jewish Culture," *Jewish Social Studies* 5 (Fall–Winter 1999), pp. 52–79; For Philadelphia, see Edwin Wolf 2nd and Maxwell Whiteman, eds., *The History of the Jews of Philadelphia from Colonial Times to the Age of Jackson* (Philadelphia: Jewish Publication Society, 1957); Murray Friedman, ed., *Jewish Life in Philadelphia, 1840–1940* (Philadelphia: American Jewish Committee, 1983). For New York, see Hyman Grinstein, *The Rise of the Jewish Community of New York, 1654–1860* (Philadelphia: Jewish Publication Society, 1945).

85. Sarna, "The Cult of Synthesis in American Jewish Culture," *Jewish Social Studies* 5 (1998/1999), pp. 52–79; Stern, "American Jewry Comes of Age," in Sarna, ed., *American Jewish Experience*.

86. It is quite striking to see the similarities between American Jewry in the early decades of the nineteenth century on the eve of the first mass migration from Central Eu-

rope and American Jewry from the end of the Civil War to the early 1880s on the eve of the mass migration from Eastern Europe. In both cases we find a relatively small community that had spent recent years strengthening, building, and transforming its institutional and communal foundations. These new and revived institutions would both enable the absorption of large numbers of new Jewish immigrants, while at the same time realize their dependence on the vitality of the newcomers for their growth and continued success. We find in both periods an affinity of American and Jewish values, forms, and institutions. Not surprisingly, it was this very Americanized Judaism that, in both periods, attracted, transformed, and yet repelled the newcomers, motivating them to define their own expressions of Judaism in their new land of adoption.

87. The process of Jewish identity transformation in response to Jewish emancipation has been well documented by scholars. See, e.g., David Sorkin, *The Transformation of German Jewry, 1780–1840* (New York: Oxford University Press, 1987); George Mosse, *German Jews beyond Judaism* (Cincinnati: Hebrew Union College Press, 1985); Marion Kaplan, *The Making of the Jewish Middle Class: Women, Family, and Identity in Imperial Germany* (New York: Oxford University Press, 1991).

88. The shift toward Jewish "renaissance" and assertion of new categories of Jewish identity from the late nineteenth century through the Weimar period has been the subject of much recent scholarship. See, e.g., Michael Brenner, *The Renaissance of Jewish Culture in Weimar Germany* (New Haven: Yale University Press, 1996); George Mosse, *Germans and Jews* (Detroit: Wayne State University Press, 1982); Jehuda Reinharz, *Fatherland or Promised Land: The Dilemma of the German Jew, 1893–1914* (Ann Arbor: University of Michigan Press, 1975); Reinharz and Schatzberg, eds., *The Jewish Response to German Culture*; Steven Aschheim, *Brothers and Strangers* (Madison: University of Wisconsin Press, 1987).

89. This is not to say that it was only American-born Jews (or post-emancipation German Jews) who were instrumental in asserting such a program. Certainly, young American-born Jews drew from the wisdom, cooperation, and projects of their foreign-born elders and peers, as well as Jewish leaders and institutions in Europe. I also would not dismiss the impact of anti-Jewish sentiment itself on motivating Jewish communities to assert their identity more positively and confidently, for the sake of defense as well as morale. Nevertheless, it seems likely that one's status vis-à-vis one's national-political entity may have as much of an impact as other factors, such as antisemitism, fear of Jewish apathy, intermarriage, ignorance of Jewish sources and rituals, upswings in missionary activity toward the Jews, communal crisis, and changing rhetoric of minority, ethnicity, or religion in the larger culture, on motivating periods of Jewish communal and cultural awakening.

GRAND REVIVAL

OF THE

Jewish National Holiday of Chanucka,

ACADEMY OF MUSIC,

TUESDAY, DECEMBER 16th, 1879.

The greatest Jewish event chronicled in Post-Biblical History, the recollection of which ever awakens the true Jewish spirit and patriotism, will be celebrated by the

Young Men's Hebrew Association,

in a manner and style never before equalled, and worthy the subject and occasion.

Living representations of the stirring scenes and glowing events of the Maccabean war and triumph will be vividly protrayed, concluding with a grand procession of the return of the victorious heroes.

The tableaux will be under the direction of Prof. CARL MARWIG, the genius of Children's Carnival Balls.

Costumes new and original, historically correct, and specially designed to illustrate the Maccabean period.

Choruses of Hebrew Melodies will be rendered by 100 children of the Hebrew Orphan Asylum.

Music by an Orchestra of 100 performers.

GRAND BALL AFTER THE TABLEAUX.

The prices of admission have been fixed to enable all to join in this Jewish National Celebration. Gentleman's ticket, $2.00; Ladies' ticket, $1.00.

Tickets for sale at the Association Rooms, 110 West 42d Street, and by the following gentlemen:

DANIEL P. HAYS, 170 Broadway.   MORRIS S. WISE, 291 Broadway.   U. HERRMANN, 67 Pine St.
H. M. LEIPZIGER, 413 E. 58th St.   M. SOLOMONS, 110 W. 42d St.   A. L. SANGER, 117 Broadway.
H. P. BINSWANGER, 43 John St.   S. J. LEVY, 564 Broadway.   J. KLABER, 223 W. 51st St.
A. E. KARELSEN, 69 Nassau St.   Dr. E. HOCHHEIMER, 315 E. 4th St.   M. LIPPMANN, 368 Broadway.
MITCHELL HERSHFIELD, 293 Broadway.

Reserved Seats and Boxes for sale at the ASSOCIATION ROOMS, and by MAX D. STERN, Treas., 32 Broadway.

Courtesy of 92nd Street Y Archives

2 On the Road to Renaissance

*The Young Men's Hebrew Associations of New York
and Philadelphia, 1877–1883*

In recent years, American Jewish historians have come to recognize that
the roots of the great institutions of American Jewish culture at the turn
of the twentieth century lay in the highly innovative, and overwhelmingly
indigenous, leadership of the so-called "Philadelphia" and "New York" Jewish intellectuals during the last quarter of the nineteenth century.[1] The great
institutions and projects that have become synonymous with twentieth-century
American Jewish cultural activity—The Jewish Theological Seminary, the
Jewish Publication Society, the American Jewish Historical Society, and the
American Jewish Year Book—grew in great part out of the inspiration and
efforts of this circle of Jewish intellectuals. Through memoir literature, correspondence, and the work of historians and biographers, we have begun to
trace the achievements of such figures as Cyrus Adler, Mayer Sulzberger,
Solomon Solis-Cohen, Philip Cowen, and others, both as individuals and as
a common group of intellectuals. What remains to be written, however, is a
group portrait of these men—not as the polished intellectual leaders and
benefactors of great cultural and intellectual institutions—but rather as young
men, reacting as young intellectuals to their environment. Even in their
youthful aspirations and projects, one can recognize the seeds of a Jewish
renaissance, which flowered in their maturity as these figures took on greater
leadership in the Jewish community in the late 1880s. In order to produce
such a group portrait of these young men, we must turn our attention toward
one particular institution of this period, one that became the common meeting point for all of these figures in their youth—the Young Men's Hebrew
Association.[2]

The first Young Men's Hebrew Associations of this period were founded
in New York and Philadelphia, in 1874 and 1875, respectively; and they soon
spread outward, westward, and southward to include nearly every major city

in the United States.[3] They all shared certain common characteristics. They emphasized Jewish character building in adolescents and young men, they provided for social encounters between young Jewish men and women from different religious or geographic backgrounds, and they all expressed a degree of concern for the welfare of the larger Jewish community.[4] Many YMHAs offered lecture courses, entertainments of music and poetry, recreational and athletic facilities, language courses, academic competitions, club meetings, and, at their core, a library and reading room. While a comprehensive and interpretive history of the Young Men's Hebrew Associations remains to be written, the following essay will examine only the YMHAs of New York and Philadelphia.[5] The decision to limit my discussion to these two associations rests on the fact that they were often the trendsetters of the larger movement, and they are most pertinent to our larger discussion of the Philadelphia and New York young intellectuals.[6] My discussion of the Philadelphia and New York YMHAs will focus on the period during which the young Philadelphia and New York intellectuals were active in the Y, from approximately 1877 to 1883. It is my contention that it was during this period that the Young Men's Hebrew Associations became an undeniable force within the Jewish community, largely due to the young and extraordinarily articulate leadership of the aforementioned Philadelphia and New York intellectuals. Armed with the powerful spokesmanship of these young intellectuals, the Young Men's Hebrew Association underwent a substantial shift in focus and direction, turning intensively toward Jewish education and what we might call Jewish "renewal" work. It was during this time that these young men began to edit new publications on behalf of the YMHAs, beginning with the very small-scale *Association Review* (1877–1878), and eventually the larger and more sophisticated *Association Bulletin* (1881–1883). At the very same time as they devoted their energies to the Y movement, they began a much larger venture, whose aims went far beyond the associations through the publication of a national weekly, the *American Hebrew*. While this paper spoke to the larger Jewish (and non-Jewish) community, its message, as well as its editors, remained firmly grounded in the YMHAs. One can see clearly the fluidity of ideas between the internal association publications and the influential *American Hebrew*. For this reason, I will refer often to the *American Hebrew* as reflective, not only of the aims and concerns of these same young intellectuals, but also of the Young Men's Hebrew Associations as they evolved under their leadership. The present essay aims to explore the ideology of the YMHAs under the leadership of these young men. It will also ask two fundamental questions.

First, in what ways can the program of the New York and Philadelphia associations under the leadership of these intellectuals be characterized as Jewish renewal work, with both ethnic and religious overtones? Second, does the period coinciding with the leadership of this group reflect a unique, temporal moment in the longer history of the Young Men's Hebrew Associations? Did the agenda and ideology of the YMHA shift dramatically once these leaders matured and eventually abandoned the associations for more sophisticated and far-reaching projects? The overarching theme of this essay will be to understand the leadership of these young intellectuals in the YMHA as an early expression of the "Jewish Awakening," which so far has been identified with this group largely as more mature members of the community from the late 1880s through the turn of the century. My focus will therefore be the *nascent* Jewish awakening, or renewal, proposed and implemented by these well-known leaders as younger men in their late teens and early twenties, during the approximate years 1877–1883, before these men emerged as the new leaders of early-twentieth-century American Jewish culture.

The founding of the Young Men's Hebrew Association, first in New York in 1874 and then in Philadelphia in 1875, introduced a new setting for the socialization and education of young, largely second-generation Jews in America. The founders of these associations, however, were not, in the main, young men themselves. Louis May was at least fifty years old at the time he helped establish the New York association, and Mayer Sulzberger founded the Philadelphia association at the age of thirty-two. These men, and most of the other original founders and officers, were already well initiated into the Jewish community, and were highly recognized as established benefactors of Jewish cultural and institutional life.[7] In addition to the prominent Jacob Schiff were to be found Philip Joachimsen, president of the Board of Delegates of American Israelites, Myer Stern, president of the Hebrew Benevolent and Orphan Society, and Myer S. Isaacs, who founded the New York United Hebrew Charities.[8] These founders also relied on the heavy support of the most esteemed rabbis of the day, including Rabbi Gustav Gottheil and Rabbi Sabato Morais. One assumes from this that the early motivations for the associations originated from the "top"—with the concern of leading members of the Jewish community for the direction and well-being of the younger next generation. Within only a few years, however, a growing number of this younger generation came to assert their own voices in the association. These young men, categorized within the associations as "Associates," as opposed to the "Active" senior members, soon began to take responsibility for the direction of the associations.[9] With the persistence and dedication of such young men as Daniel P. Hays, Solomon Solis-Cohen, Cyrus Sulzberger, Samuel Greenbaum, Max Cohen, and eventually the younger Cyrus Adler, the original older leaders of the associations gradually began to hand the reins of leadership over to the young men themselves. With this transfer of power, the leadership of the associations came to better reflect its own constituency, the young men (and eventually women) toward whom the association was directed.

A foreshadowing of this transition can be detected as early as 1875, when younger associate members of the Philadelphia association began to form an informal organization of their own, asking for new demands and greater privileges, for example, rooms for their own associate meetings, and involvement with the membership committee. The older leaders either saw no harm in this or recognized the potential of these members, and granted their requests, excluding them only from holding their own separate entertainments.[10] By 1877, the associate organization began to show signs of greater formality and confidence, when it began to publish the proceedings of its meetings as *The Association Review* (1877–1878).[11] Not surprisingly, the editors of this publication were none other than our young intellectuals, who had begun to take a larger leadership role in the association, including Solomon Solis-Cohen and Cyrus Adler.[12] At the same time as they began the *Review*, the associate organization began to make waves at the board meetings, asking at one point for an annual appropriation of twenty-five dollars for its expenses.[13] The activism of the associate members must have made an impression on the older leadership, and there are indications that tension existed between the rising "Associates" and the established "Actives." In 1878, Mayer Sulzberger, in his farewell address as president of the Philadelphia association, offered the following remarks:

> In retiring . . . I offer a word of advice to Associate members. In their zeal they are apt to mistake the coolness and discretion of older heads for apathy and incapacity, and this may generate in them a desire to elect to the Board only such as they deem more direct representatives of their wishes and feelings. They should remember that the members of the Board are Trustees of money and valuable interests.[14]

Sulzberger's words reflect both an understanding of the spirit of the rising generation of leadership as well as an awareness that the association created by the older generation was quickly moving into the hands of the young men for whom it was created. One also sees in his message the evolving concerns of the younger generation, who clearly perceived the older generation as passive and unresponsive to the needs of the younger men. This concern is central for our discussion, as it lays the groundwork for the later efforts of these young leaders in changing the direction of the association to reflect their ideals. Philip Cowen, offering his own New York perspective on this dynamic, comments in his memoirs:

> In Philadelphia, [Cyrus] Sulzberger and Solis-Cohen were prominent among the associate members—as the junior group was known—and, like some of us here in New York, they were a thorn in the side of the older members. We thought we knew it all and wanted to put some life into the organization. Thus, our Quaker City friends started the publication of a monthly paper, *The Association Review*, that was a live wire.[15]

In both New York and Philadelphia, then, one can observe the agitation among younger members for a new direction for the association. As many of the advocates of these changes moved out of the associate group and into positions of leadership in the association around the years 1879–1880, the YMHA began to show signs of substantial transformation.

This period also marked the founding of the *American Hebrew*, a weekly paper based in New York, aimed at reaching a large cross-section of the Jewish community. The editors of this new paper were the very same young intellectuals (as well as a number of older intellectuals and leaders in the community) who were at this very time emerging as the new leaders of the New York and Philadelphia Young Men's Hebrew Associations. Philip Cowen, Solomon Solis-Cohen, Cyrus Sulzberger, Daniel P. Hays, Max Cohen, and Samuel Greenbaum, all in their twenties, and sixteen-year-old Cyrus Adler had in common their active membership and leadership in the Y. While the paper was not formally affiliated with the YMHAS, its layout illustrated its strong ties to the association. Similar to the way in which Isaac Mayer Wise's *American Israelite* highlighted the activities of the International Order of B'nai Brith (IOBB) in its columns, the *American Hebrew* featured the ongoing programs and activities of the Young Men's Hebrew Associations conspicuously in its pages. Just as the *Israelite* kept a permanent section on the IOBB, the *American Hebrew* maintained its own section for the YMHA. Within this section, as well as in its editorials, the *American Hebrew* advocated the development of the movement and championed its emerging ideology, as it was recognizably consistent with that of the paper's editors. One can see this, for example, in the December 12, 1879, issue of the *American Hebrew*, in which the front-page editorial (the liveliest part of the paper, written together by its editorial board) remarks at length on the importance of Hanukkah, hailing the efforts of the Young Men's Hebrew Association for its recent introduction of a community Hanukkah festival. It then continues in its second editorial to express its admiration for the strides that the association has taken in advancing the interests of the Jewish community.[16] It is no coincidence that the idea for an annual public celebration of Hanukkah originated only with the new leaders of the association, who were the very same young intellectuals who edited the *Hebrew*.[17] In the paper's weekly column, "Friday Night"— written in the form of dialogues intended to stimulate Sabbath observance by providing material for family discussion—one would often find issues and debates relating to the Young Men's Hebrew Association.[18] The *American Hebrew* also regularly published the minutes from the New York and Philadelphia associations' annual meetings and elections, and reported on the larger events of both the New York and Philadelphia associations.[19]

It was during this time as well that the associations developed new organizational structures under the efforts of our New York and Philadelphia young leaders. In 1880, the Philadelphia association proposed the creation of a union of all YMHAs, to be named the American Hebrew Association (1880– 1883).[20] The primary aim of the organization was to publish a national periodical, which would be distributed to the members of Young Men's Hebrew Associations around the country. Through this publication, *The Association Bulletin* (1881–1883), the American Hebrew Association hoped to arouse greater interest in the YMHAs, to help smaller societies strive for higher goals in Jewish orientation and education, and to allow for the lecture series and successful programs of the larger societies to be shared with the smaller societies. In the first issue of the *Bulletin*, its editors, Solomon Solis-Cohen and Cyrus Sulzberger, outlined its goals:

> That the higher aims of the societies may be furthered, that their true objects may be understood, that they may labor unitedly and with a better knowledge of the ends they seek to accomplish, and above all that societies distant from the centres of thought and activity may share with the larger and older ones the benefits these enjoy by reason of their more favored circumstances; this is the task the American Hebrew Association has undertaken.[21]

The American Hebrew Association, largely a product of the young intellectuals of the Philadelphia group, asserted a new agenda for the associations.

Under their guidance, the YMHA sought to redefine their aims. They perceived the earlier years of the associations as something of a preparatory period, which focused on building the organization and establishing it as an important institution within the Jewish community. Once this groundwork had been laid, and the security of the institution had been established, it could turn to more important aims, and higher purposes. These new aims centered around an intensified program of Jewish education and experience, geared toward revitalizing the young Jews faced with the challenges of indifference, assimilation, antisemitism, and faithlessness. The Young Men's Hebrew Associations under this new program worked to reconnect these young Jews with their heritage and their community, and to build up their knowledge and love of the Jewish people. Lectures and courses on contemporary Jewish topics, Jewish history and literature, and Hebrew moved to the forefront of programming. Through the American Hebrew Association, the young new leaders were able to impress upon the smaller associations the value and urgency of their new agenda. As they strove to encourage young Jews to read books on Jewish topics, and to help the associations expand the Judaic collections of their libraries, they discovered a larger need in the community. This need was for more works on Jewish topics in the English language. Already among these second-generation American Jews, German was becoming less and less familiar. The rising intellectuals, even as young men, appreciated and understood that in order to reach their own generation and coming generations of American Jews, a new scholarly and popular literature on Jewish subjects, written in English, was required. Empowered by this realization, our young intellectuals announced a proposal to launch a "Publication Union" through which they would assume the task, under the auspices of the Young Men's Hebrew Associations.[22] Their suggestion came in the form of a written dialogue, through the voice of the *American Hebrew*:

> "The Young Men's Hebrew Association can be a great power in this land. If they will only realize that the time has past, when the plea of 'necessity'—the old hackneyed formula that stands in the way of all progress—can excuse their devotion to amusing the public, to the exclusion of their legitimate functions."
> "What would you have them do?" ...
> "Well, for one thing, the assumption by the YMHA of the duties of the defunct Publication Society. ... It is true that there is a lamentable lack of works on Jewish history and Hebrew literature, written in the English language from a Jewish standpoint. But the Society could begin its labors by publishing translations from the French, German, and Italian, and a proper

system of inducing original works, would meet with gratifying success. There is an immense amount of talent and knowledge among Young Israel, that awaits only a fitting encouragement to manifest itself."[23]

This early proposal, like many of the youthful projects imagined by this group, would only come to fruition several years later, in their adulthood, with the establishment of the Jewish Publication Society of America in 1888.

The development of the American Hebrew Association (AHA) was an exciting but also a complicated time in the history of the movement. It coincided with a period of tension and distance between the New York and the Philadelphia YMHAs. When the Philadelphia association proposed the creation of a union, the New York association balked, agreeing reluctantly to attend the first meeting. The New York association, represented by Daniel P. Hays, remained at odds with the goals of the Philadelphians on two major points. First, the New York Association argued that it should have greater representation in the AHA than other associations, considering its large size. Second, it demanded that congregational associations be excluded from membership. When it was decided that all associations would have equal representation and that the AHA would welcome the congregational societies as members, the New York association withdrew its membership and its support for the union.[24] While Hays and the main New York association remained outside the American Hebrew Association, other New Yorkers, in particular Cyrus Sulzberger of the Anshe Chesed Congregation YMHA, were highly active in the union. Sulzberger, whose original membership was in the Philadelphia association before his move to New York, worked as coeditor with Solis-Cohen on the *Bulletin*.

This episode of tension between New York and Philadelphia was not the only one to occur during this period. In 1880, the Philadelphia YMHA, in response to news of the persecution of Russian Jews, wrote a statement addressed to the secretary of state condemning the situation of Russian Jewry, and sent it out to the other associations for signatures of support. This statement, written "in behalf of 250,000 Jewish citizens of the United States," triggered a furious debate among the associations, as well as within the larger Jewish community.[25] The reason for the debate was that it seemed to undermine the newly created Board of Delegates on Civil and Religious Rights under the auspices of the Union of American Hebrew Congregations, whose perceived role was to issue such statements on behalf of the larger Jewish community. The New York association was divided over the question of whether to sign the Philadelphia statement and, in the end, voted not to sign.

The New Yorkers decided that, indeed, the Philadelphia association had overstepped its boundary in acting as a representative of the Jewish community, and confirmed their belief that only the Board of Delegates on Civil and Religious Rights was deemed an appropriate forum for such a statement.[26]

Underlying this conflict was another important debate, which emerged during this time, over the role of the Union of American Hebrew Congregations in the American Jewish community. In 1878, the original Board of Delegates of American Israelites merged with Isaac Mayer Wise's UAHC, in a bid to function as the primary representative of the American Jewish community to the international community, as well as to the general American community. With the growth of the Young Men's Hebrew Association movement around the country, and its rise in popularity, the young leaders of the Philadelphia and New York associations began to advocate the inclusion of YMHAs in the Union of American Hebrew Congregations. They argued that because the UAHC only represented those Jews affiliated with its congregations, it was not a truly representative body. On April 16, 1880, the editors of the *American Hebrew* commented:

> We have among us the "Union of American Hebrew Congregations," having as one of its objects the protection of Jewish interests generally: but it is rightfully urged that this is not a representative enough body, being limited to congregations only, which in reality form but a minority of the Jews of this country.[27]

The issue was hotly debated within the Jewish community, and the editors of the *American Hebrew* remained at the forefront of propaganda in favor of inclusion. In response to the criticism hurled at the Philadelphia association for its proposed letter on behalf of Russian Jewry, they wrote:

> At present there is no American Jewish body which can claim by virtue of its constitution to have the sole authority to represent the whole Jewish community throughout the country. . . . [T]he Union of American Hebrew Congregations . . . is perhaps more representative than any other organization . . . but more than this cannot be claimed for it. . . . Not only congregational Judaism but the great mass of thinking Jews, who, unfortunately perhaps, have no connection with synagogue or temple, but who are on that account none the less Jewish, are just as well entitled to a representation in a Union which claims to speak for and represent all American Jews. . . . Throughout the country, Young Men's Hebrew Associations are rapidly springing up and coming into prominence; why are not these Associations entitled to a representation in a Union such as we would see established?[28]

One can sense in the editorials of the *American Hebrew* the passion felt by the young intellectuals writing on behalf of their own Young Men's Hebrew Associations. The debate over the inclusion of the YMHAs into the Union of American Hebrew Congregations continued until 1884, when the sound of bitterness could still be heard among its advocates. In that year, in response to the semiannual convention of the UAHC Executive Committee in Niagara Falls, New York, the following editorial comment appeared in the *Hebrew*:

> The whole proceedings, emphasize and intensify the long recognized fact that the best energies and possibilities of the U.A.H.C. are lost and will continue wasted as long as it remains a pet scheme for the glorification of Mr. Wise and Cincinnati.[29]

These editorial remarks reveal the strong degree of dissatisfaction among this circle of young Philadelphia and New York intellectuals who led the YMHAs and edited the *American Hebrew*. Their attacks on the Union of American Hebrew Congregations suggest a number of interesting conclusions. First, in vehemently claiming that the Union failed to accurately represent the American Jewish community, the editors of the *Hebrew*—who we also know were simultaneously heading the American Hebrew Association—implicitly declared that the Union did not represent their particular interests. The relevance of this becomes clear when we consider that this debate was taking place in the years preceding the infamous "Trefa Banquet" of 1883—the event that was to become the proverbial "straw that broke the camel's back." In light of the defections from the UAHC that took place after this divisive event (and the subsequent Pittsburgh Platform of 1885), and the extensive involvement of the Philadelphia and New York intellectuals in the eventual creation of The Jewish Theological Seminary, the inclusion debate takes on great meaning. The debate raises the question of how long, and how intensely, this group felt dissatisfied with the Union. The above-quoted remark from 1884, stating the "long recognized fact" that the Union fell short of its aims, suggests that these sentiments were both strongly felt and emphatically spoken in the years before the "Trefa Banquet" and its eventual consequences. Second, the rhetoric of the *Hebrew* during this debate reflects the emerging power struggle between the established center of Jewish leadership in Cincinnati, represented by Isaac Mayer Wise, and the emerging leadership of the young Jewish intellectuals of Philadelphia and New York. Out of this power struggle also emerges a shift in the character of leadership. In Cincinnati, the reins of leadership were held by rabbis, reflected in the dominance of Rabbis Isaac Mayer Wise and (until his death in 1882) Max Lilienthal. In contrast, the new leadership of Philadelphia and New York came not only in the form of rabbis, who were indeed prominent, but also in the highly capable and learned *lay leadership* reflected in the intellectual figures under discussion here.[30]

Under the direction of these new leaders, the work of YMHAS came to stress a new, more serious set of priorities. The most important element of the new agenda was its focus on Jewish education rather than the popular entertainments that were so integral to the early years of the associations. "Too long have the associations been hampered by a misconception of their aims and duties," wrote Cyrus Sulzberger in the first issue of the *Bulletin*.

> Some have generated into mere social societies; others, and more especially those situated in the large cities, have become a species of cheap club; and while social societies and cheap clubs may possibly be useful and desirable, yet it cannot be denied that the title "Young Men's Hebrew Association" is a misnomer for such societies. . . . the safety of the associations is now assured, and it is time that we pay more attention to the higher purposes for which we exist.[31]

Echoing these sentiments, Daniel P. Hays submitted his own remarks to the *American Hebrew*, commenting on the state of the New York association:

> It becomes a serious consideration whether [the members of the YMHA] appreciate its true aims and objects. When its literary and intellectual features shall be encouraged and supported as they deserve, and when its membership roll is increased by those whose desire for the intellectual, moral and social advancement of themselves and their race prompts them to join, then and not till then will its pertinence and usefulness in the community be established.[32]

It is clear that the new leaders of the YMHA saw it as their goal to purify the movement, to bring out its more noble cause by encouraging the commitment and knowledge of Jewish youths. When, in 1882, the American Hebrew Association established its annual "Association Day" to promote the improvement of the associations, Solomon Solis-Cohen summarized the Hebrew-oriented goals of the movement to his Philadelphia association: "To study that language, that history, that religion, should be our fixed and determinate purpose, and entertainments, speeches and balls should be made secondary to this prime object."[33]

Consistent with these new goals, the associations during this time showed a marked increase in scholarly lectures on Jewish themes, improvement of the Judaic sections of association libraries and reading rooms, and the introduction of new courses on the Hebrew language, Jewish history, and Jewish literature. It was to the advantage of the new leadership that, in addition to arranging lectures by well-known and popular rabbis, they could rely on themselves as lecturers to various societies. Recognizing that the smaller, more distant societies would not be able to receive such lectures, the editors of the *Bulletin* reprinted the best lectures presented to the larger societies.

One can detect a number of motivations for the intensified program that these leaders proposed. The late 1870s were fraught with antisemitic episodes, both abroad and in America. The refusal of the Grand Union Hotel in Saratoga Springs to admit Joseph Seligman in 1877, and the exclusion of Jews from Coney Island in 1879, must still have been fresh wounds to the young American Jews of the period. New urgency was also felt as a result of the progressive persecution of Russian Jewry, and the growing awareness of the potential immigration crisis of the 1880s.[34] What seemed most disturbing to the young leaders of the YMHA, however, was their fear that young Jews were growing up without any sense of connection either to their Jewish faith or their Jewish community. In a lecture to the Philadelphia association on November 19, 1881, Rev. Sabato Morais spoke to this very concern, and the important role of the YMHA in providing a solution:

> You turn on one side, and hear in incisive language an all-destructive theory. The universe sprang up of itself. . . . I will remind you of the aim of a "Young Men's Hebrew Association." It is to hold up the faith by the spreading of a knowledge of its history and literature, not as an accomplishment on which to pride ourselves, but as an instrument to search out truth. To effect that manly object, pleasure has necessarily to be minimized and instruction increased. . . . Members of the Young Men's Hebrew Association! Are you in real earnest about carrying out the main purpose of your institution? Study, then; study to lay a tenaciously strong hold of the belief which is now shot at by well-trained archers.[35]

Morais touches upon the perceived faithlessness of the younger generation, which, coupled with growing fears over the assimilation of American Jewry, encouraged the new leaders to embrace many of the new tactics outlined above. These fears were also fed by the growing popularity of Felix Adler's Ethical Culture movement, which was seen by the young Philadelphians and

New Yorkers as a primary threat to the Jewish community. When the YMHA of St. Louis invited Adler to give a lecture to their association, the editors of the *Bulletin* responded with angry words, worth quoting here at length, calling Adler "a false teacher":

> The Association Bulletin has not taken, nor shall it be permitted to take, any partisan views of the various questions between what are known as the orthodox and the reform parties in Judaism. It stands on the common ground to all Jews, and, because it stands on this ground, it protests in all solemnity and earnestness against the indignity which has been offered to all Jews, and especially to all Young Men's Hebrew Associations, by the Young Men's Hebrew Association of St. Louis, in presenting to its members Felix Adler as one of its lecturers. . . . We maintain that he is not a proper person to instruct our Jewish youth. The man who has prostituted his magnificent abilities in the endeavor to break down Judaism,—the man who has spat upon and reviled the faith and observances of Israel,—the man who, within the past few months, has lamented the fact that there is arising a young Judaism which draws its inspiration from the history and literature of the Hebrews,—is eminently unfit to be selected as a Jewish teacher. The Young Men's Hebrew Association of St. Louis deserves the severest censure of its sister societies, and, if it can find no better means of performing its work, and can learn no truer conception of the nature of that work, the best service it can render to Judaism is to disband, and let a truly Hebrew association take its place.[36]

These are, perhaps, the most impassioned words to be found in the three years of the publication of the *Association Bulletin*. Through the anger that the editors directed toward one of their own associations and toward Adler, one can see that these young leaders saw Adler and his movement as a formidable enemy to their program. The intensity with which they expressed their sense of betrayal cannot be overestimated. The young leaders saw their work in the YMHAS and in the *American Hebrew* as essential to the survival of the community, and movements such as Adler's as their dangerous antithesis.

Essential to the program of these young intellectual leaders was their desire to "spark" what Jonathan Sarna has called "an American Jewish cultural revolution."[37] Indeed, both the rhetoric of their *American Hebrew* and the activities and publications of their associations reflect a strong desire to transform the status quo by kindling greater attachment to Judaism and the Jewish community among Jewish youth. The *American Hebrew* and the Young Men's Hebrew Associations were to be the primary vehicles for this transformation. Accordingly, when the editors of the *Hebrew* outlined the improved role the associations could undertake if a union of associations would exist, they expressed their belief that,

> with the impetus that union will give, with the energy that youth will infuse, with the zeal that knowledge will inspire, will the Young Men's Hebrew Association of America proceed to the accomplishment of its mission. And when, in the fullness of time, its work shall have been completed, we will find the descendants of the noble Hebrew patriarch of old again fulfilling the injunction, "Become a blessing." They will once more take their rightful place at the front of civilization and enlightenment, and invincible by reason of their knowledge and their patriotism, they will proudly carry to all the nations of the earth the banner of Eternal Truth inscribed in letters of perennial light, "The Lord is One and His name One!"[38]

These aims were not just words to the editors of the *Hebrew*, and their sentiments were supported by the innovative programming in the associations. Through their leadership, the festival of Hanukkah took on great symbolic meaning, both as a national and a religious celebration. In his analysis of the Young Men's Hebrew Associations, David Kaufman has suggested that the YMHA Hanukkah celebrations focused essentially on the festival's national symbolism. While Kaufman is correct that the emphasis on nationalism and peoplehood played an important and innovative role in these celebrations, he perhaps underestimates their equally *religious* character and symbolism.[39] The deeply religious overtones of the celebration were emphasized in the *Hebrew*, as a means of preparing and exciting the community for the coming celebration:

> The intelligent observer who has duly informed himself upon the history of our Chanuka festival, must concede that the calendar of no other faith indicates a holiday so purely religious, and at the same time, so entirely national. . . . Judah fought for religious observance. . . . No clash of steel, no battle-alarms will mark the shock of this Maccabean revival, but steadily the line of conflict will surge forward, yielding here, gaining there, slowly irresistibly onward against the legions of grasping greed, worldliness and indifference, until in a restoration of the public worship on the seventh day . . . the Hebrews of this century will have recaptured the *maoz tzur yeshuati* the rock-fortress of Judaism's lasting salvation.[40]

The editors' remarks display a clear desire to express not just the national but the religious nature of the festival as well. These editors, who it must be remembered were themselves responsible for the Y's Hanukkah celebration, also encouraged the observance of the Sabbath, and devoted much time to encouraging revived attachment to Shabbat in the home. Nevertheless, Kaufman is correct in his assertion that the YMHAs did not intend to act as religious institutions in and of themselves, and the associations saw themselves as supplementing, not supplanting, the synagogue. The *Association Bulletin* clarified its position with regard to the synagogue, stating, "it [the YMHA] certainly cannot do anything in a directly and distinctively religious way, as that would be trenching upon the province of the Synagogue. But it can and should effectively supplement the work of the Synagogue and Sunday-School by establishing classes in Hebrew language and literature, and by the delivery of essays and lectures on Jewish history."[41] Despite this formal position, however, the underlying ideology of the leadership remains. In orchestrating its enthusiastic Hanukkah celebration, it de facto encouraged participation, what we might call *observance* of the holiday, though not doing so with any explicit preference for Orthodox or Reform boundaries.[42] It is therefore not surprising that in the wake of the very successful Hanukkah celebration of that year, the *Hebrew* commented:

> The Young Men's Hebrew Association has again endeared itself to the Jewish community, which thus again becomes its debtor for the good, staunch work it has done in the cause of Judaism. It has preached Jewish worth, character, history, faith, constancy and honor with a more effective and powerful sermon than synagogue or temple ever listened to.[43]

Further evidence that the aims of the Y leaders went beyond a desire to encourage "national" feeling, to include a strong concern for religious attachment, can be seen in the creation of their annual "Association Day." It is no coincidence that the leaders chose the Sabbath as the appropriate day for Association Day to take place, for in their opinion, "the day is certainly a fit one for such an anniversary—the great Sabbath, to which tradition has assigned a special importance."[44]

Indeed, the young intellectuals who embarked on a new agenda and an improved program for the Young Men's Hebrew Associations believed that their efforts would lead to a great renewal of Judaism and the Jewish community in America. Instrumental to this belief was their faith in the importance of the emerging younger generation. It was among these young Jewish men and women that they hoped a transformation would take shape. One of the most inspiring lectures to be published in the *Bulletin*, delivered by Rabbi Jacob Voorsanger, helps to capture the spirit of the new agenda.

Prompted by the biblical story of Hannah, Voorsanger imparted to the young members of the Y an inspiring interpretation of its three main characters, Hannah—the barren mother, Eli—the aging priest, and Samuel—the child who would grow to serve the faith and the community. Voorsanger's story begins with a description of Hannah, a graceful, barren wanderer in a time "when the black clouds of idolatry and gross materialism overcast Israel's sky." She is "the personification of pure faith" amidst these forces, which "all combined to render Israel faithless to their mother, to their God." Eli is also childless, dying without the hope for a leader for the next generation, to whom he can pass along his knowledge and his priestly role. "Not alone," Voorsanger explains, "the picture of the past is this dying priest, but also the gloomy representation of indifference, awaiting nothing but a peaceful sleep in death . . . and yet his half-dead lips mutter a promise that the dead shall return to life, and the weeping mother [Hannah] find again her children. . . . And the promise came true." With the birth of Samuel, "the living representative of the future . . . Hannah is at peace. Her heart, inspired by the fealty of the new generation, sings anthems to the Lord." At the conclusion of Voorsanger's interpretive tale, he leaves no question in the minds of his readers and listeners as to its meaning:

> To the young men and women of the house of Israel living in this fair land, this article is respectfully inscribed and submitted. Already the cause of Hannah has found a hearing in their hearts. . . . The dying priest has not promised falsely, and the dry bones are becoming animated to continue the mission of Samuel. . . . Already champions are arising to contend with an obnoxious enemy for the possession of the coming generation. May the Young Men's Hebrew Associations understand that theirs is the mission to wrestle with the enemy—indifference,—as powerful coadjutors of the Synagogue,—that theirs is the task to preserve Hannah's children to Hannah's faith.[45]

Voorsanger compares the YMHA to the figure of Samuel, who renews hope and allows for the continuity of the people and their faith. The essence of Voorsanger's remarks, which are to be found in his introductory statement to the association, reflects the grand ideal envisioned by the leaders of the YMHA of this period: "And the boy Samuel . . . became a prophet, a servant of the Lord, a great teacher and reformer, who hurled the thunder of his eloquence at his indifferent people, who founded a school that sent forth teachers in Israel, and who laid the foundation to a—'renaissance.'"[46]

Having established that the young Philadelphia and New York intellectuals who led the YMHA movement in these years were indeed oriented by their hopes for a Jewish renaissance, or renewal, we turn now to our final question. To what extent was their leadership consistent with the larger history of the movement? Did the aims that they worked toward remain central to the movement after they passed their leadership to a new generation of YMHA activists? Charles Wyszkowski, discussing the YMHA in his study of the *American Hebrew*, remarks, "despite the momentary enthusiasm for Jewish-oriented activities, Y programs receded to their earlier levels with little more than a token of Jewish culture."[47] While his comment strikes me as somewhat overstated, Wyszkowski correctly sensed that the period 1879–1884—coinciding with the birth and early years of the *American Hebrew* and the rise in leadership of the young Philadelphia–New York group in the Y—was one of remarkable and unique concentration on Jewish educational and cultural activities. Indeed, one can argue that it was precisely under the influence of these young leaders that the YMHA was able to have such an important cultural impact on the community during these years. By 1883–1884, just as these figures were beginning new projects as influential adult members of the Jewish community, we can observe a shift in focus within the YMHA. The ever-increasing influx of immigrants from Eastern Europe demanded greater concentration and energy from the Jewish community. It was at this time that many YMHAS established "downtown branches" to serve the immigrant communities.[48] Employment agencies, vocational classes, and English-language courses dominated the programs. Beyond this shift in focus toward the immigrant crisis, one can observe changes in the makeup of the organization. Among the associate groups—one of the most helpful indicators of change in the organization—a new batch of leaders emerged.[49] These youths bore little resemblance to the earlier generation of associates who pushed the organization in the direction of Jewish culture and education. They, too, published their own periodicals, but unlike the high literary style and Jewish orientation of the older *Association Bulletin*, the new associates' paper, *The Associate*, concentrated on their debating societies and athletic competitions. The area of greatest excitement in the paper revolved around the rivalry between the New York and Philadelphia YMHA debating societies. But the most impressive evidence I have found to support the notion that the period 1879–1883 was a unique one in the history of the YMHA movement is an editorial comment from the *Monthly Journal of the Young Men's Hebrew Association of N.Y.C.*, January 1887:

> A dozen years ago [1875] there were probably not a dozen Jews in the United States (ministers excepted) who were competent enough to deliver an English lecture on any subject connected with Jewish history or literature. The estab-

lishment of the YMHAs has brought about something of a *renaissance*—so much that in this city, as in Philadelphia, whole courses of lectures on such subjects have been successfully given, the lecturers being entirely young laymen.... The point ... is this, that while five years ago [1882] we harvested a splendid crop of such young lecturers, since then the yield has been very sparse, and in fact, next to nothing.[50]

It is no coincidence that the two points of chronological reference given here are 1875 and 1882. In 1875, when the YMHA began, the young intellectuals of our Philadelphia and New York group were still in their mid-to-late teens. Yet once they turned the corner to young adulthood, beginning approximately in 1877–1878, these young men came to be highly articulate leaders in the movement. It was at this point that the "renaissance" began. These young men, who were on the path not to becoming rabbis but doctors, businessmen, and scholars, embodied nevertheless the knowledge and inspiration to lead the movement, and to shift its direction toward Jewish education, religious experience, and Jewish national pride. It was indeed a unique time, for just as quickly as these men became leaders of the Young Men's Hebrew Association, changing its essential ideological core, they almost immediately brought their leadership into the greater Jewish community. The *American Hebrew* and the *Association Bulletin* were instrumental in this effort. Yet, as these young men matured and their influence continued to grow beyond the movement, a void was left in the YMHA. As indicated by the editor of the *Monthly Journal*, quoted above, by 1887 there were few, if any, leaders in the movement who were willing or able to provide intellectual leadership and knowledge. The height of the lay-intellectual leadership, personified by our Philadelphia and New York intellectuals, had clearly passed. By the end of the 1880s, these intellectuals, who remained lay leaders of the community, began to pursue new, larger projects, which were to become some of the most significant and lasting contributions to American Jewish cultural and religious life.

The Young Men's Hebrew Association movement, during the approximate years 1877–1883, the period coinciding with the leadership of these young intellectuals, was a formative moment in the emergence of a Jewish renaissance culture at the end of the nineteenth-century. It provided a unique model and agenda that these leaders took with them when they left the YMHA, and which they built upon and transferred to the larger Jewish community as adults. As we seek to further understand the importance of the Philadelphia and New York intellectuals as leaders of the Jewish renaissance culture in America at the end of the nineteenth century, the history of the YMHA of this period is an essential chapter to consider. It is within the context of this institution that we are provided with a unique view into the evolution of these figures, from passionate and talented youths, to articulate and creative young men, to the sophisticated and powerful intellectual leaders they became (and tend to be remembered as) in their adult lives.

NOTES

1. Notable in this regard are the foundational study by Maxwell Whiteman, "'The Philadelphia Group,'" in Murray Friedman, ed., *Jewish Life in Philadelphia, 1830–1940* (Philadelphia: American Jewish Committee, Philadelphia Chapter, 1983), pp. 163–78; the symposium held in 1990 titled "The Philadelphia Group: The Making of an American Jewish Community," published as Murray Friedman, ed., *When Philadelphia Was the Capital of Jewish America* (Philadelphia: Balch Institute Press, 1993); and Jonathan Sarna, "The Late Nineteenth-Century American Jewish Awakening," in Walter Conser Jr., and Sumner B. Twiss, eds., *Religious Diversity and American Religious History* (Athens: University of Georgia Press, 1997). The latter essay has laid an essential foundation for understanding the far-reaching nature of Jewish renaissance work in the last quarter of the nineteenth-century. Sarna's analysis of this period, and his elucidation of the close relationship between the Philadelphia and New York intellectuals and the emergence of the new turn-of-the-century American Jewish culture, forms the basis and context for my own exploration of these intellectuals within the Young Men's Hebrew Association movement.

2. As Philip Cowen memorably stated, "The YMHA was the common bond that held all of us. There we were all active." Philip Cowen, *Memories of an American Jew* (New York: The International Press, 1932), p. 52.

3. The Young Men's Hebrew Associations existed in an earlier form in the 1850s and 1860s. The relationship between the two institutions has not yet been explained definitively. It is certain, however, that as the YMHAs of the 1870s and 1880s attempted to place their institution within a historical framework; they identified these earlier groups as precursors to their own associations. One can see this, for example, in the first issue of *The Association Bulletin* (to be discussed later in this chapter). Here the editors mention, under the heading "The Past": "The first Young Men's Hebrew Association of which we have been able to find any account, is the Young Men's Literary Association of Philadelphia," mentioned in *The Occident* in 1850, and the editors also take note of the Hebrew Young Men's Literary Association of New York's "Onward" motto of November 1852. Benjamin Rabinowitz's retrospective of the YMHA movement follows this chronology as well, viewing the earlier associations as precursors to the associations of the 1870s. Rabinowitz, however, does not adequately explain the relationship between the associations of these different periods. It seems clear that the relationship was also unclear to the young men of the later associations, who remark in this same issue of the *Bulletin*: "They then disappear from *The Occident*, and, probably, from the earth." *Association Bulletin*,

vol. 1, no. 1 (April/Iyar 1881), pp. 17–18. Benjamin Rabinowitz, *The Young Men's Hebrew Associations, 1854–1913* (New York: National Jewish Welfare Board, 1948), pp. 5–11; reprinted from the *Publications of the American Jewish Historical Society* 37 (1947).

4. The relationship between the YMHAs of this period and their Protestant precursors, the Young Men's Christian Associations (YMCAs), is an area that needs further exploration. An interesting comparison might be made between the Ys as uniquely middle-class institutions and their shared concern for so-called "character building." This question would be of particular relevance for understanding the nature of the YMHA as a second-generation American, Jewish middle-class phenomenon. This becomes especially interesting when one considers that these second-generation Americans were born of German-Jewish parents, for whom the concept of *Bildung*, or "self-cultivation" was likely to have been highly influential. David Sorkin and George L. Mosse have both placed *Bildung* at the center of their analyses of German Jewry. See David Sorkin, *The Transformation of German Jewry, 1780–1840* (New York: Oxford University Press, 1987), and George L. Mosse, *German Jews beyond Judaism* (Cincinnati: Hebrew Union College Press, 1985). It would be interesting to explore the possibility that the Jewish "character building" that was central to the program of the YMHAs of this period was, in some important respects, an American-Jewish variation of German-Jewish *Bildung*, as interpreted by second-generation American Jews of German-Jewish descent. David I. Macloud's *Building Character in the American Boy: The Boy Scouts, YMCA, and Their Forerunners, 1870–1920* (Madison: University of Wisconsin Press, 1983) is highly suggestive in its analysis of the YMCA as a Protestant, middle-class initiative in "character building" of the same period. Full development of this question, however, falls outside the scope of the present essay. I hope to pursue this comparison in a future study.

5. The only attempt at a comprehensive study of the entire YMHA movement remains Benjamin Rabinowitz's book, cited above. This book, as well as William Langfeld's monograph on the Young Men's Hebrew Association of Philadelphia—while helpful in providing essential details as to chronology, leadership, and organizational dynamics—can only be categorized as an "insider" retrospective, and therefore lacks sustained critical analysis. See William R. Langfeld, *The Young Men's Hebrew Association of Philadelphia, a Fifty-Year Chronicle* (cited hereafter as *YMHA of Philadelphia*) (Philadelphia: The Young Men's and Young Women's Hebrew Association of Philadelphia, 1928). On the other hand, David Kaufman, in his study of the Jewish Community Center movement, provides a valuable examination of the Y movement as a precursor to the Jewish Community Centers. See David Kaufman, *Shul with a Pool: The "Synagogue-Center" in American Jewish History* (Hanover, NH: Brandeis University Press/University Press of New England, 1999).

6. In dealing with the New York YMHA, I have allowed for some degree of fluidity between the representation of the New York intellectuals through the main New York City YMHA and other New York City Ys. This becomes relevant, for example, in the figure of Cyrus Sulzberger, an important member of this group, who was a member of the Anshe Chesed Congregation YMHA, also located in New York City. This situation is unique to the New York group, whereas the Philadelphia YMHA represents a much smaller and more tightly knit community. For the purpose of this essay, when referring to

the New Yorkers, I intend, for the most part, to extend representation to those in smaller New York City Ys. This rule, however, does not necessarily apply when dealing with moments of sharp disagreement between the main New York City YMHA and the smaller city associations, for example, in my discussions of the creation of the American Hebrew Association and the debate over YMHA inclusion in the UAHC.

7. Mayer Sulzberger has been appropriately viewed as the "patriarch" of the Philadelphia group, as he was instrumental in coordinating and advising nearly all of the group's major institutions. See David G. Dalin, "The Patriarch—the Life and Legacy of Mayer Sulzberger," in Friedman, ed., *When Philadelphia Was the Capital of Jewish America*, pp. 58–74. It is not clear to me, however, whether we can rightly place him among the young group of intellectuals in discussion here. Traditionally, Mayer Sulzberger, born in 1843, has been seen as representing the oldest member of the group, while Cyrus Adler, born in 1863, has represented the youngest member. My sense, however, is that there may be an important gap between Mayer Sulzberger and the younger members, born in the 1850s and early '60s. This can be seen in the fact that Sulzberger was already a prominent and successful figure in the community by the time the younger members began their activity in the Y. Also indicative is the suggestion by Ira Robinson that there was noticeable tension between the older Sulzberger and the younger Adler, whom Sulzberger took under his wing. See Ira Robinson, "Cyrus Adler, the Philadelphian," in ibid., p. 96.

8. See Rabinowitz, *Young Men's Hebrew Associations* (cited hereafter as *YMHA*), pp. 12–13.

9. Membership within the YMHAs was divided into two major categories, "Active"— those over the age of eighteen or twenty-one, paying higher dues, and holding the privileges of holding office and voting, and "Associate"—those over the age of thirteen or sixteen, paying lower dues, with the same rights as active members, with the exception of holding office and voting. These categories were often adjusted over the course of time, and within each association. See Rabinowitz, *YMHA*, pp. 58–63.

10. This debate was noted in the minutes of the Board of Managers meeting of the Philadelphia association, October 7, 1875, found in typed excerpts of these minutes at the American Jewish Historical Society, New York (hereafter AJHS), I-241, Box 1, pp. 5–6. Langfeld makes note of this meeting as well in his retrospective, *YMHA of Philadelphia*, p. 11.

11. I have not been able to locate any existing copies of this publication, and Langfeld and Rabinowitz mention them only briefly.

12. Langfeld, *YMHA of Philadelphia*, p. 13.

13. Board of Managers meeting, February 1, 1877. See excerpts from the Philadelphia YMHA, Board of Managers minutes, AJHS, I-241, Box 1, p. 18.

14. Quoted in Langfeld, *YMHA of Philadelphia*, pp. 15–16.

15. In Philip Cowen, *Memories of an American Jew*, pp. 52–53.

16. *American Hebrew*, December 12, 1879, p. 38.

17. The first of the association's grand Hanukkah celebrations took place in 1878, precisely at the time that the associates (made up of the young New York and Philadelphia intellectuals) began to have an influence over programming in the associations.

18. See, for example, the "Friday Night" columns of the *American Hebrew*, April 16, 1880, p. 103; and April 23, 1880, p. 115.

19. For examples of published minutes, see *American Hebrew*, May 14, 1880. For reports of large events, see the *American Hebrew*, December 19, 1879 (Hanukkah), p. 56; and February 27, 1880 (Purim), p. 20.

20. Incidentally, the name chosen for the new organization, the American Hebrew Association, further evidences the fluidity of the *American Hebrew* and the YMHAs.

21. *Association Bulletin*, vol. 1, no. 1 (April/Iyar 1881/5641), p. 3.

22. This proposal is raised in the "Friday Night" section of the *American Hebrew*, April 16, 1880, p. 103. It should be noted that this proposal was made in the months before the creation of the American Hebrew Association (AHA). The stress on literary productivity and the importance of publishing Jewish books was a foremost impetus in creating the AHA, as they hoped it would be able to publish internal and external pamphlets, as well as an informative monthly bulletin. See the condensed minutes of the AHA, published in the first issue of the *Association Bulletin*, vol. 1, no. 1 (April/Iyar 1881/5641), p. 16: the suggestion that "the present object of the Union to be the periodical publication of articles of interest to the associated societies" and the annual appropriation of dues, "towards a general publication fund." Jonathan Sarna discusses the continued efforts of Solomon Solis-Cohen to create an active publication society in his history of the Jewish Publication Society; see J. D. Sarna, *JPS: The Americanization of Jewish Culture, 1888–1988* (Philadelphia: The Jewish Publication Society, 1989), p. 19.

23. *American Hebrew*, April 16, 1880, p. 103.

24. This fact continued to be a stumbling block to the success of the American Hebrew Association. The editors of the *Association Bulletin* often commented on their disappointment that the large New York association, which had the capacity to strengthen the association [AHA], would not lend its support. See for example *Association Bulletin*, vol. 1, no. 3 (August/Elul 1881/5641), pp. 16–17: "All this has been done, it must be remembered, with an exceedingly limited income . . . in the face of the opposition . . . of the strong, rich and influential YMHA of New York. Were this society to unite with its kindred organizations in their unselfish and earnest endeavors to better themselves, each other and the community, success would be placed beyond peradventure. Without its assistance, the work will be more difficult, but ultimate fruition none the less certain." Rabinowitz notes, however, that tensions between the New York and Philadelphia associations "disappeared quickly," and that "amicable relations resumed." Rabinowitz, *YMHA*, p. 38.

25. *American Hebrew*, April 9, 1880. Quoted in Rabinowitz, *YMHA*, p. 42.

26. See the minutes of the New York City YMHA Board of Directors, April 13, 1880, located at the 92nd Street Y Archive, New York City. Rabinowitz also provides a description of the disagreement, Rabinowitz, *YMHA*, p. 42.

27. *American Hebrew*, April 16, 1880, p. 98.

28. *American Hebrew*, April 23, 1880, p. 110.

29. *American Hebrew*, July 18, 1884, pp. 145–49. Quoted in Charles Wyszkowski, *A*

Community in Conflict: American Jewry during the Great European Migration (New York: University Press of America, 1991), p. 105.

30. Jonathan Sarna points out this essential difference between the two centers of leadership. As he has shown, the lay character of this new leadership would mark an important shift in the Jewish community, as these young lay leaders of the Young Men's Hebrew Association and the *American Hebrew* remained outside the rabbinate, yet continued to forge ahead to become conspicuous leaders by the end of the 1880s. See J. D. Sarna, "The Making of an American Jewish Culture," in Friedman, ed., *When Philadelphia Was the Capital of Jewish America*, pp. 150–51. A slightly different picture of the YMHA is described by David Kaufman. While Kaufman rightly emphasizes the important role played by rabbis, who were indeed central to the programming of the Associations, he perhaps overlooks the even greater importance of this group of lay-leaders in the institution. He assumes, for example, that the *religious* impulse in the YMHA movement was drawn primarily from the rabbis who were involved in the institution. See Kaufman, *Shul With a Pool*, pp. 58–59, 61. It is my contention, however, that it was the *lay leadership*, represented by the young Philadelphia and New York group, that provided, not only the core of the institution as a whole during this period, but also the essence of its religious-ethnic programming and ideology. We will return to this question later in this chapter, as we turn to the role of Jewish renewal work within the Young Men's Hebrew Association.

31. *Association Bulletin*, vol.1, no. 1 (April/Iyar 1881/5641), p. 2.

32. *American Hebrew*, May 14, 1880, p. 153.

33. Excerpts from Solis-Cohen's remarks were published in the *Association Bulletin*, vol. 2, no. 4 (April/Iyar 1882/5642), p. 83.

34. See Jonathan Sarna, "The Late Nineteenth-Century American Jewish Awakening," pp. 5–7.

35. The lecture was reprinted in the *Association Bulletin*, vol. 2, no. 2, pp. 25–36.

36. *Association Bulletin*, vol. 2, no. 3 (February/Adar 1882/5642), p. 44.

37. See Jonathan Sarna, "The Making of an American Jewish Culture," in Friedman, ed., *When Philadelphia Was the Capital of Jewish America*, p. 148.

38. *American Hebrew*, May 7, 1880, p. 137.

39. Kaufman writes: "The best example of the secularization of Jewish religious practice is the YMHA approach to the holidays. Understandably, the historical holidays with the least religious and ceremonial baggage were emphasized." Kaufman, *Shul with a Pool*, p. 69.

40. *American Hebrew*, December 12, 1879, p. 38.

41. *Association Bulletin*, vol. 1, no. 1 (April/Iyar 1881/5641), p. 48.

42. Kaufman suggests that the YMHAs' Hanukkah celebrations should be seen within the context of the "secularization of Judaism." Kaufman, *Shul with a Pool*, p. 69. I question whether the new programs, regardless of their new national overtones, can truly be described as "secular." As I have hopefully demonstrated above, the programs were designed, not only to encourage attachment among young Jews to their people and their history, but also to encourage the experience, meaning, and observance of the holidays.

43. *American Hebrew*, December 19, 1879, p. 56.

44. *Association Bulletin*, vol. 1, no. 3 (August/Elul 1881/5641), p. 36.

45. Jacob Voorsanger, "A Trio of Characters," *Association Bulletin*, vol. 1, no. 3 (August/Elul 1881/5641), pp. 51–56.

46. Jacob Voorsanger, "A Trio of Characters," *Association Bulletin*, vol. 1, no. 3 (August/Elul 1881/5641), p. 53. Emphasis in the original.

47. Charles Wyszkowski, *Community in Conflict*, p. 44.

48. The New York YMHA established its downtown branch in 1883.

49. Langfeld notes that in the Philadelphia association a new "Associate group" emerged in approximately 1888. He notes that this new group was much more focused on athletics than Jewish intellectualism. Langfeld, *YMHA of Philadelphia*, pp. 25–27.

50. *Monthly Journal of the Young Men's Hebrew Association of N.Y.C.*, vol. 2, no. 1 (January 1887), p. 6.

3 A Renaissance of Jewish Readers in Victorian Philadelphia

How does one write a cultural history of Jewish reading activities?[1] In the following discussion, circumscribed by a particular location (Philadelphia) and time period (ca. 1840s–1890s),[2] I will ask in a preliminary way several questions related to such an undertaking: namely, what did Jews read; what reading materials did Jews lack that they tried to acquire or produce themselves; where did Jews read; and what functions did their reading activities serve? Scattered through this discussion of sources, sites, and reading activities, I also hope to point to some of the deeper challenges and at times counterintuitive questions scholars of the history of reading have posed about this subject.[3] Roger Chartier, the most distinguished contemporary historian of reading practices, has formulated the task as follows: first, to recognize that "reading is not always inscribed in the text; that it is not true that there is no imaginable gap between the meaning assigned to it [the text] (by the author of the text or its editor, by criticism, tradition, etc.) and the use or interpretation that readers may make of it" and second, to understand that "a text exists only because a reader gives it meaning."[4] In shifting the interpretive focus from traditional conceptions of authorship to material texts and historically contextualized audiences, Chartier follows the arguments of Michel Foucault, who redirected cultural historians' attention to the processes governing the reception of texts.[5] At the same time, Chartier, building on the work of Donald McKenzie, has demonstrated how the forms in which messages are delivered and the manner in which texts are performed shape, constrain, and otherwise affect the meanings conveyed.[6] Consequently, the physicality of reading materials and the historicity of reading activities are critical for understanding not only the ways that individuals read but also for analyzing how audiences generate meaning.

Such an approach, if it is to be comprehensive, requires us to treat not only the words on the page as symbolic carriers of meaning and to know something about the life stories of the readers themselves. It also demands that we explore the complex processes by which words, sounds, and images as texts are received and read. Recognizing the historicity of texts and the contexts in which texts and readers are located helps us to appreciate the distinctive communities to which readers belonged, the skill levels and competencies of these readers, and the manner and environment in which they read or were read to. Unfortunately, owing to insufficient empirical research, the important and underlying question of literacy levels attained by readers who can be identified as Jewish in mid-nineteenth-century Philadelphia will not be addressed.[7] Instead, I will focus here on a limited group of producers and consumers of reading materials who were highly literate, multilingual, and instrumental in building the institutional and cultural foundations for new kinds of sociability through reading. Even as they resemble in some respects their non-Jewish counterparts, these Victorian Jewish writers, editors, compilers, and readers also show distinctive characteristics that set them apart. These differences are especially evident when contrasted with models of secularization often advanced to characterize non-Jewish reading patterns during this time period.

For the sake of studying cultural histories of Victorian Jewish reading activities, it first may be useful to recall that while there is some definitional overlap between the analytical categories "Jewish" (e.g., readers) and "Judaic" (e.g., what was read), they are not identical. The fact that someone was born Jewish does not necessarily make that person a Jewish reader, and the fact that someone of Jewish parentage authored a particular work does not mean the work counts as a work of Judaica. Indeed, part of what is fascinating about this Victorian moment in vernacular cultural exchanges between Jews and non-Jews is precisely this new and rapidly expanding availability of and accessibility to a wide variety of works in multiple languages. In this context, the English vernacular helped to produce a new kind of Jewish reader, indeed, one might even argue, a new kind of non-Jewish Judaic reader.

All people who identified themselves as Jews obviously did not exclusively read "Jewish" books and serialized publications. The bibliographic concept of "Judaica," notably, can refer to publications issued by Jews *or* non-Jews, but whose content is preponderantly concerned with Jews and Judaism. As Robert Singerman put it in the introduction to his authoritative bibliography of pre-twentieth-century "Judaica Americana": "Judaic subject matter, and not the author's ancestry, is the determining factor in judging the appropriateness of a work for inclusion."[8] He includes, for example, missionary tracts as works of Judaica that target a Jewish audience even as the stated purpose of these publications is to advance the cause of Jewish conversion to Christianity.

Similarly, works printed in Hebrew may be "Judaic," if not exactly Jewish: Thomas Dobson, a Scottish-born Christian printer, published in Philadelphia in 1814 the first complete non-Masoretic Hebrew Bible in the United States (which is to say, an "Old Testament" Bible whose type font was Hebrew but lacked the Masoretic vocalization and accentuation marks). In so doing, it would seem he anticipated primarily a non-Jewish market for his Holy Scriptures. One recent bibliography reports not having found evidence of any Jews having actually owned a copy. Notably, there are two gift copies of the Dobson Bible held at the University of Pennsylvania previously owned by two of Philadelphia's Victorian Jewish leaders, David Sulzberger and Cyrus Adler. The latter copy formerly belonged to a non-Jew named Robert Dearden and may have been purchased by Adler specifically for donation, not for personal use. Interestingly, the first few pages of this unique copy have been vocalized by hand underneath the printed letters. Such notations suggest a possible Jewish owner (Adler?), but it also may have been inscribed by a Christian practicing his Hebrew grammar (Dearden?)! In any case, Penn's copies must be regarded as exceptions that prove the rule that something Judaic need not be Jewish.[9]

Background

Philadelphia's Jews, or at least those families and individuals demographers have been able to identify as Jewish, numbered fewer than 2,000 in 1840, approximately 10,000 on the eve of the American Civil War, and no more than 15,000 in 1880.[10] During that time, the total Jewish population never amounted to more than 0.5 percent of the city's general population.[11] Despite their relatively small numbers, those Jews who were active in communal affairs gave birth to a remarkable set of pioneering educational institutions.[12] Philadelphia, America's "First City," was also a city of Jewish "firsts." Philadelphia was home to the first Hebrew Sunday School,[13] established in 1838, the first American Jewish monthly journal, the *Occident and American Jewish Advocate*,[14] started in 1843, the first American Jewish Publication Society,[15] founded in 1845, the first Hebrew Education Society,[16] a kind of Jewish "high school," instituted in 1849, and the "first Jewish Theological Seminary," Maimonides College,[17] which began holding classes in 1867.[18] Forty years later, in 1907, the Dropsie College for Hebrew and Cognate Learning, the first academic institution of higher Jewish learning in the world accredited to confer PhDs in Judaic studies, was chartered in Philadelphia.[19] Jewish Philadelphians also established multiple Jewish benevolent and relief associations during this era, and in particular created some of the first Jewish literary societies, which will be discussed in detail below.[20] One scholar of this premass migration era, Lance Sussman, has described an antebellum "Philadelphia Pattern" of Jewish communal life with national repercussions. As new Jewish communities grew roots, for example, in Pittsburgh, Cleveland, Cincinnati, Chicago, and St. Louis, we find parallel literary, social, relief, and other extra-synagogal institutions sprouting up there as well.[21]

Philadelphia's Jewish cultural organizations were led by a close-knit group of people who are sometimes referred to as the "Philadelphia Group." The moniker was coined by Solomon Solis-Cohen in his "Founder's Day Address" delivered at Dropsie College on March 9, 1924. His idea was to link together a historical chain of Jewish educators and educational institutions dating from the beginnings of the Hebrew Sunday School movement in the 1830s to Dropsie College in his own time.[22] Solis-Cohen, a prominent physician, lay scholar, and translator of medieval Hebrew poetry, argued that "these men and women of vision and various phases of their activity must be studied as an organic whole. They founded synagogues as a matter of course . . . and maintained charitable associations. But their chief endeavors were directed in two lines—school and publications."[23] In so doing, Solis-Cohen lumped into one, not entirely consistent pot a multigenerational mix of rabbis, educators, teachers, scholars, legal professionals, administrators, and businessmen: Isaac Leeser, Sabato Morais, Mayer Sulzberger, Cyrus Adler, as well as Rebecca Gratz, Hyman Gratz, Solomon Solis, Moses Aaron Dropsie, Marcus Jastrow, and one non-Philadelphian—Solomon Schechter, who came to New York from Cambridge University in 1902 to head the reorganized Jewish Theological Seminary of America. With the exception of Jastrow and Schechter, all these leaders had for some period of time been affiliated with the city's historic first synagogue, the Spanish and Portuguese Congregation Mikveh Israel, and Sephardic history and culture informed their sense of history and manner of worship.

Not mentioned by Solis-Cohen but closely associated with the same Sephardic congregation was the Cohen family.[24] Henry Cohen, a prosperous merchant, originally from London, and his American-born son Charles J. Cohen, who owned a stationery company, served as presidents of Mikveh

Israel during the second half of the nineteenth century. Henry and his wife Matilda, from Liverpool, had five children, all born and raised in Philadelphia. One of them, Mary M. Cohen, became a prominent literary figure and contributor to a number of Jewish newspapers including the short-lived (Philadelphia) *Jewish Index*,[25] the (Philadelphia) *Jewish Record*, and the (Philadelphia) *Jewish Exponent*. She served as the superintendent of Philadelphia's Hebrew Sunday School and notably was among the founders of the Browning Literary Society in the 1880s. Cohen, whose career is the subject of a recent study by Dianne Ashton,[26] also served as president of the Mikveh Israel Association, a kind of congregational literary society, during the 1890s. She shared a close friendship with Nina Morais, another literary figure of note, translator, and champion of women's suffrage. Nina was the daughter of the Sephardic hazan (prayer service leader) of Mikveh Israel, Sabato Morais, and his wife Esther Clara Weil, who died tragically in 1872 when Nina was seventeen.[27]

The concept of a "Philadelphia Group" was enlarged in 1983 in a collection of essays titled *Jewish Life in Philadelphia, 1830–1840*, edited by Murray Friedman.[28] The leadership pattern was taken beyond the framework of Philadelphia Jewish educators and publishers to encompass relief workers and other communal services associated with the period of mass migration (especially from Eastern Europe to the Atlantic shores during the 1880s and 1890s through 1924, after which time the U.S. government severely restricted the arrival of new immigrants). Two such members added to this expanded conception of the Philadelphia group were Louis Edward Levy, the cofounder in 1884 of the Association for the Protection of Jewish Immigrants," and Charles Spivak, a physician and community leader. In 1993, following a conference in Philadelphia on the Philadelphia group, Friedman penned a "Collective Portrait" of them to introduce *When Philadelphia Was the Capital of Jewish America*. This was the second in a multivolume series he edited on Philadelphia Jewish history.[29]

Despite the coherence and heuristic value the concept of a "Philadelphia Group" of Jews offers, it is important to understand that this conceptualization of these individual Jewish leaders as a collective is something that postdates their communal activities and conceals more than it reveals. This Philadelphia "group" of Jews active and visible in communal affairs spanned several generations. Its different "members" did not always see eye to eye politically, had different life experiences in terms of gender, family origins, and levels of wealth, and did not always share the same religious orientation.

Perhaps the deepest social fissure that divided the first "generation" of these communal leaders active during the antebellum period can be traced to the dismissal of the Westphalia-born Isaac Leeser as the hazan of Mikveh Israel in 1850. Leeser had aroused the wrath of his congregation by demanding more autonomy, more money, and more respect. In response, the congregation that had hired him dismissed him for insolence.[30] The furor that erupted also created the job opening that brought Sabato Morais, an Italian Sephardic Jew, to Philadelphia from London. Ultimately, Morais was elected the congregation's next minister under these difficult circumstances (many of Leeser's supporters left Mikveh Israel and started a new congregation, Beth El Emeth).[31]

Leeser and Morais did not get along, differed as much in their temperaments as in their politics (the former was combative and voted Democrat, the latter self-abnegating and voted Republican), and about critical issues such as the slavery question (Leeser argued that it was not appropriate to speak out about political issues like this one, and at one point was suspected of being a Southern sympathizer; by contrast Morais adamantly opposed the institution of slavery and in 1864 was given a three-month "gag" order against preaching by his congregational board). In later years Solis-Cohen, and his teacher Morais, fiercely opposed political Zionism, while other figures such as Bernard Levinthal, an early-twentieth-century leader of modern Orthodox Judaism and a kind of "chief rabbi" of immigrant Jewish Philadelphia, became ardent advocates of the cause.[32] Marcus Jastrow, who served as rabbi of Rodelph Shalom from 1866 to 1892, today is associated with the beginnings of the Conservative movement of Judaism.[33] During his ministry in Philadelphia, he instituted several controversial reforms in the content and character of the prayer service, including mixed seating and organ music.[34] Joseph Krauskopf, among the first graduates of Hebrew Union College, the Reform rabbinical seminary started in 1875 in Cincinnati, became the leader of Philadelphia's Reform Congregation Keneseth Israel in 1887.[35] Taken together, they reflect a wide diversity of viewpoints about religion and politics that existed within the framework of Philadelphia's intergenerational Jewish leadership patterns.[36]

What these generations of individuals did share was a commitment to Jewish communal service and a noblesse oblige sense of responsibility for their brethren in Philadelphia and abroad. All were committed to some form of a ritually observant Jewish religious culture, albeit some in highly modified and voluntary forms. All learned to read in the original languages and also to translate into the English vernacular classical works of Jewish culture. To take just one example, Solomon Solis-Cohen, under Morais' tutelage, rendered into highly stylized Victorian English the medieval Hebrew poetry of Moses Ibn Ezra and Yehudah ha-Levi. He was not alone in this kind of literary activity. On the day that Morais suffered a fatal stroke in November of 1897, he and two of his students, Isaac Husik and Gershon Levi, had been reading and translating the Hebrew poetry of Yehuda ha-Levi.[37]

Figures like Morais and many of the young people he nurtured as a spiritual leader and teacher sought to rediscover and/or translate into English classics of Jewish learning. These included some of the most dazzling and difficult texts of medieval Sephardic philosophy and poetry, such as the works of Sabbatai Donnolo, Moses Maimonides, Hasdai Crescas, Immanuel of Rome, Joseph Albo, and Isaac Abravanel. Through study in the original and through translation these works were made newly accessible as part of a Judaized classical curriculum. As will be discussed below, the educational and literary associations these Jewish Philadelphians created were self-consciously intended to serve the purpose of cultivating a new kind of Jewish reader—one trained to read traditional Jewish sources, to worship in Hebrew, to speak, read, and write proper English—and to ensure that these new readers' Jewish reading activities were isomorphic with the Victorian culture in which they lived.[38]

The Production of Reading Materials

Perhaps one of the most striking features of Jewish reading activities in Victorian Philadelphia was the labor-intensive effort to print, publish, or acquire Jewish reading materials. Thanks to Robert Singerman and his bibliographical labors we learn that between 1840 and 1900 there were at least 170 monograph titles and 70 distinct periodicals of a Judaic nature published in Philadelphia.[39] The types of printed works included a variety of religious works such as prayer books and catechisms. The multiplication and diversity of these versions of Jewish liturgy offer bibliographical evidence as well as visual and textual illustrations of communal fractures in the manner of worship and character of religious reading.[40] We also find distinctively Americanized forms of Jewish publications, all reflecting a diversity of purposes and forms of reading materials: constitutions, by-laws, and minutes of synagogues, fraternal orders, and relief organizations; communal histories; books of poetry, travel books, and dramas; apologetic literature; philo-Semitic and antisemitic works; conversionist, millenarian, and internal Jewish polemical tracts.[41]

Printing and publishing not only were cultural activities but also, notably, generated business opportunities. Newspapers, books, pamphlets as well as commercial advertising and want ads were critical sources of revenue, especially for Leeser, who supplemented his ministerial salary with sales of the various publications he authored or edited.[42] Advertising also provided a practical means of communication by which distant communities were able to circulate news about job opportunities and hopeful candidates might learn about and apply to fill them. Similarly, the business of printing broadsides, circulars, invitations, and occasional works such as birthday, bar mitzvah, anniversary, and funeral addresses formed a significant part of this growing public sphere of commercial reading materials.[43]

The Jewish periodical press and printed books themselves were ready outlets for advertisements promoting the latest Judaica publications.[44] The most important antebellum Jewish newspaper, the *Occident and American Jewish Advocate*, was published in Philadelphia and edited by Isaac Leeser.[45] The *Occident* circulated news about Jews from all over the world to the scattered Jewish communities of the Western Hemisphere and beyond. At the same time, it frequently was quoted overseas, particularly in the Anglo-Jewish press, as a reliable source of information about happenings in North America and the Caribbean. The first issue of the *Occident* came out in April of 1843, and it subsequently appeared every month (not including a brief stint as a weekly from 1859 to 1861) until 1869. In the *Occident*, its founder and editor editorialized on the burning issues of the day such as Saturday closing laws, the role of religion in the public schools, the need to build up Jewish education, establish a rabbinical seminary, support charities, and otherwise strengthen Jewish communal ties.

Subscription lists demonstrate that the *Occident* circulated to the farthest reaches of the pioneer West, from Canada to the Caribbean islands, and across the Atlantic to England and Western Europe.[46] Both Jews and non-Jews subscribed to and read the *Occident*. Letters from Christian ministers, for example, posing questions about Jewish doctrines and practices can be found among Leeser's personal correspondence and in print on the pages of the *Occident*. As a news source, the *Occident* also found its way into the non-Jewish press through reprinting of its content. In short, the *Occident* provided a (semi-) neutral meeting place for Jews and non-Jewish readers as well as for Jews themselves.[47]

Philadelphia was among the most important publishing centers in the United States in the Victorian era, and this also held true for Jewish publishing.

The city's Jewish leaders maintained an almost unbroken chain of Jewish journalism, dating from Leeser's *Occident* in 1843 and continuing into the twenty-first century:

1843–1869: *The Occident and American Jewish Advocate*, edited by Isaac Leeser (Mayer Sulzberger served as editor for the final year of publication [1868–1869] after Leeser's death in fulfillment of a pledge to his mentor.)

1872–1873: *The Jewish Index*, edited by Samuel Mendelsohn and Maurice Lam under the supervision of Sabato Morais, who ultimately wound up writing most of the content

1875–1886: *The Philadelphia Jewish Record*, edited by Alfred T. Jones

1887–present: *The Philadelphia Jewish Exponent*, edited by Charles Hoffman and Henry S. Morais, inter alia

As a publisher of Victorian Jewish religious works in antebellum America, Leeser was peerless. Between 1837 and 1838, he produced an English translation, in six volumes, of the Sephardic prayer book *Sifte tsadikim* (Lips of the Righteous) bound in tooled, gold-embossed leather. Leeser's text, in turn, relied upon the first English translation, produced by David Levi, one of the leading figures of enlightened Jewish London, in the late eighteenth century.[48] In 1839, Leeser published the first American Jewish catechism,[49] and in 1848, he published an English translation of the Ashkenazic prayer book *Divre tsadikim* (Words of the Righteous), bound in red Moroccan leather and also embossed in gold.[50] Both his Sephardic and Ashkenazic liturgies moved in their pagination from right to left like a traditional Jewish text, yet were accompanied by a vernacular translation on the facing page. His Jewish Bible translations, first of the Pentateuch in 1845 and later of the entire Hebrew Bible, the famous "Leeser Bible," published in Philadelphia in 1853, became the standard Bible editions in English read by Jews in the second half of the nineteenth century.[51]

The first American Jewish Publication Society (AJPS) was established in Philadelphia by Leeser in 1845. In the AJPS's constitution, Leeser declared the purpose of this enterprise as twofold: "to obtain a knowledge of the faith and proper weapons to defend it [Judaism] against the assaults of proselyte-makers on the one side and of infidels [Reformers] on the other."[52] To launch the society, Leeser introduced a serialized publication that he titled the *Jew-*

ish Miscellany, of which seven numbers appeared between 1845 and 1848. In this series, Leeser selected for publication and/or reprinting works by notable Anglo-Jewish authors including Grace Aguilar, Charlotte Elizabeth, Marion Moss Hartog, Hyman Hurwitz, and Moses Samuels.[53]

Thus, among the key ingredients supporting the reading activities of Jews living in Victorian Philadelphia were their own entrepreneurial efforts. They printed religious and educational materials, published newspapers and monographs, purchased additional books from abroad, and established schools, libraries, and literary associations as sites for meeting, reading, and discussing what was being read.[54]

A Renaissance of Jewish Reading

Beginning with Rebecca Gratz[55] and Isaac Leeser in the 1830s, the first generation of this Philadelphia group created the educational institutional infrastructures of Philadelphia's organized Jewish community. Sabato Morais, Leeser's successor at Mikveh Israel, later infused these forms with his own Sephardic rabbinic humanist content and played a critical role in the shaping of Jewish reading activities in the second half of the nineteenth century. Where Gratz and Leeser built institutions, Morais raised disciples. To do so, Morais drew upon his own background and training in classical rabbinic, Sephardic, and Italian religious humanist sources to implement a new program of Jewish cultural regeneration.

Morais was born in the port city of Livorno on the western coast of Tuscany in 1823. After receiving his rabbinical certification, he found work in London as a teacher at the Sephardic congregation's Orphan Home from 1846 to 1851. Over the course of his six years there he became fluent in English and began delivering well-received public addresses in his adopted language. In March of 1851, he came to Philadelphia to apply for what had been Leeser's position at Mikveh Israel. Morais remained employed there, despite some periods of controversy (during the Civil War, for example, he was silenced for preaching in support of Lincoln and the Union cause), until his death in 1897 at the age of seventy-four. Morais' near half-century tenure, as Pamela Nadell has observed, was the longest continuous ministry sustained by any American rabbi during that time.[56]

Over time, Morais emerged as the mentor, teacher, guiding force, and religious leader of a group of young activists who took up the call to produce what he called a "regenerated" version of observant Judaism planted in

American soil. From the first year of his arrival in 1851 until his death in November of 1897, Morais programmatically advanced his Italian Sephardic heritage as a basis for this version of Jewish religious Americanization. In particular, he turned to literary associations to cultivate this new generation of young people and instruct them how to be ritually observant and culturally refined, how to be pious and enlightened, in essence how to be a modern citizen and preserve Jewish tradition.

But why would young Jews trying to be modern and American want to imitate a medieval European model? And what did this group mean by the seemingly oxymoronic phrase "enlightened orthodoxy" eventually adopted to characterize its outlook? Superficially, one might think anyone living under the sway of the Enlightenment by definition would always reject revealed religion as irrational, as superstitious, and as a threat to freethinking, and would regard oneself as unbound by the traditions of the past. By contrast, is not a religiously observant Jew committed to a belief in divine revelation and historically obligated to practice *mitsvot* (that is, God's commandments, as transmitted to Moses on Sinai and as interpreted by Jewish sages across the millennia) and not to freely choose his or her own lifestyle?

Here we find a set of tensions that goes to the heart of the meaning of "renaissance" in this Victorian Jewish context of reading. For our purposes, I would like to suggest that the term "renaissance" refers to a specific kind of appeal to the past and a specific set of activities—teaching, reading, translating, printing, publishing, preaching, and otherwise publicly communicating classic works of Judaism and Jewish thought. In Philadelphia, beginning in the 1850s, we find Morais programmatically transmitting traditional forms of Jewish religious learning in a new setting outside the synagogue and *beit midrash* (house of study): the literary association. It would be a mistake to characterize the literary association as a secularized form of the *beit midrash*. Sephardic culture did not require such a dichotomy between the synagogue and the world outside it, and such a harmonization had deep roots, both historically and intellectually, in Morais' thinking. Indeed, there is clear and consistent evidence that Sephardic history, religion, and culture occupied a paradigmatic place in Morais' neoreligious humanist curriculum as a basis for religious Americanization. And significantly, some of the most important non-Jewish sources informing Morais' thinking hark back to the intellectual heritage of the Italian renaissance in which he was raised—a legacy marked by the attempt to synthesize religious and humanist currents. Above all, this renaissance heritage, Jewish and non-Jewish, was intensely preoccupied with activities of reading, including the recovery of classical literary sources for study and publication and the critical preparation of manuscripts for printing. In speaking about the early Hebrew printers in Venice, for example, Morais once referred to the "critical minds" that revised the Masoretic Bible and its traditional commentaries, "freed them from the blunders of copyists," and "disclosed in the Jews of Italy abilities of the highest order."[57] In these sentiments we find the pride he felt for his native Italian Jewish heritage as well as evidence of his early education in Livorno, where he was infused with this religious- humanist sensibility. The educational program Morais advanced in Philadelphia reflected his Sephardic-Italian upbringing. In his teachings, he rejected the more radical philosophies of secular Enlightenment otherwise pervasive in Continental Europe and America, which preached the autonomy of reason unbound by the demands of traditional religious authority. At the same time, he affirmed the critical role reason and historical criticism should play in shaping Jewish religious culture in America.

Common to the early Jewish leaders of the "Philadelphia Group" and their young pupils was precisely this embrace of classical learning—Jewish and non-Jewish—undergirded by a belief in reason in harmony with God's revelation. They shared a belief in a forward-looking, progressive, messianic view of history but also believed in the binding character of the distinctive historical practices of Judaism and the obligation to preserve a separate Jewish national identity, charged with a special divine mission. Taken together, their programmatic efforts sought to give rebirth to observant Judaism in the open, democratic, voluntary environment of the United States. The term Morais introduced in 1851 to capture the spirit of this proposed rebirth was "regeneration."[58] He spoke of the "virgin soil" of America "in which the ritual system governing Judaism would be regenerated." And he turned to the voluntary, social form of literary associations to help achieve this ambitious goal.

Historically, the concept of "regeneration" had already become widespread by the late eighteenth century.[59] In relation to Jews, it referred especially to calls for their occupational diversification and social rehabilitation as a precondition or at minimum a preliminary step toward their political integration into European society. The term itself can be found in writings of a variety of different Enlightenment writers, including religious philosophes such as the Abbe Gregoire, who championed Jewish political emancipation.[60] In Philadelphia, beyond the walls of the synagogue, literary societies would become a new site for promoting regeneration as a cultural and religious undertaking. Reading, it must be emphasized, was an extension of their religious identities, not a rejection or a secularization of them. Reading activities would be one of the most important means envisioned to help attain this fusion of the sacred and the putatively secular. In short, reading, as well as the production and/or importation of suitable reading materials, was crucial to the Philadelphia group's pedagogic efforts to realize this internal harmonization of the classical and the contemporary, the particular and the universal, the revealed and the rational, the Jewish and the American.

Victorian Jewish Readers and Their Literary Associations

One distinctive feature of Victorian culture in general was a particular style of reading. Mary Kelley, in her study of reading habits among antebellum American women, has examined some of the characteristic features of their experiences.[61] Kelley discovered, through a close study of diaries, letters, autograph albums, and journals, the hidden world of what she calls "reading women." She has shown how women made the activity of reading into "a vehicle for what the Renaissance scholar Stephen Greenblatt has called 'self-fashioning,' namely the achievement of a distinctive personality, a particular address to the world, a way of acting and thinking." Reading, Kelley explains, could be serious or playful, inward or political, private or public. In particular, Kelley writes, "sometimes books confirmed an already familiar identity. Sometimes, [books] became catalysts in the fashioning of alternative selves."[62] To get a sense of what was read, Kelley surveyed the variety of reading materials women reported selecting (in their diaries, letters, and other sources) and argued for discontinuity between the revolutionary and Victorian reading eras: "in contrast to their seventeenth- and early-eighteenth century counterparts who devoted themselves primarily to religious literature, women readers active after the revolution began to immerse themselves in secular literature. The traditional 'steady sellers,' the Bibles, psalm books, and devotional works to which colonial Americans had devoted themselves still constituted an important share of their reading. Simultaneously, however, they read widely in history, biography, and travel literature."[63]

In a master's thesis titled "'Better and Wiser Daughters in Israel': The Diaries of Fannie and Amelia J. Allen," completed at the University of Pennsylvania in 1997, Idana Goldberg studied the phenomenon of reading as "self-fashioning" in the diaries of two Jewish sisters, Fannie and Amelia Allen.[64] These sisters, living in mid-nineteenth-century Philadelphia, were committed to observing Jewish traditions and maintaining a distinctive Jewish identity even as they acculturated into the American middle classes. According to Goldberg, we find the Allen sisters reading precisely in order to fashion their own identities as Jews, as women, and as Americans. In contrast to the processes of secularization and individualization implied by Kelley's interpretation, the Allen sisters used reading to advance their social commitments, both to their religious/ethnic particularism and to the project of acculturation and refinement.

In Dianne Ashton's pioneering study of Mary M. Cohen, based in part on a scrapbook Cohen kept, we find another example of a highly educated Victorian Jewish woman engaged in performative reading activities. The act of scrapbooking, like diary keeping, both of which were so much in vogue during the Victorian period, preserved material traces that document aspects of her reading practices.[65] Unlike diaries, which contain handwritten, intensely personal reflections, scrapbooking was a visual medium, a compilation of acquired sources such as newspaper clippings, keepsakes, calling cards, holiday memorabilia, broadsides, invitations, as well as more intimate, handwritten letters. In scrapbooks, in other words, we find not only excerpts and references to the bound, commercially available forms of what people read (i.e., books and serialized publications) but also the ephemeral contents of everyday life. These acts of reading, clipping, annotating, reordering through compilation and arrangement, pasting, and patterning generated new meanings as well as entirely unforeseen associations. By illustration, consider what can be gleaned from a handful of pages from Mary M. Cohen's scrapbooks: on one sheet we find pasted a handwritten letter, dated June 1877, to her from Cyrus L. Sulzberger praising her for her "excellent article on "Jane Austen and her works." In a second scrapbook volume she kept, we learn that Mary published this piece about Austen under the pseudonym "Coralie" in the [North American] "Review." On the reverse side of the first scrapbook page where she pasted Cyrus Sulzberger's letter, we find a program for the "Sixth Entertainment" of the Young Men's Hebrew Association in Philadelphia held two months earlier on March 20, 1877, publicizing a duo performance by "Miss Mary M. Cohen and Mr. William Stoll, Jr. on piano and violin, performing Osborne and De Beriot's 'I Puritani.'"[66] And on another page, we find "Coralie" publishing her own rendering of Psalm 65 into English.[67] In just a few juxtaposed pages we learn that "Miss Mary Cohen," who was single, received flattering letters from her male admirers, that she played the piano (or violin), and that she did so well enough to perform contemporary "high culture" non-Jewish musical compositions at public entertainments for like-minded Jews. We learn that she was capable of reading and translating biblical verse from the original Hebrew, and that she not only read Jane Austen but published essays about her novels in nationally circulating non-Jewish newspapers. Perhaps most significant for our purposes is the discovery that, as an author, Cohen frequently published under a pseudonym.

Mary Cohen's teacher, Sabato Morais, also acquired the Victorian habit of clipping and pasting. Thanks to his scrapbook, we now know of hundreds of articles he anonymously published in a variety of Jewish and non-Jewish newspapers and which he carefully annotated by hand and commented on in a ledger-size volume he kept. We also know, exclusively from marginal annotations he inscribed in his scrapbook, of the episode during the Civil War when he was forced to stop preaching and of the details of his plan for a uniform Jewish liturgy that he propounded in the 1870s.[68] Common to both writers was the habit of publishing pseudonymously or anonymously.[69] Though intensely public in their activities, they concealed their literary authorship. This self-abnegating habit, ironically, argues against the individualist notion that reading and writing activities were private and self-fashioning and suggests rather that the outward-directed selfless act of educating, rather than fame, was regarded as the most important virtue.

Recognizing the social dimensions and functions of Victorian Jewish reading activities is crucial to understanding the lived experiences of Jews in Philadelphia during this time. Though not quantifiable, it seems reasonable to assume that many American Jews, as an aspect of their acculturation, were engaged in practices similar to those of the Allen sisters, Mary M. Cohen, and Sabato Morais. At the immigrant level, reading offered an entrée into the unfamiliar world into which newcomers arrived as they adjusted to a new language and new surroundings. For native-born, English-speaking American Jews, the habit of reading (and the flood of discussions and debates that reading provoked) furthered the absorption of the mores, the morals and manners, and the expectations of the surrounding society. It also deepened the connections between these Jews and their non-Jewish neighbors. Through books and broadsides, through newspapers and literature, through translations and catechisms, and by clipping and pasting Jewish readers learned about themselves, tried to figure out who they wanted to be collectively and how they wanted to be seen. In short, reading provided Jews with a mode of "self-fashioning" both as individuals and as a community. Reading activities could be instructive or adaptive, purposeful or entertaining, silent or out loud, private or social. Reading activities ultimately served as social glue that

bound together the Jewish community, with all its internal fractures and differences, as each individual groped to make sense of his or her local environment and, consequently, what it meant to be Jewish collectively in America.

To do so, people of all kinds, both Jews and non-Jews, regularly sought
out new forms of literary association outside traditional, especially religious,
settings. Perhaps it should be recalled that the Victorian period in American
history predates Andrew Carnegie and the building of the great system of
public libraries at the end of the nineteenth century. Before then, it is not
self-evident when and where people met to talk and read outside the marketplace, churches, and synagogues. And yet, as Alexis de Tocqueville was famous for observing in his *Democracy in America*, whose first edition appeared in 1835,[70] Americans exhibited an unbelievable passion for associating
and creating voluntary organizations of all kinds. Tocqueville defined the
American penchant to "join" and to form voluntary associations of all kinds—
"political, industrial, commercial, or even literary or scientific"—as one of
the unique features of American democracy. "Americans," he wrote, "of all
ages, all stations in life, and all types of dispositions," "are forever forming
associations. . . . In every case, at the head of any undertaking, where in
France you would find the government or in England some territorial mag-
nate, in the United States you are sure to find an association."[71] In Tocqueville's liberal understanding of American democracy, Jurgen Habermas explains, these "educated and powerful citizens were supposed to form an elite
public (in view of the lack of aristocracy by birth) whose critical debate determined public opinion."[72]

The cultural life of Jews outside the American synagogue emerged in this
public sphere under unprecedented conditions: Constitutional guarantees
separating church from state; mass migration; opportunities for social mobility and voluntary affiliation; pluralism and lay-driven leadership patterns.[73]
Precisely because Jews in the United States historically enjoyed legal protec-
tions to associate voluntarily without interference from the state, new kinds
of questions arose about the imperative to join Jewish organizations. As the
level of affiliation with the chosen people in America became a matter of individual choice for Jews, a rationale was needed to explain and otherwise
justify the meaning of that choice. The greater the openness of the American
milieu to individual Jews (in terms of opportunities for social integration and
material betterment), the greater became the perception by Jewish leaders of
a threat to Jewish communal cohesion and survival. A new kind of question
began to haunt Jews in America: "why be Jewish?" The answer was no lon-

ger a simple matter of birth and belief nor a consequence of being excluded from the majority culture. Even while many Jews believed in America as a land of freedom, in fact, America's freedoms threatened the cohesion and the very existence of these Jews as an organized community.

In his 1845 circular announcing the American Jewish Publication Society, Leeser sought to remedy the problem through the medium of publishing as a form of association: "as associationalism has been found to produce a remarkable degree of success where individual efforts have failed, it was deemed highly probable that if Israelites were to unite for the encouragement of their own literature, they might speedily witness many beneficial effects of their union."[74] In contrast to Leeser's relatively impersonal publishing efforts, Morais' preferred solution—literary associations themselves—provided intimate, direct physical sites of sociability and orality beyond the printed page and unburdened by the demands of congregational affiliation to think about these questions.

The first (non-Jewish) reading society in Philadelphia, the "Junto," was organized by Benjamin Franklin in 1727. In the colonial period leading up to the American Revolution (declared of course in Philadelphia in 1776), reading societies served a subversive, political function. In the case of the Junto, the names of its members and the subject matter discussed were often kept secret or just secret enough to attract the attention of potential members. As Scharf and Westcott record in their three-volume encyclopedic *History of Philadelphia*, published in 1884: "The artful founders knew the value of secrecy, and this was made on its elements, yet only to appear to stimulate interest among those who were admitted and lead outsiders to conjecture that it was of much importance. It existed until the war of the Revolution. . . . Morals, politics and natural philosophy were its themes."[75] There was more to it than that, as we now know. The Junto's members played substantial roles in the rebellion against British rule. After the Revolution, the Junto was transformed into a more open institution, the subscription library.[76]

While Jews had joined non-Jewish associations such as the Freemasons and learned institutions such as the American Philosophical Society in the eighteenth century, Jewish-identified voluntary associations beyond the walls of the synagogue only began to flourish later, in the setting of Victorian Philadelphia under the impact of population growth and cultural change. There were three generations of Victorian Jewish literary gathering, with some overlap in their orientations: antebellum literary associations for mutual improvement; postbellum literary associations for educational uplift and social entertainment; and thirdly, in the 1880s amidst the rising tide of mass migration, elite literary societies (as they then began calling themselves, shedding the earlier, more egalitarian language of association) named after cultural icons, as well as congregational literary societies, and the beginnings of immigrant literary societies.

The first generation appeared during the 1840s, and we have very little information about these societies, except to observe that they were coterminous with the rise of other, non-Jewish literary societies during the same time. In the antebellum period, reading societies ceased to function as subversive instruments of revolution. In fact, a strange inversion and inward turn occurred as the stated aims of reading societies were domesticated to serve the social needs of individuals and their self-improvement. Nonetheless, reading itself at times could function as a vehicle for social protest, if not revolution. Sam Warner, in his *Private City: Philadelphia in Three Periods of Its Growth*, shows how books and newspapers sensitized people to social inequities and injustices afflicting the working poor (e.g., working conditions in the needle trades) by "shaping the sentimental consciences of readers" and spurring them to take action (e.g., the growth of unions during this time, ca. 1830s–1850).[77]

The earliest Jewish literary societies in Philadelphia were less political and more internally focused than the kinds of societies that existed in the eighteenth century. According to Henry Morais in his history of the Jews of Philadelphia, published in 1894, the city's first Jewish literary association, a "Young Men's [Literary] Society[,] was started in 1841 . . . [and another] society, bearing the Hebrew name of Ohabe Lemudah [Lovers of Religious learning], whose object was the 'mutual improvement of its members' was formed in May [of] 1844." Morais also mentions a "Hebrew Literature Association," started in 1850, and another called the Young Men's Hebrew Literary Association, organized in 1855.[78] As noted earlier, it was Henry Morais' father who first turned to this generation of literary societies to cultivate a vanguard of young Jewish leaders.

What then did this teacher and regular speaker at literary societies read and impart? Part of the answer is easily traced from secondary works he drew upon in his published and unpublished writings, as well as from his correspondence, in which he cites or otherwise alludes to a wide-ranging variety of works of a Jewish and general nature. Another source is Morais' personal library, albeit keeping in mind that not every book in one's library has been read, and not everything one reads is found in one's library.[79] One of the few extant sources documenting the actual contents of Morais' library collection, at least as it stood in the 1860s, is a pocket notebook he kept listing book purchases.[80] Though limited to a few pages of brief entries, his notes reveal a thorough awareness of the most important works and currents that circulated in English-speaking Jewish intellectual circles. The notebook is inscribed "Catalogue of Religious Works (more particularly in the Jewish Religion)," but the fragmentary information shows that Morais possessed a large variety of volumes of a Jewish and a general nature. According to the list (which does not identify the specific editions),[81] Morais purchased, inter alia, the seventeenth-century Dutch Sephardic printer Menasseh ben Israel's famous biblical commentary *Conciliador*;[82] the English translation of the *Phaedon*, a dialogue on the immortality of the soul by Moses Mendelssohn, the eighteenth-century icon of Jewish enlightenment; the English translation of "Letters of [Certain Jews to Monseiur] Voltaire" (an apologetic response to Voltaire's attack on the Jews); David Levi's "Dissertations" and "Letter to Joseph Priestly," on the limits of deism and in defense of religious liberty; Robert Lowth's "Isaiah" and "Hebrew Poetry"; Johann Herder's "Spirit of Hebrew Poetry" (in English translation), treating the aesthetic dimensions of sacred scripture; Bernard Picart's "Religious Ceremonies of All Nations" (in English translation); the "Political and Literary History of the Jews in Spain," by Don Joseph Amador de Los Rios (in English translation); Georges-Bernard Depping's "History of the Jews in the Middle Ages" (in English or French translation), with his notable sections on the economic history of the Jews; and various types of belles lettres, such as the Victorian Jewish poet and novelist Grace Aguilar's "Women of Israel," as well as a work by the famous American orator Edward Everett. Morais subscribed to various Jewish periodicals published in England and America (the *Voice of Jacob*, the *Hebrew Review*, the *Occident*, and the *Asmonean*). According to the notebook, he sought and may have acquired a copy of Julius Fuerst's *Bibliographica*,[83] one of the most important bibliographies of Hebrew printed books available in the nineteenth century. His notebook shows that he purchased many of these works from booksellers abroad in London, Paris, and Italy, as well as in the United States.[84]

There also appear entries for works concerning biblical philology, archaeology, and geology, including a clipping of an advertisement for "An Answer to Hugh Miller and Theoretic Geologists," by Thomas Davies, and other works, mostly on the Bible, such as Sir Edward Strachey's "Hebrew Politics in the Times of Sargon" and Isidore Kalisch's "Historical Critical Commentary on the Old Testament Hebrew and English." Intriguing is a purchase note for "One Thousand and One Arabian Nights" in the original Arabic published in four volumes, along with an Arabic grammar by Faris El Shidac, which suggests that Morais had some facility with Arabic. Morais also kept abreast of Christian missionary and polemical tracts, such as Joseph Frey's "Letters and Articles on Judaism." Frey was a Jewish-born convert to Christianity and founder in April 1820 of the American Society for Meliorating the Condition of the Jews, a Christian missionary group.[85] These kinds of reading materials formed the core of his personal library; he also made them available to visitors to his home, which served as a kind of informal literary salon where he tutored students.[86] His daughter Nina continued this practice after moving to Minneapolis, where she hosted a weekly Sabbath study group at her home.[87]

A leather-bound notebook containing the loan entries made for the Hebrew Education Society "Maimonides College Library" during the 1880s discloses additional information about what Morais was reading and teaching.[88] In August of 1880, for example, Morais borrowed a copy of "Mishnah Nezikin" (which contains, notably, the beloved ethical tractate called "Pirke Abot"), presumably for study and teaching. The latter purpose appears to be confirmed by his student Solomon Solis-Cohen's renewing the same title in November of 1880. Additional entries show Morais having in his possession French and Hebrew editions of the travels of Benjamin of Tudela as well as the French translation of volume one of Maimonides' *Moreh Nebukhim* (Guide of the Perplexed), with Salomon Munk's notes. More surprising, perhaps, are notations during 1883 showing Morais borrowing a copy of Spinoza's *Ethics*, providing evidence that he knew his work firsthand.[89] To the right of the entry appears the number "546," which was Morais' home address on Fifth Street, suggesting he took the book home with him and did not merely consult it as a day loan in the Hebrew Education Society building. On August 28, 1884, we find on loan to Miss Gertrude Hahn, a member of Congregation Mikveh Israel, an unspecified work about the Inquisition, and in June of 1885, Cyrus Adler, a Morais disciple, borrowed the poetry of Dryden, and the works of Locke and Milton on education. This highly abbreviated list of reading materials speaks not only to what presumably was being read but also what was being discussed through direct instruction, public address, publications, and indirectly by allusion to the various sources and via informal conversation.

In the years following the Civil War a second generation of Jewish literary associations formed in Philadelphia, and with them came a broader mission. In this period, the emphasis shifted from small-scale mutual improvement to strengthening Jewish community ties in general, both through opportunities for young, single Jews to meet and socialize with their coreligionists and through the acquisition of a more advanced, sophisticated understanding of Jewish history, culture, and learning. The establishment and development of these youth-oriented cultural and educational institutions, however, remained central to Morais' implementation of his programmatic Sephardic vision of Jewish regeneration. There is clear historical evidence for his continuous efforts in this regard after the Civil War.

The first postbellum Jewish literary society in Philadelphia, named the "Hebrew Association," appeared in 1873 and received Morais' approbation and "active assistance." Reportedly, Morais served as its president "for a while"[90] and addressed the association's members at all its meetings.[91] On the broadside promoting the Hebrew Association, printed in Philadelphia in a variety of bold and italicized fonts of different sizes and dated December 15, 1873, we learn that its stated purpose was to "gain an insight into the Jewish learning of the past" through the study of all subjects that "may expand the range of human thought and impart a knowledge of what is good and useful."[92] The rallying cry at the end of the broadside summed up the spirit, if not the reality, of the association: "Fellow Israelites: Let us endeavor to rekindle the love of letters among those who have inherited a rich and varied literature."[93]

The social composition of the membership, which "gradually increased until it numbered about fifty or more," is not exactly known, but from the association's published list of officers, we know that women did not hold leadership positions. Membership was not based exclusively on class, though clearly the association appealed to the wealthier members of Philadelphia Jewish society. Most telling perhaps was the relatively high subscription fee charged to help maintain the Hebrew Association's library of "Standard works and Journals": an "initiation fee of ONE DOLLAR [caps in original] and a yearly subscription of three dollars payable by instalments [sic!] the first week of every month."[94]

Nathan Weissenstein, the association's founder, first president, and a student of Morais from the city's Jewish Foster Home, was an exception to the social profile. The majority of the officers included the sons of prominent Jewish leaders. These young men, such as Lewis W. Steinbach, Hyman P. Binswanger, Harry B. Sommer, and David Solis-Cohen, also happened to be

Morais' students from Congregation Mikveh Israel. Another officer, Jacob Voorsanger, would later become a prominent rabbi in San Francisco. Marcus E. Lam, a student of Morais from Maimonides College, served as secretary.[95]

Members met at different locations every two weeks, where they regularly heard lectures with a "Jewish tinge" and attended a variety of musical performances and recitals. Formal debates and informal, sometimes fiery arguments were also part of the social experience: "On a certain occasion, a Mr. Pearsall delivered a lecture,[96] in which he gave a clever expose—by means of stories—of Spiritualism. The address was exceedingly entertaining but it aroused the wrath of a certain Professor Rehn [Isaac Rehn was the president of the "Harmonial Society of Philadelphia"],[97] a Spiritualist, who was at that time giving a series of séances at Handel and Haydn Hall. He [Rehn] argued against the speaker, and said that he had long been convinced of the truth of Spiritualism. This led to his engagement to speak at a subsequent meeting of the Association."[98]

A more famous and direct outgrowth of the Hebrew Association was the Young Men's Hebrew Association (YMHA), established two years later in May of 1875. Many of the YMHA programs, according to its founders, were patterned on the activities of the Hebrew Association.[99] The YMHA also drew its inspiration from the establishment of a YMHA in New York the previous year. In Philadelphia, most though not all (some Hebrew Association members did not embrace the new institution)[100] of its founders previously belonged to the Hebrew Association. In the "Preamble to the Constitution and By-Laws" of the YMHA we learn that membership was by subscription and that the purpose of the society was "to promote a higher culture among the young men and to unite them in a liberal organization which shall tend to their moral, intellectual, and social improvement, hereby agree to form the Young Men's Hebrew Association." Women were not offered formal membership as "Active members," a category reserved for "male Israelites" over the age of twenty. Still, women were quite active in its programming, both as planners and as speakers. Morais' daughter Nina Morais, for example, received a prize for an essay she wrote and publicly delivered.[101] Other women known to have been involved include the aforementioned Mary M. Cohen, her sister Katherine Cohen, Ida Casseres, Bessie Davidson, Freda Jonas, Clara Kaufman, Esther Solis, Ida Sternstein, and Julia Weiler. The YMHA regularly presented lectures "on Jewish and current topics," held "entertainments of a social, musical, dramatic, and literary character," and had an "Associate Organization or branch, composed of junior members between the ages of 16 and 21 years"—a group that included young women. The YMHA, thus, was a meeting place outside the synagogue where Jewish teenagers and young men and women in their twenties could socialize, read, perform, debate, and promote their distinctive cultural and religious identities.

Reading in these public settings was often out loud or performed, especially in the form of public addresses and musical entertainments, in which sheet music reading played a critical role.[102] In Mary M. Cohen's scrapbook, we find a program for the "Young Men's Hebrew Association. Season 1877–78," whose opening entertainment on "Tuesday Evn'g, October 2d, 1877 at Musical Fund Hall" featured Franz von Suppe's comic opera *Fantanitza* arranged by H. Hahn, with accompanying orchestra; an address by Mayer Sulzberger, followed by Miss C. Long singing "Bliss Forever Past"; then a performance of the French composer Daniel Francois Espirit Auber's overture *Le Cheval de Bronze* (The Bronze Horse); A. Roggenburger performed a violin solo composed by the Belgian composer Charles August De Beriot, and Julius Kaufman gave a recitation of "The Ghost" by Gaetano Donizetti, another famous composer, from Bergamo, near Milan. Between Auber's overture and De Beriot's "6th Air" violin solo, Emanuel Cohen, the future husband of Nina Morais, read his first-prize essay, "The Philosophy of Carlyle," to the audience. By 1877, two years after its founding, the association already was hosting such extravagant programs and publishing its own monthly literary review. Beginning in 1881, the YMHA began publishing a bimonthly called the *Association Bulletin*, but it only survived two years.[103]

As the title of the "Young" Men's Hebrew Association explicitly states, and as its constitution and by-laws confirm, these Jewish literary societies clearly represented a youth-driven push for new forms of sociability. Note, however, that the early officer and membership lists of the YMHA demonstrate that the preponderance of the young men and women active in the Philadelphia YMHA were affiliated with Congregation Mikveh Israel, or otherwise knew Morais from his involvement with them at the Hebrew Association, as a teacher at the Hebrew Sunday School, at the Hebrew Education Society, at the Jewish Foster Home, and/or at Maimonides College.[104] The YMHA librarians, for example—first Jacob Voorsanger, followed by Lewis Steinbach, on the recommendation of Ellen Philips, the superintendent of the Hebrew Sunday School Society—were both former Hebrew Association members. The leading spirit of this generation's keeper of the books was Nathan Weissenstein, "an alumnus of the Jewish Foster Home, intensely religious, full of Hebraic zeal, but of frail physique." (He died three years later in 1878.) Weissenstein also had served as the first librarian of the Hebrew Sunday School Society when it launched its library.[105]

Weissenstein, Morais' Foster Home pupil, reportedly was credited by the majority of his peers as being the chief founder of the YMHA. Nonetheless, Mayer Sulzberger, the first president of the YMHA, a disciple of Isaac Leeser, and witness to the controversies of the 1850s that divided Leeser and Morais loyalists, is generally recognized to have been the most important intellectual and administrative figure in the growth of the Philadelphia YMHA. At the same time, Morais remained a behind-the-scenes mentor and supporter of the YMHA and also delivered innumerable public lectures before its members.

By the end of the 1870s, the literary associations had taken on a new role as the locus for planning public events. During this time, organized missionary activities and anti-Jewish discrimination was growing. The evangelical preaching of Moody and Sankey, for example, at mass outdoor events that attracted thousands, was the most visible face of these Protestant revival movements.[106] These revivals did not leave Philadelphia's Jewish community unaffected, and the young people involved with the YMHA launched a counteroffensive for what they called a "revived Judaism."[107] Speaking out from their literary societies, they pledged to defend Jews and Judaism against the newly intensifying threats of conversion and other forms of anti-Jewish hostility.[108]

According to documents discovered by Jonathan Sarna, a select group of members of the YMHAs of Philadelphia and New York joined together in October of 1879 to form a secret society called Keyam Dishmaya (from the Aramaic, meaning roughly "rise up for the sake of Heaven")[109] with the aim of promoting Sabbath observance, reviving Jewish ritual observances, and resisting these new threats to Jewish life. These young activists called for a "Grand Revival of the Jewish National Holiday of Chanucka" to be held at the Academy of Music in Philadelphia on December 16, 1879.[110] In subsequent years, Sarna points out, Cyrus Adler (a Morais disciple) would refer to their "revival of Jewish learning" as an American Jewish "renaissance" that pointed back to the events of 1879.[111]

This revival of Jewish learning, I would like to suggest, did not stem only from resistance to imminent threats and forces. In Philadelphia, at least, it also harked back to and reflected the decades of religious and cultural education Morais self-consciously nurtured in the young activists. The program Morais launched in the 1850s to cultivate a new generation of young Jewish leaders, to inculcate in them a sense of duty toward Jewish traditions, and to regenerate through them ritual observances in America preceded and conditioned the forms of resistance we find at the end of the 1870s. This is not to argue for a "great man" version of Victorian Jewish acculturation in Philadelphia, however charismatic and beloved Morais may have been; rather, it reinforces the argument for the isomorphic appeal of his teachings with the cultural situation of the time.

During the 1880s, a third generation of Jewish literary societies came to the fore in Philadelphia. These societies often were named after famous literary and political figures that were becoming canonical during the last two decades of the century. Acculturated Victorian Jews exhibited a clear desire to identify themselves with these non-Jewish icons. Among the names of this generation's Jewish literary societies were the "Irving," named after the author Washington Irving, whose presidents, David Solis-Cohen and Harry B. Sommers, formerly served as officers at the original Hebrew Association; the "Whittier Society," after the poet James Greenleaf Whittier; the "Longfellow," after Henry Wadsworth Longfellow; the "Tennyson," after Lord Alfred Tennyson; and the "Robert Browning Society." There were also Jewish literary societies and social clubs named explicitly after Jews, suggesting that already in the 1880s the formation of a kind of parallel Jewish cultural canon was under way. These included a "Leeser Society" (it would seem that Leeser was already becoming a canonical figure for American Jews within twenty years of his death); and nearby, in Lancaster, Pennsylvania, we find a Moses Mendelssohn literary society. Among the Jewish social clubs that existed in Philadelphia during the 1880s, we find the "Montefiore Social" and the "D'Israeli Society," named, respectively, after nineteenth-century England's most famous Jew and Jewish convert (who nonetheless was claimed as "Jewish" for the political successes and heights he attained). In addition to these extra-synagogal literary associations, there were also a number of associations connected with Philadelphia's synagogues. Among them were the Auxiliary Association of Rodeph Shalom, which then became the Jewish Culture Association; the Mikveh Israel Association; Adath Jeshurun's "Our Students of Jewish History"; and the "Knowledge Seekers," attached to the Reform congregation Kenesset Israel (under the leadership of Rabbi Joseph Krauskopf, the first American-born ordained Reform rabbi) and which later was called the Lyceum.[112] Perhaps the most innovative change within the Victorian Jewish cultural model was the founding of an immigrant "Hebrew Literature Society" in 1888, which itself was an outgrowth of a library established by garment workers and cigar makers in 1887.[113]

As part of their stated mission, all these literary societies began building libraries to supply their reading rooms. Perhaps the single most important private collection of books and pamphlets of Judaica Americana assembled in the nineteenth century belonged to the aforementioned editor of the *Occident*, Isaac Leeser. His personal collection grew over the years as he became a well-known personality to whom various works were sent for publication or review. After Leeser's death in February of 1868, the lifetime bachelor bequeathed his collection to Maimonides College, one of his most cherished achievements as an institution builder.[114] For Leeser, the building up of the college's library was of prime importance. Leeser's personal library came to form the core collection of the college's holdings, supplemented by new acquisitions. When Maimonides College closed in 1873, five years after Leeser's death, the Maimonides College Library, also known as the "Leeser library," was transferred to the Hebrew Education Society, another of Leeser's pioneer institutions. The Hebrew Education Society/Leeser Library continued to grow until 1912, when, in a public ceremony, it was formally transferred to the newly established Dropsie College for Hebrew and Cognate Learning, with Cyrus Adler, the college's first operating president, presiding. The Leeser Library/HES Library today forms the core of the Dropsie collection of Judaica Americana, which now belongs to the library at the Herbert D. Katz Center for Advanced Judaic Studies at the University of Pennsylvania.[115]

Today, the two most important private collections of nineteenth-century Judaica Americana—those of Leeser and Joshua I. Cohen—are held under one roof at the Library at the Katz Center at the University of Pennsylvania. Together with the collections at Gratz College, the Philadelphia Jewish Archives Center at Temple University, the Historical Society of Pennsylvania, the Library Company, the Rosenbach Museum and Library, the American Philosophical Society, the Free Library of Philadelphia, and in conjunction with many of the historic synagogue archives in the city, Philadelphia is home to the incunabula of Victorian Jewish cultural production. In short, what was read and what was printed in Philadelphia forms the basis for any serious inquiry into the history of reading and Jewish readers in the Victorian world.

Postscript

The Leeser Library and personal papers collection are how I came to know Leah Levitz Fishbane. Early on in her graduate career Leah came to Philadelphia to research the Philadelphia group and the renaissance and revival of Jewish learning associated with them. In 2006, the Penn Libraries hired her to work on our newly formed "American Genizah Project," whose pilot archival collection for cataloging, transcription, and digitization was that of Isaac Leeser. Leah made significant contributions to the development of our cataloging template and was the first to provide transcriptions in Hebrew font of original material. Her participation in our project will not be forgotten, and her memory will remain for a blessing.

NOTES

1. I would like to express my deep appreciation to Eitan Fishbane, Adam Mendelsohn, and Jonathan Sarna for their insightful criticisms and great encouragement in helping me to complete this essay.

2. This time period is often designated by the adjective "Victorian," roughly corresponding to the reign of Queen Victoria (1837–1901). Scholars such as Carl Degler and Michel Foucault have enlarged the term's scope to encompass social life in America and France during the same time period. See Carl Degler, "What Ought to Be and What Was: Women's Sexuality in the Nineteenth Century," *American Historical Review*, vol. 79, no. 5 (December 1974), pp. 146–90; Michel Foucault, *Discipline and Punish: The Birth of the Prison*, trans. Alan Sheridan (New York: Pantheon Books, 1977; 2nd edition, Vintage Books, 1995); idem, *The History of Sexuality, Vol. 1: An Introduction*, trans. Robert Hurley (New York: Pantheon Books, 1978; 2nd edition, Vintage Books, 1990). In a broad sense, the term has come to refer to a geographical and cultural space, what has been called an "Atlantic community, a translatlantic culture that tells us more about Victorian attitudes and institutions than we could learn from a single nation." See the introduction to *Victorian Women: A Documentary Account of Women's Lives in Nineteenth-Century England, France and the United States*, ed. Eran Olafson Hellerstein, Leslie Parker Hume, and Karen M. Offen (Stanford, CA: Stanford University Press, 1981). In speaking about a Victorian period in American history during the mid-nineteenth century, scholars like Daniel Ward Howe point to the emergence of American middle-class occupational patterns, such as entrance into the liberal professions (law, medicine, ministry and teaching); cultural phenomena such as fraternalism, voluntary and literary associations; and a variety of reform movements aimed at moral improvement and social control (e.g., the creation of asylums for the insane and the orphaned; penitentiaries and penal reform; the abolition of slavery, corporal punishment, and the death penalty; and the temperance movement). See the special issue on "Victorian Culture in America" edited by Daniel Walker Howe, *American Quarterly*, vol. 27, no. 5 (December 1975), and especially Howe's essay, "American Victorianism as a Culture," pp. 507–32, reprinted with some modifications and additions as *Victorian America*, edited with an introductory essay by Daniel Walker Howe (Philadelphia: University of Pennsylvania Press, 1976).

3. On the history of reading, see especially Roger Chartier, "Texts, Printings, Readings," in *The New Cultural History*, ed. Lynn Hunt (Berkeley and Los Angeles: University of California Press, 1989), pp. 154–75; *Reading in America: Literature and Social*

History, ed. Cathy N. Davidson (Baltimore and London: Johns Hopkins University Press, 1991); Robert Darnton, "History of Reading," in *New Perspectives on Historical Writing*, ed. Peter Burke (University Park: Pennsylvania State University Press, 1992; 2nd ed. 2001), pp. 140–67; *Readers in History: Nineteenth-Century American Literature and the Contexts of Response*, ed. James L. Machor (Baltimore and London: Johns Hopkins University Press, 1993); Richard H. Brodhead, *Cultures of Letters: Scenes of Reading and Writing in Nineteenth-Century America* (Chicago: University of Chicago Press, 1993); Roger Chartier, *Forms and Meanings: Texts, Performances, and Audiences from Codex to Computer* (Philadelphia: University of Pennsylvania Press, 1995); Alberto Manguel, *A History of Reading* (New York: Viking Press, 1996); Anthony Grafton, "Is History of Reading a Marginal Enterprise?" *The Papers of the Bibliographical Society of America*, vol. 91 (1997), pp. 139–57; *A History of Reading in the West*, ed. Guglielmo Cavallo and Roger Chartier, trans. Lydia Cochrane (Amherst: University of Massachusetts Press, 1999).

4. Chartier, introduction to *A History of Reading in the West*, pp. 3–5.

5. Michel Foucault, "What Is an Author?" in *Textual Strategies: Perspectives in Post-structural Criticism*, ed. Josue V. Harari (Ithaca, NY: Cornell University Press, 1979), pp. 141–60, as cited and discussed by Chartier in Roger Chartier, *The Order of Books: Readers, Authors, and Libraries in Europe between the Fourteenth and Eighteenth Centuries*, trans. Lydia Cochrane (Stanford, CA: Stanford University Press, 1994), pp. 29–32. The essay has been reprinted several times, including perhaps most conveniently in *The Foucault Reader*, ed. Paul Rabinow (New York: Pantheon Books, 1984), pp. 101–20.

6. Chartier, *Forms and Meanings*, pp. 2–5, 89, and p. 28, and p. 99, n. 8, citing Donald F. McKenzie, "The Book as an Expressive Form," *Bibliography and the Sociology of Texts: The Panizzi Lectures 1985* (London: The British Library, 1986), pp. 1–21.

7. I refer here to literacy levels for Hebrew and/or English, both of which were assigned the status of literary languages during this time, unlike Yiddish, for example, which was treated by many in the acculturating classes as an unrefined "jargon."

8. Introduction to *Judaica Americana: A Bibliography of Publications to 1900*, comp. Robert Singerman, 2 vols. (New York; Westport, CT; London: Greenwood Press, 1990), p. xxviii.

9. On the Dobson Bible, see most recently Yosef Goldman, *Hebrew Printing in America, 1735–1926: A History and Annotated Bibliography*, research and editing by Ari Kinsberg, 2 vols. (Brooklyn, NY: Yosef Goldman, 2006), vol. 1, p. 1, and entry four, p. 6. Goldman writes in his introduction to his first subject section (on Bibles), "We have not seen any copies of Dobson's Bibles that contain evidence of Jewish ownership" (Goldman, *Hebrew Printing*, vol. 1, p. 1). For the copies at the University of Pennsylvania previously owned by Jews (call number: BS715 1814), see the Penn Libraries Catalog (www.franklin.library.upenn.edu):

> TITLE: Biblia Hebraica Torah, nevi'im ketivim; secundum ultimam editionem Jos. Athiae, a Johanne Leusden denuo recognitam, recensita variisque notis latinis illustrata ab Everardo van der Hooght, V. D. M.
>
> PUBLISHER: Philadelphiæ: cura et impensis Thomae Dobson edita ex Ædibus lapideis. Typis Gulielmi Fry. MDCCCXIV.

DESCRIPTION: Book 2 v. 22 cm.

NOTES: First Hebrew Bible printed in America. v. 1–2 are from the collection of David Sulzberger, v. 1–2, c. 2 are From the collection of Robert Dearden. c. 2 is a gift of Cyrus Adler.

LOCAL NOTE(S): v. 1–2 (c. 1–2) is a gift of Cyrus Adler.

Similarly, among Judaica bibliographers, a distinction is sometimes made between Judaica and Hebraica. A modern Israeli publication written in Hebrew that is not preponderantly concerned with Jews or Judaism, therefore, would not fall into the category of "Judaica."

10. For the population statistics cited here, see Jacob Rader Marcus, *To Count a People: American Jewish Population Data, 1585–1984* (Lanham, NY; London: University Press of America, 1990):

Jewish Population of Philadelphia and the United States, 1830–1900

YEAR	PHILADELPHIA	UNITED STATES	PERCENTAGE OF U.S. POPULATION
1830	750	5–6,000	0.05
1860	10,000	150,000	0.47
1880	15,000	250,000	0.50
1900	40,000	1,058,000	1.39

11. For Jewish population figures for Philadelphia, and in comparison with other Jewish and general American population figures, see the figures collected in Marcus, *To Count a People*, pp. 193–194 and pp. 237–241; Edwin Wolf 2nd, "The German-Jewish Influence in Philadelphia's Jewish Charities," in *Jewish Life in Philadelphia, 1830–1940*, ed. Murray Friedman (Philadelphia: Ishi Publications/Institute for Human Issues, 1983), p. 325, n. 4; Harry S. Linfield, *Statistics of Jews and Jewish Organizations: Historical Review of Ten Censuses, 1850–1937* (New York: American Jewish Committee, 1939); and *Statistics of the Jews of the United States, Compiled under the authority of the Board of Delegates of American Israelites and the Union of American Hebrew Congregations* (Philadelphia: [BDAI and UAHC], 1880), p. 5. See Julius L. Greifer, "Neighborhood Centre—a Study of the Adjustment of a Cultural Group in America" (PhD diss., New York University, 1948), pp. 104–10, for a discussion and figures for general population trends in Philadelphia and the United States, compiled from the U.S. Census, between 1790 and 1940.

12. For a discussion of some of these institutions, see *Jewish Life in Philadelphia, 1830–1940*, ed. Friedman. On the history of the Jewish Publication Society, including its forerunner, the American Jewish Publication Society, see Jonathan D. Sarna, *JPS: The Americanization of Jewish Culture* (Philadelphia: The Jewish Publication Society of America, 1989).

13. On the founding of the Hebrew Sunday School, see Dianne Ashton, *Rebecca Gratz: Women and Judaism in Antebellum America* (Detroit: Wayne State University Press, 1997), pp. 121–69, and more generally Anne M. Boylan, *Sunday School: The Formation of an American Institution* (New Haven and London: Yale University Press, 1988).

14. There have been a number of studies of Leeser and the contents of the *Occident*. See Lance J. Sussman, *Isaac Leeser and the Making of American Judaism* (Detroit: Wayne State University Press, 1995), passim, for the most authoritative study, and see further below.

15. On the American Jewish Publication Society, see *Constitution and By-Laws of the American Jewish Publication Society, (founded on the 9th of Heshvan). Adopted at Philadelphia on Sunday, November 30, 1845, Kislev 1, 5605* (Philadelphia, 5606 [1845]), copy at the Library at the Herbert D. Katz Center for Advanced Judaic Studies, University of Pennsylvania (henceforth CAJSL); Henry Samuel Morais, *The Jews of Philadelphia: Their History from the Earliest Settlements to the Present Time* (Philadelphia: The Levy-type Company, 5654/1894). pp. 175–76; Solomon Grayzel, "The First American Jewish Publication Society," *Jewish Book Annual* (1944), pp. 42–44, which provides a list of the projected series of publications and the statement of purpose; and especially the authoritative study by Sarna, *JPS*, pp. 1–4, as well as Sussman, *Isaac Leeser*, pp. 152–54.

16. *Constitution and By-Laws of the Hebrew Education Society of Philadelphia. Adopted at a Town Meeting of Israelites on Sunday, Sivan 3, 5608, June 4, 1848* (Philadelphia, 5608 [1848]), copy at the CAJSL. Morais anonymously wrote the first history of the Hebrew Education Society (HES), in Hebrew, sometime between 1889 and 1893, and signed it in the name of Moses Aaron Dropsie, at that time "Chief Director" of the institution. See Menahem M. Glenn, *Rabbi Sabato Morais' Report on the Hebrew Education Society of Philadelphia* (Cincinnati, 1958), reprinted from *Essays in American Jewish History, to Commemorate the Tenth Anniversary of the Founding of the American Jewish Archives under the Direction of Jacob Rader Marcus* (Cincinnati: American Jewish Archives, 1958), pp. 407–24, for the Hebrew text and English translation. See also *Fifty Years of the Hebrew Education Society of Philadelphia, 1848–1898* (Philadelphia, 1899), p. 20, for a reprinting of the act of incorporation, and also see H. S. Morais, *Jews of Philadelphia*, pp. 154–60, for an early sketch of the history of the HES.

17. Bertram Wallace Korn, "The First American Jewish Theological Seminary: Maimonides College, 1867–1873," in *Eventful Years and Experiences* (Cincinnati: The American Jewish Archives, 1954), pp. 151–213.

18. On Philadelphia's Jewish "firsts," see Bertram Wallace Korn, "1655–1901," in *Seventy-Five Years of Continuity and Change: Our Philadelphia Jewish Community in Perspective*, reprint of the seventy-fifth anniversary supplement published by the (Philadelphia) *Jewish Exponent*, March 12, 1976, pp. 3–16. Korn credits Isaac Leeser as the leading force behind what he calls a "program of Jewish revival: introducing changes into the pattern of the congregation's life, publishing original works and translations as well, and stimulating the organization of agencies for the strengthening of American Judaism."

19. On Dropsie College, see Arthur Kiron, "The Professionalization of Wisdom: The Legacy of Dropsie College and Its Library," in *The Penn Library Collections at 250: From Franklin to the Web* (Philadelphia: The University of Pennsylvania Library, 2000), pp. 182–201, and additional sources cited there. Also available online at http://www .library.upenn.edu/exhibits/rbm/at250/dropsie/ak.pdf.

20. For general information about Philadelphia's Jewish literary associations, see

H. S. Morais, *Jews of Philadelphia*, pp. 162–72; also see J. Thomas Scharf and Thompson Westcott, *History of Philadelphia, 1609–1884*, 3 vols. (Philadelphia: L. H. Everts, 1884), 2:1099–1224, for a detailed history of the (non-Jewish and Jewish) literary culture and associations in Philadelphia up to 1884.

21. See Lance J. Sussman, "Isaac Leeser and the 'Philadelphia Pattern,'" in *When Philadelphia Was the Capital of Jewish America*, ed. Murray Friedman (Philadelphia: The Balch Institute Press; Toronto: Associated University Presses, 1993), pp. 24–26.

22. Solomon Solis-Cohen, "The Philadelphia Group," *Judaism and Science with Other Addresses and Papers from the Writings of Solomon Solis-Cohen* (Philadelphia: Privately printed, 1940), pp. 246–52. On Solis-Cohen, see also Philip Rosen, "Dr. Solomon Solis-Cohen and the Philadelphia Group," in *When Philadelphia Was the Capital of Jewish America*, ed. Friedman, pp. 106–25.

23. Solis-Cohen, "The Philadelphia Group," pp. 246–47.

24. For information about the Cohen family, see H. S. Morais, *Jews of Philadelphia*, pp. 64–69, and the Charles J. and Mary M. Cohen Collection at the CAJSL, MS 3, and the finding aid to the collection, Box 1, FF 1.

25. Letter from Samuel Mendelsohn (coeditor of the *Jewish Index*) to Mary M. Cohen, Philadelphia, November 22, 1872, written on the letterhead of the "Office of the Jewish Index, 413 Chestnut Street." See Mary M. Cohen scrapbook, Charles and Mary M. Cohen Collection, CAJSL, Box 4.

26. Dianne Ashton, "Crossing Boundaries: The Career of Mary M. Cohen," *American Jewish History*, vol. 83, no. 2 (1995), pp. 153–76.

27. On Nina Morais Cohen, see the entry by Judith E. Endelman in *Jewish Women in America: An Historical Encyclopedia*, ed. Paula E. Hyman and Deborah Dash Moore. 2 vols. (New York; London: Routledge, 1999), 1:248–49 and additional bibliography provided there, and note H. S. Morais, *Jews of Philadelphia*, pp. 319–20, who recounts how the burden of domestic responsibilities shifted to Nina, the oldest of seven children, upon the loss of their mother.

28. *Jewish Life in Philadelphia, 1830–1940*, ed. Friedman (see n. 11).

29. *When Philadelphia Was the Capital of Jewish America*, ed. Friedman, pp. 9–21. In conjunction with these ongoing efforts to study the "Philadelphia Group," Dianne Ashton produced an invaluable research bibliography of primary and secondary sources: *The Philadelphia Group: A Guide to Archival and Bibliographic Collections* (Philadelphia: The Feinstein Center for American Jewish History at Temple University, 1993).

30. On Leeser and his break with Mikveh Israel, see *A Review of the Late Controversy Between the Rev. Isaac Leeser and the Congregation Mikveh Israel* (Philadelphia: n.p., 1850) and *A Review of "The Review" of the Late Controversy Between the Rev. Isaac Leeser and the Philadelphia Congregation "Mikve Israel" by an Israelite* (Philadelphia: Published at the Office of the Asmonean, 1850) (*Judaica Americana*, comp. Singerman, 1:227, nos. 1158 and 1159), copies held in the Leeser Library at the CAJSL. See Sussman, *Isaac Leeser*, pp. 155–78; Maxine Sellers, "Isaac Leeser, Architect of the American Jewish Community" (PhD diss., University of Pennsylvania, 1965), pp. 19–20.

31. Sellers, "Isaac Leeser," pp. 19–20.

32. Philip Rosen, "Orthodox Institution Builder: Rabbi Bernard Lewis [*sic*] Levinthal," in *When Philadelphia Was the Capital of Jewish America*, pp. 126–44.

33. See Moshe Davis, *The Emergence of Conservative Judaism: The Historical School in Nineteenth Century America* (Philadelphia: The Jewish Publication Society of America, 1963), passim and esp. pp. 342–44 for a biographical sketch.

34. For additional background about Marcus Jastrow and his tenure at Rodeph Shalom, see H. S. Morais, *Jews of Philadelphia*, pp. 76–78, and Edward Davis, *The History of Rodeph Shalom Congregation Philadelphia, 1802–1926*, with an Introduction by Rabbis Louis Wolsey (Philadelphia: Press of Edward Stern & Co., 1926), pp. 81–98.

35. Martin P. Beifield Jr., "The Americanization of Reform Judaism: Joseph Krauskopf—a Case Study," in *When Philadelphia Was the Capital of Jewish America*, pp. 156–72.

36. For other examples of conflicts, such as between Sulzberger and Krauskopf, see Sarna, *JPS*, pp. 53–54. My thanks to Jonathan Sarna for pointing out this example to me.

37. For the account of Morais' last moments of reading, see Charles Hoffman, "Memorial Tribute," (Philadelphia) *Jewish Exponent*, November 19, 1897, p. 2.

38. This discussion of the social history of reading builds on previous research that I published: Arthur Kiron, "Varieties of Haskalah: Sabato Morais' Program of Sephardi Rabbinic Humanism in Victorian America," in *Renewing the Past, Reconfiguring Jewish Culture: From al-Andalus to the Haskalah*, ed. Ross Brann and Adam Sutcliffe (Philadelphia: University of Pennsylvania Press, 2004), pp. 121–45, and especially pp. 133–37 regarding translation and the Sephardic cultural paradigm.

39. *Judaica Americana*, comp. Singerman, see esp. index, 2:1263–64, from where these statistics have been compiled.

40. Sharona Wachs, *American Jewish Liturgies: A Bibliography of American Jewish Liturgy from the Establishment of the Press in the Colonies through 1925*, historical introduction by Karla Goldman, liturgical introduction by Eric L. Friedland (Cincinnati: Hebrew Union College Press, 1997).

41. *Judaica Americana*, comp. Singerman, index, s.v. "Philadelphia."

42. See the rare advertisers to the *Occident*, a bound volume of which is held at the CAJSL.

43. Ibid.

44. On American Jewish journalism and publishing during this time, see the comprehensive bibliography of nineteenth-century serials (in English, German, Hebrew, Yiddish) in *Judaica Americana*, comp. Singerman, 2:931–1070. On the American Jewish press in Philadelphia in the nineteenth century, see H. S. Morais, *Jews of Philadelphia*, pp. 356–59; on the Jewish press in the United States in the nineteenth century, see Mayer Sulzberger, "Jewish Journalism," *Occident*, vol. 26, no. 6 (September 1868), pp. 241–49; Albert M. Freidenberg, "American Jewish Journalism to the Close of the Civil War," *Publications of the American Jewish Historical Society*, no. 26 (1918), pp. 270–73; Robert Singerman, "The American Jewish Press, 1823–1983: A Bibliographic Survey of Research and Studies," *American Jewish History*, vol. 73, no. 4 (June 1984), pp. 422–44; Arthur A. Goren, "The Jewish Press," *The Ethnic Press in the United States: A Historical Analysis and Handbook*, ed. Sally M. Miller (New York; Westport, CT; and London:

Greenwood Press, 1987), pp. 203–28; and for additional comparative perspective, see most recently *Outsiders in Nineteenth Century Press History: Multicultural Perspectives*, ed. Frankie Hutton and Barbara Strauss Reed (Bowling Green, OH: Bowling Green State University Popular Press, 1996).

45. On Leeser, see Sussman, *Isaac Leeser.*

46. On the subscribers to the *Occident* and subscription lists to other antebellum American Jewish periodicals, see Rudolf Glanz, "Where the Jewish Press Was Distributed in Pre–Civil War America," *Western States Jewish Historical Quarterly*, vol. 5 (1972–73), pp. 1–14. According to Glanz, "254 settlement points in thirty-three states and territories were reached by the Occident during the eighteen years of its antebellum existence." I am grateful to Arthur Aryeh Goren for calling to my attention and sending me a copy of this article.

47. On Leeser and the *Occident*, as well as his other publishing ventures, see Sussman, *Isaac Leeser*, pp. 136–48, and Arthur Kiron, "An Atlantic Jewish Republic of Letters?" *Jewish History*, vol. 20 (2006), pp. 171–211, esp. pp. 178–81; for examples of non-Jewish readers of the *Occident*, see, e.g., C. D. Oliver (Pastor of M. E. Church, Montgomery, Mass.) to Isaac Leeser, 20 October 1852, found in the Isaac Leeser Collection, CAJSL, Box 9, FF 14; Henry W. Ducachet (Rector of St. Stephen's Church) to [Isaac Leeser?], August 21, 1840; John Bilton ONeill to Isaac Leeser, August 8, 1848. The last two letters are held in the private collection of Arnold Kaplan and are cited with his permission.

48. *Sidur Sifte tsadikim. kolel seder ha-tefilot mi-kol ha-shanah ke-minhag kehilat ha-kodesh sefaradim. . . . The Form of Prayers According to the Custom of the Spanish and Portuguese Jews. Edited and with the Former Translations Carefully Compared and Corrected by Isaac Leeser*, 6 vols. (Philadelphia, 5597–98 [1837–38]). Cf. Kiron, "An Atlantic Jewish Republic of Letters?" p. 181. Interestingly, Leeser refers to himself in Hebrew on the title page as the "*shaliah tsibur*" (public emissary [to the divine], i.e., the reader of prayers) of Congregation Mikveh Israel, not as the hazan. On the early history of English translations of the Jewish liturgy, see S. Singer, "Early Translations and Translators of the Jewish Liturgy in England," *Transactions of the Jewish Historical Society of England*, vol. 3 (1896–98), pp. 36–71, and pp. 56–71 on David Levi. See also Sussman, *Isaac Leeser*, pp. 55, 159. On David Levi in particular and the Anglo-Jewish turn to vernacular translation in the eighteenth century in general, see Richard H. Popkin, "David Levi, Anglo-Jewish Theologian," *Jewish Quarterly Review*, vol. 87, nos. 1–2 (1996), pp. 79–101, and especially David Ruderman, *Jewish Enlightenment in an English Key: Anglo-Jewry's Construction of Modern Jewish Thought* (Princeton, NJ: Princeton University Press, 2000), pp. 57–88 and 215–268.

49. [Isaac Leeser], *Catechism for younger children: designed as a familiar exposition of the Jewish religion* [1st ed.] (Philadelphia: Printed for the author by Adam Waldie, 5599 [1839]).

50. *Sefer Divre tsadikim. . . . The Book of Daily Prayers for Every Day in the Year. According to the Custom of the German and Polish Jews*, ed. Isaac Leeser (Philadelphia, 5608 [1848]). In both editions (i.e., *Sidur Sifte tsadikim* and *Sefer Divre tsadikim*), whose pagination went from right to left, the English translation faced the Hebrew text on the

opposite page, almost as if Leeser meant to imitate Jews in America proudly facing their heritage. See also Sussman, *Isaac Leeser*, pp. 13, 157–59, and 283, n. 3.

51. On the "Leeser Bible" see Lance J. Sussman, "Another Look at Isaac Leeser and the First Jewish Translation of the Bible in the United States," *Modern Judaism*, vol. 5 (1985), pp. 159–90.

52. *Constitution and By-Laws of the American Jewish Publication Society, (founded on 9th of Heshvan). Adopted at Philadelphia on Sunday, November 30, 1845, Kislev 5605* (Philadelphia: C. Sherman, 5606 [1845]).

53. [Isaac Leeser]. "Address of the Jewish Publication Committee to the Israelites of America," preface to the *Jewish Miscellany* [no. 1 Caleb Asher] (Philadelphia, 5605 [1845]), p. 2. See Paul Mendes-Flohr and Jehuda Reinharz, eds., *The Jew in the Modern World: A Documentary History*, 2nd ed. (New York and Oxford: Oxford University Press, 1995), pp. 461–63, for an annotated reprinting of this address. On this early moment in Anglo-Jewish literary production, in particular the works of Aguilar and Elizabeth, see Nadia Valman, *The Jewess in Nineteenth-Century Jewish Literary Culture* (Cambridge; New York: Cambridge University Press, 2007), and Ruderman, *Jewish Enlightenment in an English Key*, pp. 261–68, regarding Hurwitz' *Hebrew Tales*, a rabbinic anthology in English, which first appeared in London in 1826. Unfortunately, Leeser's early venture to institutionalize Jewish publishing in America suffered a disastrous fate when a fire in December of 1851 destroyed his inventory. See especially Sarna, *JPS*, pp. 3–4, and his evaluation of the logistical and commercial difficulties Leeser's failed efforts also faced.

54. The relationship between the reading activities under discussion here, private library collecting, and the growth of Jewish libraries is a critical topic still in need of investigation. In the American context, the pioneering study of what Robert Singerman calls "Jewish library culture" is that of his article "Books Weeping for Someone to Visit and Admire Them: Jewish Library Culture in the United States, 1850–1910," *Studies in Bibliography and Booklore*, vol. 20 (1998), pp. 99–144.

55. For the authoritative study of Rebecca Gratz, see Ashton, *Rebecca Gratz*.

56. On Morais, see Arthur Kiron, "Golden Ages, Promised Lands: The Victorian Rabbinic Humanism of Sabato Morais" (PhD diss., Columbia University, 1999). Original documents from the Sabato Morais Papers, held at the Library of the Herbert D. Katz Center for Advanced Judaic Studies at the University of Pennsylvania, will be cited below as SM-CJS, Box, and File Folder (FF). Regarding Morais' tenure, see Pamela S. Nadell, *Conservative Judaism in America: A Biographical Dictionary and Sourcebook* (New York: Greenwood Press, 1988), p. 192.

57. See Sabato Morais, *Italian Hebrew Literature*, ed. Julius H. Greenstone, with a foreword by Henry S. Morais (New York: The Jewish Theological Seminary of America, 1926), pp. 68–69.

58. Sabato Morais, "A Sermon Delivered on Thanksgiving Day, November 27th, 1851 by the Rev. S. Morais, Minister of Congregation Mikve Israel, Philadelphia," printed in the *Asmonean* (New York), December 12, 1851, p. 181; a clipping of this printed sermon is pasted into Morais' personal scrapbook, p. 2. For further discussion, see Kiron, "Varieties

of Haskalah," p. 124. For a different view, attributing this to Leeser, see Sarna, *American Judaism: A History* (New Haven: Yale University Press, 2004), pp. 76ff. Leeser, as well as the rhetoric of regeneration, clearly preceded Morais' arrival in America; however, the argument being made here is that while Leeser is to be credited for pioneering the institutional forms discussed here that were meant to regenerate Jewish life in America, Morais came to fill those forms with his own intellectual presence and Sephardic rabbinic humanist learning, which he programmatically transmitted to the young people who came under his care.

59. On the various ideas regarding regeneration, amelioration, rehabilitation, occupational diversification, and productivization of the Jews in European social, political, and economic thought during the eighteenth and early nineteenth centuries, see Jonathan Karp, *The Politics of Jewish Commerce: Economic Thought and Emancipation in Europe, 1638-1848* (Cambridge: Cambridge University Press, 2008), pp. 94-134, 145-47, 150, 160-62, 202-7. For the French example, see Alyssa Goldstein Sepinwall, *Regenerating the World: The Abbe Gregoire and the French Revolution: The Making of Modern Universalism* (Berkeley: University of California Press, 2005).

60. On the Abbe Gregoire and regeneration, see Alyssa Goldstein Sepinwall, "Strategic Friendships: Jewish Intellectuals, the Abbe Gregoire, and the French Revolution," in *Renewing the Past, Reconfiguring Jewish Culture*, pp. 189-212, and her book-length monograph, *Regenerating the World*.

61. Mary Kelley, "Reading Women/Women Reading: The Making of Learned Women in Antebellum America," *Journal of American History*, vol. 83, no. 2 (September 1996), p. 403.

62. Ibid.

63. Kelly, "Reading Women," pp. 404 and 406-9; notable authors and works included Hannah Adams, Cervantes, Shakespeare, David Hume, Elizabeth Barrett Browning, sermons of Theodore Parker, antislavery newspapers, Thomas Macaulay's *History of England*, John Greenleaf Whittier's poetry, and of course the Bible. Reading was sometimes done aloud at home, sometimes at female academies, and sometimes alone.

64. Idana Goldberg, "'Better and Wiser Daughters in Israel': The Diaries of Fannie and Amelia J. Allen" (MA thesis, University of Pennsylvania, 1997); see also Idana Goldberg, "Gender, Religion and the Jewish Public Sphere in Mid-nineteenth Century America" (PhD diss., University of Pennsylvania, 2004).

65. Susan Tucker, Katherine Ott, and Patricia P. Buckler, eds., *The Scrapbook in American Life* (Philadelphia: Temple University Press, 2006). See also Ellen Gruber Garvey, "Imitation Is the Sincerest Form of Appropriation: Scrapbooks and Extra-Illustration," *Common-Place*, vol. 7, no. 3 (April 2007), pp. 1-13. See online at www.common-place.org; and most recently, Jessica Helfand, *Scrapbooks: An American History* (New Haven: Yale University Press, 2008).

66. Mary M. Cohen Scrapbook, Charles and Mary M. Cohen Collection, CAJSL, Box 4.

67. Ibid.

68. For the Civil War incident, see the Sabato Morais Ledger, p. 23; for Morais' ex-

panded views on liturgical reform, see Ledger, p. 80, CAJSL. Viewable online at http:// sceti.library.upenn.edu/morais/.

69. Cohen and Morais both published under their own names, but the interesting question here—why and when they chose to publish under their own names, rather than pseudonymously or anonymously—requires further investigation.

70. Alexis de Tocqueville, *De la democratie en Amerique*, 1st ed. (French), 2 vols., 1835. Translated from the French by Henry Reeve, 4 vols. in 2 pts. (London: Saunders and Otley, 1835-40). Newly translated by George Lawrence as Alexis de Tocqueville, *Democracy in America*, ed. J. P. Mayer (New York, 1969), p. 513.

71. Tocqueville, *Democracy in America*, trans. Lawrence, ed. Mayer, pp. 513, 644-645.

72. Jurgen Habermas, *The Structural Transformation of the Public Sphere: An Inquiry into a Category of Bourgeois Society*, trans. Thomas Burger with Frederick Lawrence (Cambridge, MA: Harvard University Press, 1991), p. 137. Habermas' understanding of what he calls "the public sphere," thus, is that area of social existence not centered in the operation of either government or private commercial activity nor in the intimacy of the home where public opinion is shaped. See also Jurgen Habermas, "The Public Sphere: An Encyclopedia Article (1964)," trans. Peter Hohendahl in *New German Critique*, vol. 3 (Fall 1974), pp. 45-55; and David Sorkin, "The Ideology and the Public Sphere," in *The Transformation of German Jewry, 1780-1840* (New York and Oxford: Oxford University Press, 1987), pp. 79-104.

73. See Abraham J. Karp, "What's American about American Jewish History: The Religious Scene," *American Jewish Historical Quarterly*, vol. 52 (1962-63), pp. 283-94; Salo W. Baron, "The Emancipation Movement and American Jewry," in *Steeled by Adversity: Essays and Addresses on American Jewish Life* (Philadelphia: Jewish Publication Society of America, 1971), pp. 80-105, for an overview of some of these fundamental features of the American Jewish experience.

74. [Isaac Leeser], *Circular, of the American Jewish Publication Society to the Friends of Jewish Literature, Philadelphia, December 10, 1845*, copy at CAJSL.

75. Scharf and Westcott, *History of Philadelphia*, 2:1114.

76. On Ben Franklin and the Junto, and the emergence of (non-Jewish) literary societies in Philadelphia, see Scharf and Westcott, *History of Philadelphia*, 2:1190-1214. It may be worth noting here that the term "junto" also was used by Sephardic Jews to name their board of synagogue officials, the "adjunta," e.g., at Philadelphia's Congregation Mikveh Israel.

77. Sam Bass Warner, *The Private City: Philadelphia in Three Periods of Its Growth* (Philadelphia: University of Pennsylvania Press, 1971), p. 76, n. 28.

78. H. S. Morais, *Jews of Philadelphia*, p. 163.

79. See Darnton, "History of Reading," p. 145.

80. Sabato Morais Papers, AJHS, *P-55, Box 1, FF 5.

81. The following information is based on a fragmentary list. It is not clear if Morais actually acquired all the books listed. I have not listed every work but only some of the most important titles relevant to understanding the concerns and reading materials circulating at that time. Because in some cases it is unclear which particular edition Morais

acquired (or wanted to acquire), I have not tried to supply precise bibliographic description. I have supplied some probable information about the language of a given work (i.e., in French or English translation), based on the fact that Morais did not read German and that he listed these entries with English titles. So, for example, though he read French, he apparently owned the English translation of the De Pinto exchange with Voltaire called "Letters to Voltaire." For the first English edition, see *Letters of Certain Jews to Monseiur Voltaire containing an apology for their own people and for the Old Testament with Critical Reflections and A short Commentary Extracted From a Greater. In Two Volumes. Translated by the Rev. Philip Lefanu* (Philadelphia, 1777). A 1795 edition, from the library of the nineteenth-century Baltimore Jewish doctor and bibliophile Joshua I. Cohen, is found in the CAJSL collection.

82. *Conciliador de la convencia da los Lugares de la S. Escriptura, que repugantes entre si parecen*, pt. 1 (Frankfort or Amsterdam? 1632); pt. 2 (Amsterdam, 1641); pt. 3 (Amsterdam, 1650); pt. 4 (Amsterdam, 1651). See Cecil Roth, *A Life of Menasseh ben Israel* (Philadelphia, 1934), pp. 87–89 299, for the bibliographical information. In this biblical commentary, Ben Israel tried to reconcile contradictory biblical passages that had become a matter of controversy among skeptical ex-conversos. Morais' friend from London, E. H. Lindo, translated the work into English in 1842. See Roth, *A Life*, pp. 87, 89.

83. Cf. Julius Fuerst, *Bibliographica Judaica*, 2 vols. (1st ed., 1849–51; 2nd ed., 1863).

84. Regarding Morais' means of acquiring reading materials, see also SM-CJS, Box 1, FF 8, letter from Abraham Hart to SM, August 20, 1851, offering to lend him his copies of Grace Aguilar's works, and SM-CJS, Box 1, FF 10, for a letter from Solomon Sebag to SM, April 11, 1853, telling Morais that he would "send some of my books at the earliest opportunity" to him from London.

85. On Joseph S.C.F. Frey, see George L. Berlin, *Defending the Faith: Nineteenth Century American Jewish Writings on Christianity and Jesus* (Albany: SUNY Press,1989), pp. 7–10, 17–18, 81–92, and 177, n. 1, for additional information.

86. The extent of his knowledge of the contents of these works, whether he actually read them, is a separate matter, which cannot be treated here. Morais eventually donated some 1,200 volumes of his own library to The Jewish Theological Seminary (JTS) in 1894. For news of Morais' donation of his books to the JTS, see (Philadelphia) *Jewish Exponent*, April 6, 1894, and June 22, 1894, and chapter 6 of Arthur Kiron, "Golden Ages, Promised Lands: The Victorian Rabbinic Humanism of Sabato Morais" (PhD diss., Columbia University, 1999). In his will Morais bequeathed to "the Jewish Theological Seminary, wherever it is located, if conducted according to the principles expressed in its constitution, all my Hebrew books, and books connected with Hebrew literature." He willed his "liturgical works" to his children or grandchildren or to be lent to his Philadelphia congregation for the use of its "attendants." Morais singled out his daughter Nina in his will to receive his books in French and Italian, and to his son Henry he left other books in English (perhaps allowing for the language ability of each). To my knowledge no catalog exists of Morais' library, which came to form part of the nucleus of the seminary's original collections. Librarians at The Jewish Theological Seminary adopted the practice of stamping books from the original collection, which comprised Mo-

rais' volumes as well as the David Cassell collection of Berlin (purchased in 1894), with a special identifying mark, such as that found on the seminary's copies of issues of the Italian Jewish journal *Vessillo Israelitico* stamped "Morais Library." On the Morais Library now held at the Library of The Jewish Theological Seminary of America, see Hasia R. Diner, "Like the Antelope and the Badger: The Founding and Early Years of the Jewish Theological Seminary, 1886–1902," *Tradition Renewed: A History of the Jewish Theological Seminary*, ed. Jack Wertheimer (New York: Jewish Theological Seminary of America, 1997), pp. 3–42 and especially pp. 18–19.

87. Judith E. Endelman, "Cohen, Nina Morais," in *Jewish Women in America: An Historical Encyclopedia*, 1:248–49.

88. "Maimonides College Library," circulation record book, Miscellaneous Manuscript 35, CAJSL.

89. Additional confirmation of this can be found in two letters from Morais to the editor of the *American Hebrew*, published on February 23, 1883, and March 9, 1883, in which Morais places his criticisms of Spinoza in relation to the views of the Italian Jewish biblical exegete Samuel David Luzzatto. According to Morais, these letters to the editor were prompted by an unidentified address he heard at the Philadelphia YMHA. He chose to submit his response to the *American Hebrew*, a nationally circulating Jewish weekly, edited and published in New York City.

90. "Maimonides College Library," circulation record book, p. 7, CAJSL.

91. Broadside, titled "Hebrew Association," dated "Philadelphia Dec. 15th, 1873." A copy is found in the Sabato Morais Collection, CAJSL, Box 16, FF 4. Printed at the bottom of the broadside is the following approbation from Morais: "I approve of the efforts made to give origin to this Association, and solicit in its behalf the cooperation of my Philadelphia co-religionists." Another copy of this broadside can be found pasted into a scrapbook kept by Mary M. Cohen in the Charles and Mary M. Cohen Collection, CAJSL, Box 4.

92. Ibid.

93. See "Hebrew Association" broadside, ibid.; *Jewish Messenger*, December 11, 1874; May 21, 1875; *American Israelite*, May 21, 1875; H. S. Morais, *Jews of Philadelphia*, pp. 163–67; William R. Langfeld, *The Young Men's Hebrew Association of Philadelphia: A Fifty-Year Chronicle* (Philadelphia: The Young Men's and Young Women's Hebrew Association, 1928), p. 7; Benjamin Rabinowitz, "YMHA, 1854–1913," *Publications of the American Jewish Historical Society*, no. 37 (1947), p. 230.

94. "Hebrew Association" broadside, December, 15, 1873, SM-CJS, Box 16, FF 4.

95. Ibid.

96. Jonathan Sarna has kindly suggested to me the possible identification of "Mr. Pearsall" with the highly regarded writer Logan Pearsall Smith, who indeed grew up in the Philadelphia area prior to 1894, when Henry Morais' book was published, and may very well have been the subject of Morais' recountal.

97. See Frank Podmore, *Modern Spiritualism: A History and Criticism*, 2 vols. (London: Metheun & Co.; New York: Charles Scribner's Sons, 1902), 1:243, regarding Isaac Rehn, "President of the Harmonial Society of Philadelphia."

98. H. S. Morais, *Jews of Philadelphia*, p. 163.

99. See the extended analysis of this phenomenon in Leah Levitz Fishbane, "On the Road to Renaissance," chapter 2 of the present volume.

100. H. S. Morais, *Jews of Philadelphia*, p. 164.

101. Langfeld, *Young Men's Hebrew Association of Philadelphia*, p. 15.

102. Ibid.

103. H. S. Morais, *Jews of Philadelphia*, p. 165.

104. Korn, "The First American Jewish Theological Seminary," pp. 151–213.

105. See H. S. Morais, *Jews of Philadelphia*, pp. 151 and 162–71, esp. p. 163; Langfeld, *Young Men's Hebrew Association of Philadelphia*, p. 6; Rabinowitz, "YMHA, 1854–1913," pp. 221–326 (reprinted as idem, *Young Men's Hebrew Association, 1854–1913* [New York, 1948]); and see Scharf and Westcott, *History of Philadelphia*, 2:1099–1224, for a detailed history of the literary culture and associations in Philadelphia up to 1884.

106. For the local Jewish reaction in Philadelphia to the Moody and Sankey revivals, see (Philadelphia) *Jewish Record*, January 14, 1876; Scharf and Westcott, *History of Philadelphia*, 1:840. For background, see Marion L. Bell, *Crusade in the City: Revivalism in Nineteenth-Century Philadelphia* (Lewisburg, PA: Bucknell University Press, 1977), pp. 200–53 and p. 282 for a bibliography of sources; Naomi W. Cohen, *Encounter with Emancipation: The German Jews in the United States, 1830–1914* (Philadelphia: Jewish Publication Society of America, 1984), p. 256. For background on the intensification of hostility in America toward Jews during this time, see John Higham, *Send These to Me* (Baltimore: Johns Hopkins University Press, 1975; revised ed. 1984), pp. 95–152; and Cohen, *Encounter with Emancipation*, pp. 249–65.

107. Jonathan D. Sarna, "The Making of an American Jewish Culture," in *When Philadelphia Was the Capital of Jewish America*, ed. Friedman, p. 148; idem, "The Late Nineteenth-Century American Jewish Awakening," in *Religious Diversity and American Religious History: Studies in Traditions and Cultures*, ed. Walter H. Conser Jr. and Sumner B. Twiss (Athens, GA; London: University of Georgia Press, 1995), pp. 1–25; idem, *A Great Awakening: The Transformation That Shaped Twentieth Century American Judaism and Its Implications for Today* (New York: Council for Initiatives in Jewish Education, 1995), pp. 12–15; idem, *American Judaism*, pp. 135–38.

108. Sarna, *American Judaism*, pp. 135–38.

109. The exact source of this Aramaic phrase, *keyam dishmaya*, is obscure. Eitan Fishbane has pointed out to me several sources in the Zohar, though none with the exact formulation transliterated by the group. Jonathan Sarna suspects that a section of the commentary on the Zohar by Moshe Hayim Luzzatto (RaMHaL), an eighteenth-century Italian kabbalist, may have been the source. See http://www.ramhal.net/doc/ketoret.html. Eitan Fishbane has made the point that the phrase is better translated as "in support of heaven" (rather than "for the sake of heaven," as I have rendered it here), especially in the context of this secret society. Despite his good advice, I hesitatingly but deliberately retain the term "for the sake of heaven" even though it is inexact, because my sense is that the group was working within a kind of "martyrological" cultural framework that Morais imparted to them. In other words, the translation "for the sake of" first references the

actors (those young men bound in secret covenant), *not* the object of their actions (i.e., the heavens). If that is so, the translation "for the sake of heaven" is not intended here to mean *lishmah* or *le-shem shamayim* ("for its own sake" or literally "in the name of heaven") but is closer to the idea of *kidush ha-shem/le-shem shamayim*—in this case being more of a metaphor of willingness to sacrifice one's self-interests for the sake of heaven. I briefly discuss this "Sephardic" martyrological sensibility of duty that Morais popularized in (Arthur Kiron), "Livornese Traces in American Jewish History: Sabato Morais and Elijah Benamozegh," in *Atti del Convegno Internazionale di Studi nel Centenario della morte di Elia Benamozegh* (Milan: De Pas Editrice, 2002), pp. 56ff. I also talk about it in idem, "Varieties of Haskalah: Sabato Morais' Program of Sephardic Rabbinic Humanism in Victorian America," in *Reconfiguring Jewish Culture*, ed. Sutcliffe and Brann, pp. 130–31.

110. Sarna, *American Judaism*, pp. 135–39, and p. 137 for the reproduction of the broadside.

111. Ibid., p. 138.

112. H. S. Morais, *Jews of Philadelphia*, p. 164.

113. Greifer, "Neighborhood Centre," p. 149.

114. See Korn, "Maimonides College," pp. 151–213.

115. On the fate of the Leeser Library and Maimonides College, see ibid., pp. 182–85.

4 Preserving the Past to Fashion the Future

The Editorial Board of the Jewish Encyclopedia

A merican Jews in the twenty-first century take for granted the richness of Jewish cultural life. Institutions dedicated to Jewish life abound: those dedicated to Judaism, to Israel, to promoting justice, to defending Jewish interests, to Jewish learning, and to the arts. Some organizations promote specific religious denominations while others focus on serving the needs of subcommunities of Jews—Syrians, Russians, Israelis, intermarrieds, elderly, singles, gays and lesbians. In the early twenty-first century, this evolution continues with Jewish groups that coalesce around organic farming, meditation, and alternative music, to name just of a few of the organizing venues for contemporary Jewish culture. The proliferation of Jewish film and arts festivals and the expansion of gourmet kosher food products are other ways in which contemporary Jews experience the breadth of Jewish cultural life.

As "People of the Book," Jews have always been especially attuned to the literary riches of Jewish culture and to the power of the written word to disseminate it. Not surprisingly, the explosion of resources at the turn of the twenty-first century in this arena is astounding. The translation of sacred texts into English[1] has rendered accessible so much of Jewish learning, and the publication of analytical works in Jewish history, thought, Bible studies, mysticism, literature, rabbinics, and more has made it possible for readers of all backgrounds and levels to gain access to Jewish knowledge. Scholarly works consider popular as well as high culture, with books on Jewish food, film, humor, comics, and theater found in bookstores alongside those on biblical wisdom literature or medieval liturgical poetry. Novels and short stories also abound, and Jewish children's literature has come into its own. Whereas eighty years ago parents were hard-pressed to find picture books or English-language Jewish stories to tell their children, nowadays one can choose from hundreds of esthetically pleasing, enticingly told stories that introduce children to Judaism and Jewish life.

The breadth of publications makes it possible to find ones that best match one's religious or political outlook or one's specific life circumstances. From children to adults, beginners to experts, lay or professional, secular or religious, any reader can gain entrée into Jewish culture from a particular perspective through the written word. While the quality of these books varies widely, their sheer volume is staggering. If one types "Jewish books United States" into Google, it will, in 0.28 seconds, produce 5,980,000 results![2]

The above statistic points to the dramatic shift in the way individuals find, store, and retrieve information in the contemporary world. Words are more and more frequently accessed electronically—via computer, BlackBerry, or the iPhone. One finds Daf Yomi on iPods, podcasts of lectures on Jewish topics, YouTube videos of Jewish life cycle moments—the possibilities for Jewish learning are limitless. As for Internet sites themselves, MyJewishLearning. com, for example, claims to be

> the central Internet site for learning about Judaism. . . . the trans-denominational website of Jewish information and education geared toward learners of all ages and educational backgrounds. . . . Content rich and pedagogically sound—to invite and facilitate site visitors' engagement in ever-deeper levels of learning; Relevant to adult audiences of diverse backgrounds and learning objectives— from novice learners, who know little about Judaism, to experienced learners, who know a great deal but want to learn much more; Accurate, well written, and visually engaging.[3]

Whether one agrees with this hyperbolic assessment is debatable, but with a staggering amount of information out in cyberspace, any interested individual can gain unlimited access to information about Jews and Judaism.

The impulse motivating the creators, purveyors, and marketers of such groups, books, sites, and media is not new. On a prosaic level, their desire to make knowledge accessible stems from an age-old desire to earn a living by meeting the needs of the Jewish people (though the financial viability of Internet sites remains an open question). On a loftier level, it echoes the goal of rabbinic scholars of early in the first millennium who inherited the mantle of leadership from the priests. They wanted to ensure that Jewish religious leadership would depend on learning not lineage, and that the quest for knowledge would theoretically be open to all. Though in reality, Jewish learning remained accessible only to a minority of Jews—men with demon-

strated aptitude, inclination, and time to devote to intensive study of traditional texts—the ideal of open access to Jewish learning inspired Jewish leaders throughout our history to spread Jewish knowledge to a broader audience.

In the modern world, encyclopedias have exemplified the desire to collect
and disseminate knowledge to a wide group of individuals. For example, in
the eighteenth century, Colin Macfarquhar, a printer, and Andrew Bell, an
engraver, decided to publish the *Encyclopædia Britannica* to spread the
scholarship of the Enlightenment.[4] Over time, the number of encyclopedias
proliferated, and eventually certain encyclopedias focused on specialized
topics, groups, or fields of study. One can consult encyclopedias of women,
blacks, and professions such as medicine.[5] These encyclopedias seek to re-
dress what were seen as omissions or imbalances of knowledge in the more
general works.

This inclination is in large measure what impelled a group of men, over a
hundred years ago, to devote several years to compiling the *Jewish Encyclopedia*, which was published by Funk & Wagnalls beginning in 1901. The
Jewish Encyclopedia was the first comprehensive collection of all the available information pertaining to the Jews—their history, literature, philosophy,
ritual, sociology, and biography. It is remarkable that this encyclopedia was
published in New York at the turn of the century, for at that time, New York
was hardly the hub of Jewish intellectual and cultural life that it later became.
In the United States as a whole, American Jewish learning was in its infancy.
In the mid-nineteenth century, a few individuals, such as Isaac Leeser, took
initial steps to make Jewish texts accessible to American Jews by translating
the Bible into English and issuing textbooks for children and prayer books
for adults.[6] Yet, as late as the 1870s, there was no successful Jewish publication society, there were no academic journals, and scholarly output remained
quite meager. Isaac Mayer Wise, the Reform Jewish leader, remarked in 1887
that American Jews "are no literary people as yet."[7]

But this began to change in the last quarter of the nineteenth century,
when Jewish leaders felt the need to promote Jewish heritage in the United
States. They were responding in part to the rising antisemitism in western
Europe that culminated in the Dreyfus affair, and the increasingly precarious
situation of Jews who suffered impoverishment, pogroms, and dislocation as
a result of antisemitic policies in czarist Russia. In a more positive vein, many
of these individuals had been exposed to the richness of *Wissenschaft des
Judentums*—nineteenth-century, modern critical scholarship on Jews and
Judaism, and they hoped to spread that knowledge to the United States.[8]

These individuals differed in background, institutional loyalty, and motivation: some were religious reformers and others traditionalists; nascent Zionists, staunch anti-Zionists, and non-Zionists; rabbis and laypeople. Despite their differences, they all shared a vision of promoting American Jewish culture, and they worked together to usher in what they referred to as a "renaissance" of Jewish life in America. Some, like Cyrus Adler, were born in the United States and committed to the growth and development of American Jewry throughout their lives. But what catapulted this renaissance to a larger canvas and enhanced its impact was the involvement of respected Jewish scholars, men born and educated in Europe who brought a wealth of Jewish learning and tradition to this effort of enriching Jewish life and learning in America.

Above all, these men shared a belief in the centrality of Jewish knowledge to their endeavors, and they were convinced that the key to Jewish culture was serious Jewish learning. Because of this, they worked together to establish the United States as the new center of Jewish scholarship. No accomplishment better signified the success of their efforts than the *Jewish Encyclopedia*. As this achievement was part of a broader effort on the part of many Jewish leaders to enhance American Jewish life that Leah Fishbane *z"l* was drawn to study in her doctoral dissertation, it seems especially appropriate for me to honor her memory by focusing on these men and the encyclopedia that they produced.

The *Jewish Encyclopedia* was published thanks to a meeting of the minds between its managing editor and publisher. Isidore Singer, a writer and editor, had recently arrived in the United States from Europe. He wanted to produce an encyclopedia as a way of combating the growing antisemitism that he had witnessed firsthand in Germany and France, particularly as a result of the Dreyfus affair. By presenting a comprehensive collection of rational, objective information about Jews and Judaism, Singer believed optimistically that this would give people the knowledge that would disabuse them of the antisemitic stereotypes that they held. Singer approached the Funk & Wagnalls Company about publishing the work for two reasons. First, the company had established a reputation for publishing excellent reference works with its 1894 *Standard Dictionary*. Second, Singer thought that its president, Isaac Funk, would be receptive to his goals. Singer was right. Funk was a Lutheran minister who shared with Singer altruistic motivations for the project: Funk hoped that the *Jewish Encyclopedia* would help end prejudice against Jews and also foster better understanding between Christians and Jews.[9]

Finally, they were both businessmen. Louis Ginzberg, a world-renowned rabbinics scholar who, when he first arrived in the United States, served on the *Jewish Encyclopedia*'s editorial board before joining the faculty at The Jewish Theological Seminary, recalled that Funk was a very shrewd man who "recognized the possibility of getting very large funds from the Jews." Ginzberg thought this about Singer too: "His idea was to incorporate in his encyclopedia the biographies of Jewish prize fighters and big businessmen." If prominent individuals who wanted to be included would pay $500 for a half-page entry or $1,000 for a full-page entry, Singer would earn a small fortune for himself.[10] While Ginzberg's cynical assessment may reveal more about his fears of scholarship being compromised by financial concerns, it nevertheless points to the practical considerations that surely underlay the decision of both publisher and editor to move forward with the project.

It took such entrepreneurs to get the project off the ground. But it took preeminent Jewish scholars to make the work worth publishing and to give the *Encyclopedia* its first-rate reputation. Because of this, Singer reluctantly agreed to form a board of editors consisting of world-renowned Jewish scholars, many of whom now resided in the United States: Kaufmann Kohler, Joseph Jacobs, Solomon Schechter, Herman Rosenthal, Louis Ginzberg, Emil G. Hirsch, Marcus Jastrow, Richard Gottheil, Morris Jastrow, and Gotthard Deutsch.[11] They were joined by George Foot Moore, a scholar in the history of religion and an ordained Presbyterian minister. While the editors shared with Singer the goal of ending antisemitism by educating the world about the Jews, the Jewish editors also hoped to collect and disseminate the fruits of a century of *Wissenschaft des Judentums*. They also wanted to flex their muscles as American Jewish scholars and ensure the passing of the mantle of Jewish scholarly hegemony from Europe to America.

In addition to these broader goals, the editors understood that the encyclopedia could be a powerful tool to educate Jews about their heritage and to promote Jewish pride. They felt that by collecting the range of Jewish knowledge in one twelve-volume set that would hopefully be found in all Jewish homes and libraries, they would enrich the Jewish identity of American Jews. In this way the *Jewish Encyclopedia* would become a potent catalyst for Jewish renaissance in the United States.

Transforming these sweeping goals into one twelve-volume encyclopedia proved to be a challenging process. Since this encyclopedia was the first of its kind, there was no precedent for how to describe Jews and Judaism in encyclopedic form. The editors had to reach consensus on what to include, how each topic should be treated, how long each article should be, and who should be assigned to write it. Through their choices on each of these issues, the editors presented the richness of Judaism and the Jewish experience as they understood it: a view of Jewish life as complex, multifaceted, and changing. This perspective not only reflected the breadth of Jewish scholarship of the time, but it also mirrored the varied outlooks of the editors themselves. In so doing, the editors shaped the state of Jewish knowledge for decades to come, for the encyclopedia—as the sole comprehensive reference work— became the foundation upon which subsequent Jewish scholarship in America was built.

Examples of the way the editors both reflected the state of Jewish knowledge and shaped it can be found on every page of the encyclopedia—from the illustrations to the entry authors. For example, because the editors wanted to reach beyond a scholarly audience to educate a lay Jewish readership as well as non-Jews about Jewish life, they included their understanding of the origins, significance, and current practice of Jewish customs and rituals. As Joseph Jacobs explained, one of the functions of the encyclopedia was to satisfy "those who follow the customs of their fathers [who] may at times desire to consult it for guidance in the hallowing of the Jewish home."[12] Thus, many articles—even those written by the Reform leader Kaufmann Kohler— include details about how Jews traditionally mark holiday life-cycle moments. One also finds pages of musical notation to help readers chant both synagogue and home prayers. The rich offerings of the encyclopedia in this area demonstrated to its readers that Jewish life had much that could engage a varied and eclectic group of Jews.

The editors also wanted the encyclopedia to combat antisemitism, and to do so, they strove to debunk racial stereotypes as they pertained to Jews. Above all, they stressed the crucial impact that the environment has played in shaping the Jew. Incorporating the latest scholarship in the burgeoning field of physical anthropology, Maurice Fishberg, a physician and physical anthropologist, acknowledges the existence of many inferior traits among the Jews but tries to demonstrate that they stem from environmental conditions. For example, in peculiarly titled articles such as "Girth of the Chest," "Stature," "Nervous Diseases," and "Morbidity," he acknowledges that Jews are shorter, scrawnier, and more susceptible to disease than the general population. But, according to Fishberg, this is because Jews have been mostly town dwellers, engaged in indoor occupations, and they suffered persecution for two thousand years.

Similarly, Fishberg notes that the prevalence of hemorrhoids among Jews can be traced to their habit of sitting for long periods on hard benches while studying Talmud. Also, "derangements of the function of digestion," which, many physicians concur, are common on Sunday, are often caused by the consumption of cholent on the Sabbath. And nervous diseases that often afflict the Jews may be due partly to their early induction in heder education. In his words:

> The Jews are more nervous, have a larger proportion of insane, etc., from social causes, not because the structure of their nervous systems is in any way peculiar anatomically or physiologically. All their pathological characteristics can be shown to be due to the peculiar social and economic conditions under which they live.[13]

Fishberg's perspective emerges clearly from his review of the facts. He shares the views of Jewish detractors who claim that many Jewish characteristics are "pathological." However, Fishberg attributes these characteristics not to race but rather to environmental causes: now that Jews have changed their surroundings by moving to the United States, they also have the opportunity through education, hard work, and perseverance to change these undesirable characteristics. Fishberg hopes his articles will demonstrate beyond doubt that antisemitic sentiment is wrongheaded because the negative characteristics described in the encyclopedia are not intrinsic to Jews as a race. Environmental in origin, they will disappear in the modern world as conditions inevitably improve.

On a theological level, the encyclopedia editors chose to convey the complex, multifaceted, and changing nature of Judaism by offering different viewpoints. Kohler "sees in revelation and inspiration as well as in tradition a spiritual force working from within rather than a heavenly communication coming from without." But Jacob Z. Lauterbach, a traditionally educated scholar with a doctorate from the University of Göttingen,[14] offers a more traditional perspective in his article "Theology," explaining that "revelation on Mt. Sinai is therefore the chief foundation of the Jewish faith."

The inclusion of different perspectives such as these in the encyclopedia demonstrates not only the diversity of Jewish thought, belief, and practice among Jews but also their underlying unity. Traditionalist collaborators differed from their more liberal counterparts in their commitment to Jewish peoplehood, their personal observance of mitzvot, and their uneasiness with Reform. But they shared with their Reform collaborators a modern, historical conception of Judaism. They joined forces as editors because of their shared commitment to strengthening Jewish life and scholarship in America, recognizing that the publication of this comprehensive work was just what the era required. What united them—a love of Jews, Judaism, and Jewish life; a commitment to the Jewish future; and a desire to minimize negative attitudes toward the Jews—was far greater than what divided them. Thus, though the editors continued to differ sharply on the specifics of belief and practice, and though privately some of their leaders expressed disapproval and disappointment with each other,[15] they continued to work together on the encyclopedia and other substantive projects, especially the Jewish Publication Society's Bible translation.[16] In this way, the collaborative enterprise undertaken by this group of encyclopedia editors broadened the boundaries of Jewish life for American Jews both on the pages of the encyclopedia and in the communities and institutions that these individuals helped sustain.

The *Jewish Encyclopedia* became the reference book of record for sixty years until the *Encyclopaedia Judaica* was published in the 1970s. As Joshua Bloch, head of the Jewish division of the New York Public Library from 1923 to 1956, noted, "There is not a day when we . . . do not have occasion to make use of the volumes of the Encyclopedia and to send numerous readers to its pages."[17] The *Jewish Encyclopedia* also contributed to the formation of adult Jewish study classes in synagogues and women's groups. One gets a sense of the importance of this twelve-volume work in Jewish homes through an anecdote in a children's textbook, the Union of American Hebrew Congregations' *Hillel's Happy Holidays*. When the character Hillel needed information on Sukkot, he explained:

> "I had to look in the Jewish Encyclopedia for my answer. That is the biggest book we have in our house."
> "That is a good place to look for answers," said Aunt Sophie.[18]

Ironically, the *Jewish Encyclopedia*—which lacks an index—has gained increasing visibility and usage in the early twenty-first century because one can now easily consult a searchable edition on the World Wide Web. It describes itself as "the only free Jewish encyclopedia on the Internet." Of course, the *Jewish Encyclopedia* no longer retains any claim to comprehensiveness. On the contrary, the home page of the website notes that "since the original work was completed almost 100 years ago, it does not cover a significant portion of modern Jewish History (e.g., the creation of Israel, the Holocaust, etc.)," a necessary disclaimer lest anyone using the site imagine that such omissions reflect a deliberate political decision to exclude such information.[19] The *Jewish Encyclopedia*—even on the Web—has been surpassed in so many ways, not only because it lacks information on the Jewish experience in the twentieth century, but also because so much more needs to be included in a contemporary reference work in order to do justice to claims of comprehensiveness. Scholarship has expanded exponentially over the past one hundred years to include new fields of study, including cultural history, women's studies, literary criticism; new primary sources, including texts, archeological discoveries, and material culture; new outlets, including film, video, and the Internet itself; and new categories of interpretation, including feminist analysis and literary deconstruction.

Much of this new material—primary sources, music, illustrations, speeches, critical reviews and analyses, and so forth—is now easily available at one's fingertips anywhere in the world with Internet access and at no cost. On the one hand, the democratization of information that is the hallmark of the Internet far surpasses the wildest dreams of the encyclopedia editors to disseminate information about Jews and Judaism to as wide an audience as possible. Jacob Schiff, the primary benefactor responsible for the completion and distribution of the encyclopedia, would undoubtedly be thrilled, for it far surpasses his admirable but inadequate efforts to make such information widely available by donating copies to libraries throughout the Unites States.

On the other hand, the editors took pride in including signed articles from world-renowned experts and carefully editing the content of the work as a whole for accuracy and quality. In contrast to this, today there is no one authoritative source—in print or on the Web—of information on all things Jewish. The Internet includes infinite amounts of data, but the reader cannot be certain of its reliability. Information often appears anonymously and without any critical or analytical perspective. Other material is presented as objective, but on closer look, one can discern the website's narrow agenda, which may not be readily apparent to the casual reader. For example, if one googles "Jew," the third result is a site call "jewwatch," a rabidly antisemitic site that purports to present a "scholarly Library of Facts about domestic & worldwide Zionist criminality."[20]

Finally, the Internet lacks the sense of time so essential to developing historical perspective and to making meaning out of experience. For example, an organization's regularly updated Web page provides a continually refreshed view of the company, but it obscures the evolution of the organization and its message. How did the organization present itself five years ago, how does that differ from today, and what does that tell us about its evolving image? It is virtually impossible to discern this information by looking at a website.

Encyclopedias are wonderful *primary* sources as well as reference works, for they capture the state of knowledge at the time of publication. Thus, today, scholars still consult the *Jewish Encyclopedia* to reference its classic articles, such as Louis Ginzberg's "Law, Codification of"; to learn about a small European town that no longer exists as a Jewish community in the post-Holocaust era; or to read about a nineteenth-century European Jewish custom that is no longer observed. As we think through the possibilities for using the written word to enrich Jewish life today—whether through printed books, virtual archives, Internet publications, or blogs—we would do well to consider how best to ensure the quality and specificity of Jewish knowledge in time and space. For just as the *Encyclopedia* editors subscribed to the axiom that "Knowledge is Power," so too can we draw inspiration from recalling just how much a small group of dedicated individuals was able to accomplish in working together despite differences in belief, temperament, and institutional loyalty to harness Jewish scholarship to tackle the broader challenges of the era and to fertilize a renaissance just a century ago.

NOTES

1. Most notable are the translations into English of the Babylonian Talmud by Adin Steinsaltz and by the Artscroll Publishing Company.

2. Accessed 29 June 2009.

3. About MyJewishLearning.com (accessed 28 February 2008).

4. http://corporate.britannica.com/company_info.html (accessed 29 June 2009). Its chief virtue would be, in the editor's word, "utility." The first edition of the *Britannica* was published one section at a time, beginning in 1768. The three-volume set, completed in 1771, quickly sold out. Encouraged by this success, the publishers issued the second edition in ten volumes (1777–84).

5. *Encyclopedia of African American History, 1896 to the Present*, 5 vols. (New York, 2008); *The Oxford Encyclopedia of Women in World History*, 4 vols. (New York, 2007); and *American Medical Association Complete Medical Encyclopedia*, ed. Jerrold B. Leikin and Martin S. Lipsky (New York, 2003).

6. Lance Jonathan Sussman, *Isaac Leeser and the Making of American Judaism* (Detroit, 1995), 80–104.

7. Wise, "American Judaism," *American Jews' Annual* (1887): 35–47.

8. Jonathan D. Sarna, *JPS: The Americanization of Jewish Culture, 1888–1988* (Philadelphia, 1989), 13–17; idem, "The Great American Jewish Awakening," *Midstream* 28

(Oct. 1982): 33–34; Moshe Davis, *The Emergence of Conservative Judaism: The Historical School in Nineteenth Century America* (Philadelphia, 1965), 231–33, 235–38, 241–49; Solomon Schechter, *Seminary Addresses and Other Papers* (New York, 1959), 35; Cyrus Adler, *I Have Considered the Days* (Philadelphia, 1945), 77–79; and idem, *Cyrus Adler: Selected Letters,* ed. Ira Robinson (Philadelphia, 1985), 1:20–24.

9. For more on the history of the publication of the *Jewish Encyclopedia,* see Shuly Rubin Schwartz, *The Emergence of Jewish Scholarship in America: The Publication of the* Jewish Encyclopedia (Cincinnati, 1991).

10. Eli Ginzberg, *Louis Ginzberg: Keeper of the Law* (Philadelphia, 1966), 66.

11. For biographical information on the editors and their role in the encyclopedia, see Schwartz, *Emergence of Jewish Scholarship.*

12. Joseph Jacobs, *The* Jewish Encyclopedia: *A Guide to Its Contents, an Aid to Its Use* (New York, 1906), 77.

13. http://www.jewishencyclopedia.com/view.jsp?artid=763&letter=M&search= morbidity (accessed 29 June 2009).

14. Kohler was so impressed with Lauterbach that he later invited him to serve as professor of Talmud at Hebrew Union College, a position Lauterbach held until his retirement.

15. For example, see Schwartz, *Emergence of Jewish Scholarship,* 157–58.

16. *The New English Translation of the Bible* (Philadelphia, 1917).

17. Abraham Berger, "Bloch, Joshua," in *Encyclopaedia Judaica,* ed. Michael Berenbaum and Fred Skolnik, vol. 3., 2nd ed. (Detroit, 2007), 764; Gale Virtual Reference Library, Jewish Theological Seminary of America, http://go.galegroup.com/ps/start.do? p=GVRL&u=nysl_me_jethsoa (accessed 24 July 2009); and *Twenty-fifth Anniversary of the Jewish Encyclopedia, Congratulations and Commendations* (New York, [1926]).

18. Mamie G. Gamoran, *Hillel's Happy Holidays,* new ed. (New York, 1955), 68.

19. http://www.jewishencyclopedia.com (accessed 29 June 2009).

20. http://www.jewwatch.com (accessed 29 June 2009).

5 Leah's Hope

The Legacy of German-Jewish Humanism in America

The last time I saw Leah was at the sukkah of her in-laws. She sat across from me, gently embracing her young daughter Aderet. Leah's vibrant eyes sparkled with the joy of motherhood. Indeed, most vividly etched in my memory of Leah are her soft eyes, ever glistening with a disarming innocence, affirming all that is pure and decent. Appropriately, she spoke that evening of what the Israeli philosopher Avishai Margalit called, in a volume she was then reading, *The Decent Society*[1]—that is, a society that actively seeks to enhance human dignity by minimizing the humiliation that its members may suffer from the scourge of poverty, disabilities, and invidious prejudices.

With restrained passion she accordingly appealed to us in the midst of celebrating the holiday to remain compassionately alert to the anguish of all those who are degraded by misfortune and social injustice. Imperceptibly the conversation eventually broached our shared interest in German Jewry and its legacy of religious humanism.

It is this legacy that Leah had hoped to honor through her scholarship. She was drawn, undoubtedly by both intellectual affinity and personal disposition, to the German-Jewish ethic of *Bildung*, which when wedded to Jewish commitments yielded the concept of ethical monotheism. Coined apparently by nineteenth-century Protestant biblical scholars, this concept was quickly assimilated into the German-Jewish lexicon.[2] Across the denominational spectrum, from Reform to Neo-Orthodoxy, German Jews highlighted the prophetic ethical message of Judaism, according to which the one universal God enjoins all human beings to share in the divine work of ensuring that goodness and justice will reign in the world. In fulfilling this task as God's elect, Israel is to serve as an ethical exemplar. German Jews transplanted this conception of Judaism to America, where it found a strong resonance in the ideals of the republic as a tolerant and inclusive democracy that secures the "inalienable rights" of its citizens in constitutional law. They thus found in America fertile ground for what Ralph Dahrendorf has felicitously called "applied Enlightenment."[3]

The fusion of the liberal, humanistic ethos of America with the German-Jewish conception of ethical monotheism was given a learned and eloquent formulation by Rabbi Emil Gustav Hirsch (1851–1923), a graduate of the first class of the Hochschule für die Wissenschaft des Judentums,[4] founded in 1872 in Berlin by Abraham Geiger (1810–1874) to promote the academic study of Judaism and the training of Liberal rabbis.[5] Upon completing in 1876 his rabbinic studies, while earning a PhD from the University of Leipzig,[6] Hirsch assumed pulpits at various Reform congregations in the United States; from 1880 until his death he served as the rabbi at Chicago's Temple Sinai, the bastion of radical Reform Judaism in America. He was also one of the consulting editors of *The Jewish Encyclopedia*, which appeared from 1901 to 1906 in twelve volumes and brought the fruits of German *Wissenschaft des Judentums* to the English-reading public.[7] Among the many entries Hirsch wrote for the *Encyclopedia* was an article on "modern" Jewish ethics, which may be read as a scholarly affirmation of ethical monotheism, but with a distinctly American twist. Noting that according to biblical faith God granted human beings "stewardship" of the world for one's personal benefit and for that of one's fellow human beings, Hirsch observes:

> On this basis [of human stewardship] Jewish ethics rests its doctrines on duty and virtue. Whatever increases the capacity of man's stewardship is ethical. Whatever use of time, talent, or treasure augments one's possibilities of human service is ethically consecrated. Judaism, therefore, inculcates as ethical the ambition to develop physical and mental powers, [for the] enlargement of service is dependent upon the measure or the increase of man's power. Wealth is not immoral, poverty not moral. The desire to increase one's stores of power is moral provided it is under the consecration of the recognized responsibility for larger service. The weak are entitled to the protection of the strong. Property entails duties, which establish its rights. Charity is not a voluntary concession on the part of the well situated. It is a right to which the less fortunate are entitled in justice (*tzedakah*). The main concern of Jewish ethics is personality. Every human being is a person, not a thing. Economic doctrine is unethical and un-Jewish if it ignores and renders illusory this distinction. Slavery is for this reason immoral. Jewish ethics on this basis is not individualistic; it is not under the spell of otherworldliness. It is social. By consecrating every human being to the stewardship of his faculties and forces, and by regarding every human soul as a person, the ethics of Judaism

offers the solution of all the perplexities of modern political, industrial, and economic life. Israel as the "pattern people" shall be exponential among its brothers of the world human family, of the principles and practices, which are involved in, pillared upon, and demanded by, the ethical monotheism, which lifts man to the dignity of God's image and consecrates him the steward of all his life, his talent, and his treasure. In the "Messianic kingdom," ideally to be anticipated by Israel, justice will be enthroned and incarnated in institution, and this justice, the social correlative of holiness and love, is the ethical passion of modern, as it was of olden, Judaism.[8]

Rabbi Hirsch's article palpitates with the humanistic optimism of the post-Enlightenment liberal ethos as anchored in the dual virtues of *Besitz* and *Bildung*—property and education—that had informed German-Jewish self-understanding. Economic success entailed a commitment to *Bildung*—education as an ongoing, never-ending process of aesthetic and intellectual refinement—as charitable acts promoting the common good. German-Jews excelled in philanthropic support of general and Jewish causes, particularly within the realm of culture, education, and health, and did so far beyond their demographic proportion in society,[9] as would later be the case for Jewish charitable giving in the United States.[10]

At the turn of the century, Chicago—as virtually everywhere else in the United States, North and South—was de facto a segregated city; the festering wounds of slavery deeply scarred the social tissue of the city. Rabbi Hirsch urged his congregants not only to acknowledge African-Americans to be their fellow human beings but also to work actively to secure their economic and cultural dignity. In a sermon delivered on the eve of Yom Kippur, he beseeched his congregation to remember the cardinal Jewish virtue of pursuing justice:

> Let them [the non-Jews] preach love and toleration, we will—every Jew will fight for justice. . . . Our civilization is deficient, because justice is not done. Is that just to men that they must sell themselves as goods are sold? Is that just to men that they must live in squalor in the slums, in sweat-shops and in what not? Is that just to the child of man that, having to choose between starvation and shame, must elect to walk the path of degradation of a slavery blacker than which "darkest Africa" never knew? Is that justice to humanity? Is that civilization?[11]

This was more than a mere sermonic appeal, as is exemplified by his collaboration with Julius Rosenwald (1862–1932), a member of his congregation and a son of Jewish immigrants from Germany. A senior partner of Sears, Roe-buck and Company, the department store chain that pioneered mail-order consumerism, Rosenwald resolved to employ his considerable wealth to ad-vance the common good of the downtrodden African-American commu-nity.[12] Together with Rabbi Hirsch he traveled to Alabama to visit Booker T. Washington,[13] the indomitable principal of Tuskegee "Normal and Industrial Institute," founded in 1881 to train black teachers and industrial workers.[14] Rosenwald and Washington established an immediate rapport and a fast friendship. The Jewish entrepreneur was invited to join the Institute's Board of Directors, and used that position to solicit the support for the institution of Jewish friends, such as Paul J. Sachs (1878–1965), at the time a senior part-ner of the New York investment firm of Goldman and Sachs. The two friends shared the conviction that the plight of the African-Americans was America's most serious and exigent social issue. To relieve Dr. Washington from the tedium of fund-raising and to enable him to devote himself to the academic affairs of the Tuskegee Institute, Rosenwald undertook to finance fully the school's activities. Undoubtedly his greatest and most enduring contribution on behalf of the disinherited black citizens of the United States was the estab-lishment together with Dr. Washington of more than 5,300 schools through-out the South for African-American children who were otherwise deprived of a proper education.[15] Known duly as the "Rosenwald schools," they were largely built and maintained with funds provided by Rosenwald.[16] The proj-ect met with the trenchant criticism of W.E.B. DuBois, who argued that not only did these "black" schools in effect perpetuate racial segregation but, rather, that all efforts should be placed on the struggle for full civil rights for African-Americans. Rosenwald held his ground and, perhaps drawing upon the German-Jewish legacy, insisted that education was the high road to full equality.

Back in Chicago, Rosenwald was joined by Rabbi Hirsch and other prom-inent Jews in helping to found in 1909 the NAACP (National Association for the Advancement of Colored People).[17] His commitment to the advancement of African-Americans—and, one must underscore, in a period in which seg-regation and Jim Crowism still characterized race relations in the Untied States—was sustained by his self-understanding as a Jew. As he explained, "The horrors that are due to race prejudice come home to the Jew more forcefully than to others of the white race, on account of the centuries of per-secution which they have suffered and still suffer."[18] With unflagging devo-tion to this cause Rosenwald also developed an elaborate fellowship program to promote talented African-American artists, writers, dancers, actors, and musicians. In the twenty years of its existence this program, established in 1928, granted close to six hundred fellowships rendering Rosenwald "the largest and most influential single patron of African American arts and letters in the twentieth century, perhaps ever."[19] Similarly, he initiated and financed the building of housing estates for indigent blacks of Chicago as well as schools. Rosenwald also took special interest in the medical health of all citizens of "inadequate financial means." The Rosenwald Fund thus developed a program to promote low-cost medical and dental care throughout the country. In this context, the Rosenwald Fund undertook to subsidize the salaries of African-American physicians to enable them "to serve as members of the state health departments in the South. It also aided Negro nurses in obtaining post-graduate courses in public health.[20]

The Jewish sensibility inspiring these ramified projects on behalf of the African-American community was eloquently acknowledged by W.E.B. Du-Bois in a eulogy he published in the organ of the NAACP commemorating Rosenwald's passing in January 1932:

> The death of Julius Rosenwald brings to an end a career remarkable for its significance to American Negroes. As a Jew, Julius Rosenwald did not have to be initiated into the methods of race prejudice, and his philanthropic work was a crushing arraignment of the American white Christians. Knowing that the YMCA discriminated grossly against Negroes, Rosenwald calmly offered to help pay for Negro Association buildings. To this end, he gave large sums, and few people had the wit to smile at his slap in the face of white Christianity. Seeing again that the white South did not propose to build decent schoolhouses for colored children, Rosenwald again offered to help pay for such schoolhouses, provided they were real schoolhouses and on modern lines. The South accepted his gift effusively, and never even to this day has apparently grasped the failure of democracy which permitted an individual of a despised race to do for the sovereign states of a great nation that which they had neither the decency nor justice to do for themselves. Beyond this, Rosenwald reached out toward public libraries and hospitals, and endowed a great fund to carry on his work after his death. He was a great man. But he was no mere philanthropist. He was, rather, the subtle stinging critic of our racial democracy.[21]

Rosenwald's generosity also extended to the Jewish people. Among the many Jewish charities and causes he supported,[22] his bequest to the Joint Distribution Committee (JDC) became legendary.[23] In the midst of World War One, the JDC launched an emergency campaign to collect funds for the relief of the hundreds of East European Jews displaced and wandering "aimlessly like so many hunted animals . . . , diseased-ridden, cholera racked, emaciated by starvation, . . . herded hither and thither, thousands of them dying in their tracks."[24] Given the enormity of need, the directors of JDC set the goal of collecting funds to an amount hitherto unheard of in American Jewish philanthropy. To meet the challenge it was proposed to solicit "a deed of philanthropy so gigantic and epochal that it would move the hearts of the people as they had never been moved before."[25] With great trepidation, the director of JDC, Jacob Billikopf, approached Rosenwald, the one person who it was felt had "the means and the spirit" to make the spectacular donation of one million dollars—which would be the equivalent of more than twenty million dollars in today's terms. Upon detailing to Rosenwald the plight of East European Jewry, Billikopf reported that Rosenwald asked him, "Do you think it will do any good?" In response to Billikopf's embarrassed but affirmative nod, Rosenwald laconically replied, "Very well, I will do it."[26] Duly publicized, his "unparalleled act" had the desired effect of galvanizing the American Jewish community to contribute generously to the campaign. Among those who were inspired by Rosenwald's magnanimity was President Woodrow Wilson, who dispatched a telegram to him:

> Your contribution of one million dollars to the Ten Million Dollar Fund for the Relief of Jewish War Sufferers serves democracy as well as humanity. The Russian Revolution has opened the door of freedom to an oppressed people but unless they are given life and strength and courage the opportunity of centuries will avail them little. It is to America that these starving millions look for aid and out of our prosperity, the fruit of free institutions spring a vast and ennobling generosity. Your gift lays an obligation even while it furnishes inspiration.[27]

President Wilson's esteem for Rosenwald had been sealed even before his unprecedented philanthropic gesture. In October 1916 Rosenwald was appointed chairman of the Advisory Commission to the National Council of Defense, which was charged with the task to advise the president on strategic placement of industrial goods and services should America enter the world war.

Rosenwald's capacious sense of civic duty was also nurtured by Rabbi Hirsch, who taught his congregants that social justice was sustained by *Bildung*. Thus, Rosenwald was also among the members of Temple Sinai whom Rabbi Hirsch recruited to further the cultural and educational life of Chicago. Led by Rosenwald, Hirsch's congregants generously contributed to adorning Chicago with public libraries, museums, an opera house, and a symphony orchestra. They were also among the most passionate philanthropic devotees of the University of Chicago, which opened its doors in 1892. Rabbi Hirsch himself was one of the first five full professors of the fledgling institution. He held a chair in "rabbinic literature and philosophy" until his death in 1923. In this capacity he exemplified the virtues of *Besitz* and *Bildung*, the social obligations attendant to the gift of material success. Reputed to be the highest-salaried cleric in the United States at the time, he forwent his professorial salary and earmarked it instead for student fellowships. He similarly donated considerable sums to launch the university library's Judaica collection. Concurrent with his duties as a congregational rabbi, he taught a full range of courses in Talmud, Midrash, and medieval Jewish philosophy.[28] The significance of his professorship is highlighted by the fact that among the more than forty senior and consulting editors of *The Jewish Encyclopedia* he was the only to hold an academic appointment in postbiblical Judaism at a secular institution of higher learning. Despite the concerted efforts of the founders of *Wissenschaft des Judentums*, especially as spearheaded by Leopold Zunz and Moritz Steinscheider, to secure for the study of postbiblical Judaism a place in the curriculum of German universities, it was not until 1912 that a lectureship in Jewish studies was established at the University of Leipzig—a full twenty years after Hirsch assumed his professorship.[29] Aside from a few sporadic, usually part-time and nonsalaried appointments in the years of the Weimar Republic, it was only after the Shoah that Jewish studies were recognized as belonging to the university's scholarly agenda, not only in Germany but in Europe as a whole.[30] Indeed, the University of Chicago with Rabbi Hirsch's appointment was among the very first secular universities to institute a program of Jewish studies, the symbolic import of the appointment underscored by the fact that it was one of the school's first five full professorships.[31]

The philanthropic ethic attendant to *Besitz und Bildung* is firmly rooted in Jewish tradition. Summarizing biblical and rabbinic rulings on charity, the fourteenth-century halakhic scholar Jacob ben Asher observes in his Code of Jewish Law, which had a seminal impact on Ashkenazic Jewry, that "one is to regard one's capital (*mammon*) as but a trustfund (*pikadon*), which one is to use in accord with the wishes of the one who had entrusted the funds in one's care (*ha-mafkid*, namely, God) and to distribute it to those poorer than oneself; this will be the portion of the fund from which one derives the greatest benefit."[32] As interpreted through the prism of German humanism, particularly as inflected by Kant, Goethe, and Schiller, these values became the hallmark of Central European Jewry. Even for Jews who no longer felt themselves bound to the *halakhah*, indeed, especially for them, these values became a salient feature of their Jewish religious identity. The values attached to *Besitz und Bildung* gained perhaps a fuller expression when transplanted to the United States, where they became the twin pillars of American Jewry.

Subsequent to our meeting at the sukkah of her in-laws, Leah and I corresponded about George Mosse's recently published memoirs. In his volume he provides a vivid account of his family, one of the wealthiest in Germany, and its religiosity as expressed primarily through its philanthropic support of Jewish institutions and general humanistic culture.[33] Leah's own religious humanism was not so much focused on philanthropy as it was on what Franz Rosenzweig called "knowledge as service,"[34] to pursue scholarship in order to address with maximum intellectual integrity the existential and spiritual questions of both her contemporary Jews and fellow human beings.

NOTES

1. Avishai Margalit, *The Decent Society* (Cambridge, MA: Harvard University Press, 1996).

2. The most systematic and widely cited formulation of the concept of "ethical monotheism" was by the Dutch biblical scholar Abraham Kuenen (1828–1891). See his Hibbert Lectures of 1882: "What was ... revealed to the eye of their [the prophets'] spirit was no less that the august idea of the *moral governance of the world*. ... The name 'ethical monotheism' describes better than any other the characteristics of their point of view, for it not only expresses the character of the one God whom they worshipped, but also indicates the fountain whence their faith in Him welled up." A. Kuenen, *National Religions and Universal Religion* (New York: Charles Scribner's Sons, 1882), pp. 124–25 (emphasis in original). Even prior to the emergence of the concept of ethical monotheism, German Jewry tended to identify Judaism with the ethical idealism of Kant and his votaries, which deemed ethics to be the essence of religion. Cf. Franz Rosenzweig's critical dismissal of German-Jewish religious thought, "God gave us the Torah, not ethical monotheism." Rosenzweig, *On Jewish Learning*, ed. N. N. Glatzer (New York: Schocken Books, 1965), p. 123.

3. Cited in Peter Graf Kielmansegg, introduction to P. G. Kielmannsegg et al., eds., *Hannah Arendt and Leo Strauss: German Émigrés and American Political Thought after World War II* (Cambridge: Cambridge University Press, 1995), p. 5.

4. Bertram Wallace Korn, *German-Jewish Intellectual Influences on American Jewish Life, 1824–1972*, The B. G. Rudolf Lectures in Judaic Studies (Syracuse, NY: Syracuse University Press, 1972), p. 18, n. 13.

5. Cf. Hirsch would later "speak appreciatively of the influence upon him in his student days [at the Hochschule] of Abraham Geiger, Moritz Lazarus and Hermann Steinthal." Gerson B. Levi, introduction to Emil G. Hirsch, *My Religion* (New York: Macmillan Co., 1925), p. 12.

6. According to the registry of the University of Chicago, Hirsch earned his PhD in 1876 and rabbinic ordination in 1877. See *The University of Chicago Annual Register: July 1, 1892–July 1, 1894* (Chicago: University Press of Chicago, 1893), p. 11.

7. Cf. "With the publication of *The Jewish Encyclopedia* a serious attempt is made for the first time to systematize and render generally accessible the knowledge [of the intellectual and social history of the Jews] thus far obtained. That this has now become possible is due to a series of labors carried on throughout the whole of the nineteenth century and representing the efforts of three generations of Jewish scholars, mainly in Germany." Preface, *The Jewish Encyclopedia: A Descriptive Record of the History, Religion, Literature, and Customs of the Jewish People from the Earliest Times to the Present Day* (New York/London: Funk and Wagnalls, 1901), vol. 1, p. ix. See chapter 6 of the present volume.

8. S.v. "Ethics (in modern times)," E. G. Hirsch, *The Jewish Encyclopedia*, vol. 5 (1903), pp. 257–58.

9. See Derek J. Penslar, "Philanthropy, the 'Social Question' and Jewish Identity in Imperial Germany," in *The Leo Baeck Institute Yearbook*, vol. 33 (1993), pp. 51–74.

10. Gary Tobin and Mordecai Rimor, "Jewish Giving to Jewish and Non-Jewish Philanthropy," in Robert Wuthnow, Virginia A. Hodgkinson, et al., eds., *Faith and Philanthropy in America* (San Francisco: Jossey-Bass Publishers, 1990), pp. 134–64. Also see Tobias Brinkmann, "Praise Be Upon You: Jewish Philanthropy and the Origins of the First Jewish Community in Chicago, 1859–1900," in *The Shaping of a Community: The Jewish Federation of Metropolitan Chicago,* ed. Rhoda Rosen (Chicago: Spertus Institute of Jewish Studies, 1999), pp. 24–39.

11. Emil G. Hirsch, "Alone with Thee, My God. A Yom Kippur Eve Sermon," in idem, *My Religion*, compilation and biographical introduction by Gerson B. Levi (New York: Macmillan Co., 1925), 336. The date of the sermon is not given.

12. For a comprehensive study of Rosenwald's business and ramified philanthropic activities, see the biography by his grandson Peter M. Ascoli, *Julius Rosenwald: The Man Who Built Sears, Roebuck and Advanced the Cause of Black Education in the American South* (Bloomington: Indiana University Press, 2006). Rosenwald often acknowledged that his philanthropic activities were inspired by Rabbi Hirsch's conception of *tzedakah* as an essential tenet of Judaism, which obliges particularly those blessed with wealth to attend to the needs of the less fortunate who are "entitled to justice" (*tzedek*). Ibid., p. 54.

13. Cf. "At first, [Rosenwald] donated money primarily to Jewish causes, but after reading Booker T. Washington's *Up from Slavery* and then meeting the author, he began donating funds to black causes as well." Peter M. Ascoli, "Julius Rosenwald: Unconventional Philanthropist," in Daniel Schulman, ed., *A Force for Change: African American Art and the Julius Rosenwald Fund*, Catalogue of Exhibit Sponsored by Spertus Museum (Chicago: Northwestern University Press, 2009), p. 19.

14. Ascoli, *Julius Rosenwald*, p. 88.

15. Cf. "Mr. Rosenwald's interest in Negro education was stimulated by Booker T. Washington's autobiography [*Up from Slavery*, 1901]. Dr. Washington described his tours of rural schools in the South in which he found inadequate facilities. In one Southern state where Negroes formed one-half of the population, only 20 per cent of the colored children were enrolled in schools, as compared with 60 per cent of white children, and no Negro rural school operated for longer than five months during the year compared with a seven-month term for white children. Dr. Washington was convinced that education and practical training in agriculture and industry were essential for his people. Mr. Rosenwald felt it was dangerous for ten million citizens of the United States to grow up in ignorance." Press release, July 16, 1962, Office of Public Relations, University of Chicago, announcing plans to commemorate "the 100 anniversary of the birth of the philanthropist Juilus Rosenwald."

16. Ascoli, *Julius Rosenwald*, pp. 135–53. On the effect of the Rosenwald schools on the education of blacks in the South, see James D. Anderson, *The Education of Blacks in the South, 1860–1935* (Chapel Hill: University of North Carolina Press, 1988), and Eric Anderson and Alfred A. Moss Jr., *Dangerous Donations: Northern Philanthropy and Southern Education, 1902–1930* (New York: Columbia University Press, 1999).

17. Until the 1970s the leadership of the NAACP was predominantly white and Jewish. On Jewish involvement in the civil rights movement, see Howard M. Sachar, *A History of the Jews in America* (New York: Alfred A. Knopf, 1992), pp. 801–5. In 1914 Joel Elias Spingarn (1875–1939), professor emeritus of comparative literature at Columbia University, was elected chairman of the NAACP "and recruited for its board such Jewish leaders as Jacob Schiff, Jacob Billikopf, and Rabbi Stephen Wise" in addition to Julius Rosenwald and Rabbi Emil Hirsch. Ibid., p. 803.

18. Cited in *Wikipedia*, s.v. "Julius Rosenwald," http://en.wikipedia.org.

19. Daniel Schulman, introduction" to idem, ed., *A Force for Change*, p. 13. The Rosenwald Fund also granted fellowships to 278 white southerners in such diverse fields as education, public health, agriculture, sociology, economics, the humanities, and the sciences. On the Rosenwald Fund, see Jayne R. Beilk, "To Render Better Service: The Role of the Julius Rosenwald Fund Fellowship Program in the Development of Graduate and Professional Opportunities for African-Americans" (PhD diss., School of Education, Indiana University, 1994).

20. Press release (see n. 15 above).

21. W.E.B. Dubois, editorial, *Crisis* (February 1932), 41/2:58. Cited in Ascoli, *Julius Rosenwald*, p. 385.

22. Rosenwald was the honorary president of the Jewish Charities of Chicago. For a full list of the many charities and causes he supported, see Press release (n. 15 above).

23. To pool and coordinate various existing efforts on behalf of distressed Jewish communities in Europe and Palestine, the JDC was established in 1914 as an ad hoc and temporary collective of three existing religious and secular Jewish organizations: the American Jewish Relief Committee, the Central Committee for the Relief of Jews Suffering Through the War, and People's Relief Committee.

24. Henry H. Rosenfelt, *This Thing of Giving: The Record of a Rare Enterprise of Mercy and Brotherhood* (New York: Plymouth Press, 1924), p. 31.

25. Ibid., p. 37.

26. Ibid., p. 40.

27. Cited in ibid., pp. 40–41.

28. The register for the University of Chicago's inaugural year lists Hirsch as a professor of rabbinical literature and philosophy within the Department of Semitic Languages and Literatures. His prospective teaching agenda consists of eighteen different courses ranging from an Introduction to Talmudic Literature to Maimonides' "Guide" in Arabic Hebrew. *Annual Register: July 1, 1892–July 1, 1893*, pp. 54–55.

29. The first incumbent of this lectureship in rabbinics was Israel Isaac Kahn (1858–1924); in 1918 he was promoted to a full professorship. Alfred Jospe, "The Study of Judaism in German Universities before 1933," *Leo Baeck Institute Year Book* 28 (1982): 310.

30. For a comprehensive historical survey of Jewish Studies in Germany, see Jospe, "The Study of Judaism in German Universities before 1933," 295–319; Henry Wassermann, *False Start: Jewish Studies at German Universities during the Weimar Republic* (Amherst: Prometheus Books, 2003).

31. Full documentation of Hirsch's appointment, course offerings, and efforts to foster Jewish Studies at the University of Chicago is found in the University Archives, housed in the Department of Special Collections at the University's Regenstein Library.

32. Jacob ben Asher, *Arba'ah Turim: Yoreh Deah*, Siman 247.

33. George Mosse, *Confronting History: A Memoir* (Madison: Wisconsin University Press, 1999).

34. See Nahum N. Glatzer, *Franz Rosenzweig: His Life and Thought*, reprint (Indianapolis/Cambridge: Hackett Publishers, 1998), p. 97.

6 Revival through Celebrity

American Fame, Jewish Identity, and the Early 1960s

In his 1989 study of the Jewish Publication Society, Jonathan Sarna first made the case for the phenomenon of religious revival in American Jewish history. In that work he writes:

> The late nineteenth century religious revival in American Jewish life began, as most such movements do, with a core group of young, idealistic, and highly motivated men and women who banded together to work for change. Fired with the enthusiasm of youth, these young people vowed to uplift American Jews from their spiritual malaise. They marked assimilation as their enemy and threw themselves into battle against it.[1]

Indeed, every revival in American Jewish life has been sparked by the activism of such a vanguard group. Sarna would later describe the late-nineteenth-century revival as the "Great American Jewish Awakening,"[2] borrowing once again from the language of American religious history. And most recently, he has employed the notion of religious revitalization as a central theme of his landmark history of American Judaism, emphasizing that "over and over again for 350 years one finds that Jews in America rose to meet the challenges . . . that threatened Jewish continuity."[3] It is, he notes, an optimistic rendering of American Jewish history, countering "those interpretations that posit inevitable declension ('assimilation') as Judaism passes down from one generation to the next."[4] Sarna's comment reiterates Marcus Hansen's famous "law" of ethnic revival—that "the third generation will seek to remember what the second had tried to forget." This idea of a generational reversal of assimilatory trends provides a key to understanding the nature of American Jewish revivalism. What constitutes "revival" in American Jewish history?—one simple answer: *when one generation is more Jewish than the one before.*

But what does "more Jewish" mean in this context? Jewish identity is a complex affair, comprising ethnic as well as religious elements. Insofar as

Jonathan Sarna has applied the theme of revivalism to American Jewish religion, allow me to suggest that it can be related just as well to the history of Jewish ethnic identity and secular Jewish culture. Here too, we have seen a cyclical pattern of rise and decline, and then revival. The creation of nineteenth-century communal organizations such as B'nai B'rith and the Young Men's Hebrew Association were clearly expressions of Jewish ethnic identification, instances in which the younger generation developed new models of Jewish life in order to become "more Jewish" than the current norm. In the twentieth century, first the Jewish labor movement and later the Zionist organization served this same purpose, both making Jewish education a core commitment of their otherwise political programs. In fact, the past century has seen a series of such ethnic Jewish revivals, just as in the realm of religion. How odd, therefore, that so many contemporary observers have rushed to proclaim the death of Jewish ethnicity, foreseeing the permanent disappearance of the secular Jewish culture that had pervaded twentieth-century American Jewish life. But just as religious Judaism has proven able to regenerate itself, so too has ethnic Jewishness reappeared and reasserted *it-self*. A number of scholars, Jonathan Sarna among them, have recently begun to observe the reemergence of a secular Jewish culture—not in place of a religious revival, but parallel to it. Yet the question remains as to why the development was so unexpected—perhaps some study of the last ethnic Jewish revival can shed some light on the current one.

The last revival of secular Jewish identity occurred not, as some would have it, in the 1920s and '30s, but just a generation ago, in the 1960s. Just as the countercultural '60s spurred greater ethnic identification across the board (one need only recall slogans such as "Black is beautiful" and "Kiss me, I'm Irish"), so too would Jews emerge from the decade more Jewishly identified than before. The eventful year of 1967 is often pointed to as the watershed moment in this development, and indeed, both the advent of a Jewish youth culture in that year and the increased activism following the Six Day War are rightly cited as the principal manifestations of Jewish revival in the late '60s and beyond. But on closer examination, it is the decade preceding 1967 when a vanguard laid the ground-work for this revival. That pivotal decade, from 1957 to 1967, began with the demise of McCarthyism and the rise of the civil rights movement. The sense of new possibility—a "new frontier" if you will—for outsider groups in this country reached new heights with the election of John F. Kennedy in 1960. The examples of the black community and a Catholic president both fighting for acceptance in America must have affected Jews in powerful ways—as evidenced by the heavy Jewish participation in both these campaigns. At the same time, the purported "religious revival" of postwar Jewry started to wear thin in the late '50s, and a new generation raised in suburbia began to reject the shallow Judaism and embarrassed ethnicity of their parents. Several years before the Six Day War, American Jews had already begun to recover a sharper sense of "Jewish peoplehood," evoked largely by a burgeoning pride in Israel and an ever increasing consciousness of the Holocaust, and thus began to reengage with their own Jewishness. Both external and internal factors were at play, therefore, and change was in the air. Perhaps the best indicator of the new tendency lay in the nexus of internal and external, the arena in which Jews aired their particular experience for a universal audience—the arena of popular culture.

The Jewish ethnic revival of the post-1967 era had its roots in the popular culture of the early 1960s. In one of the great ironies of American Jewish history, the very cultural space in which so many Jews attempted to "make it" in America—show business—became the medium through which they injected an explicit Jewishness into the general culture, a development which then helped make it possible for the majority of Jews to find their way back to Jewish identification. As J. Hoberman comments, "it's fair to say that popular culture plays a leading role in defining what being Jewish is for many American Jews."[5]

Some of the earliest adumbrations of the revival were the highly publicized Jewish conversions of popular stars. In the same era when most Hollywood Jews sought to avoid public Jewish identification, some high-profile non-Jews actually joined the fold by converting to Judaism. The famous new recruits were Sammy Davis Jr., who converted informally in 1955 (and formally in 1960), Marilyn Monroe in 1956, and Elizabeth Taylor in 1959—together suggesting, very publicly, that Jewish identification was a respectable and acceptable option for all. Of course, starlets Monroe and Taylor converted expressly for the purpose of marrying Jewish men, and so their newfound Jewishness should be read primarily as an endorsement of such marital choice—and we are led to wonder whether their examples may have helped prompt the later dramatic rise in the rate of intermarriage. But in the 1950s such rarified Jewish matings were more harbingers of the future than signs of the times.

More reflective of the revivalist trend was a growing consciousness of the Holocaust. As Hasia Diner has argued persuasively, the production of Holocaust memory began immediately after the Second World War.[6] Jewish leaders and educators in numerous sectors of the community attempted as best they could to introduce the subject to both their fellow Jews and the general population. But not until later in the 1950s would the Holocaust reach mass consciousness through popular culture. The *Diary of Anne Frank* is a case in point. First published in English in 1952, it was dramatized on radio and on television later that same year. The stage version premiered on Broadway in 1955, Anne and her diary made the cover of *Life* magazine in 1958, and her story was ultimately made into a major Hollywood film (by Twentieth Century Fox) in 1959. As Mrs. Van Daan, Shelley Winters won the Oscar for best supporting actress. Anne Frank had arrived, and all Americans were watching. Two years later (1961), another major Holocaust film arrived, Stanley Kramer's *Judgment at Nuremberg*. But as with the *Diary*, Holocaust memory often first appeared in literary form. In 1959, a young Jewish writer named Philip Roth published his first work, *Goodbye, Columbus*, a collection of short stories that included a classic titled "Eli, the Fanatic"—it was the story of a suburban Jewish community confronted with the presence of a group of Holocaust survivors in their midst. Holocaust literature gained its seminal work in the following year when Elie Wiesel published an English edition of his memoir, *Night*, in 1960. Still, popular awareness of the Holocaust only reached its apogee in the next few years, as the capture of Adolf Eichmann and the subsequent televised trial in Jerusalem galvanized viewers around the world in 1961 and 1962.

Concurrent with the rise in Holocaust consciousness, American Jews became ever more focused on the existence of Israel—again, by virtue of popular culture. In 1958, Leon Uris published a riveting novel about the birth of the Jewish state. *Exodus* was an immediate best seller, ranked number one for nineteen straight weeks. As historian Deborah Dash Moore writes: "Its vision of the creation of the State of Israel influenced an entire generation of American Jews."[7] One critic explained its appeal as telling "a new kind of story about a *new kind of Jew.*"[8] Those who didn't read the book certainly saw the film, which came out in 1960. Directed by the German-Jewish Otto Preminger and starring the young Paul Newman (whose father was Jewish), the film version became a major hit and a cultural touchstone for American Jews. The film's key moment in this regard was a scene between Newman's Ari Ben-Canaan, the Sabra freedom fighter, and his American love interest, the very blonde and very gentile Kitty, played by Eva Marie Saint. Showing Kitty the biblical landscape, Ben-Canaan proclaims, "I just wanted you to know I'm a Jew. This is *my* country." Eva Marie Saint's character replies with a typically American sentiment, "All these differences between people are made up. People are the same no matter what they're called." To which Newman emphatically responds,

> Don't ever believe it. People are different. They have a right to be different. They *like* to be different. It's no good pretending that differences don't exist. They do. They have to be recognized and respected.[9]

It was the classic dialectic between assimilation and cultural pluralism, and Newman's words reflected the new cultural confidence of American Jews. Responding to the popularity of *Exodus*, Philip Roth stated in late 1960, "I find myself living in a country and in a time in which the Jew has come to be—or is allowed to think he is—a cultural hero."[10] Of course the true cultural hero of the moment was the recently elected president, John F. Kennedy; yet some Jews, emboldened by the spirit of the times, saw the election in Jewish terms. Rabbi Albert Vorspan, for instance, published a "whimsical fantasy" just in time for Purim of 1961—as he wrote: "The election of our first Roman Catholic President has affected me strangely. Last night I had a dream—that a Jew became President of the United States."[11] Others, also humorously, began to project Jewishness into the American cultural arena. During Kennedy's first year in office, two former members of the Sid Caesar show, Carl Reiner and Mel Brooks, released a record album highlighting their comedy routine about a "2000 Year Old Man." As performed by Brooks, the character was the quintessential *alter kocker*, speaking in a thick New York Jewish accent and complaining about his thousands of children who "never once come to visit!" The record was a runaway hit and made Reiner and Brooks household names. An even bigger hit came out in the following year, 1962—a comedy album of parody songs called *My Son, the Folksinger*. Like Reiner and Brooks, Allan Sherman had been performing his take-offs of popular songs at parties but never thought the material was commercially viable. It was too patently ethnic, that is to say, "too Jewish"—the traditional Hollywood lament. The phrase "too Jewish," and the sentiment behind it, had served to forestall public Jewish identification for decades. But Sherman's hit albums belied the anxiety—his Jewishly flavored tunes became so widely popular, even President Kennedy was heard humming one in the White House. Just two years later, the ultimate rejoinder to "too Jewish" appeared on Broadway. The first musical theater production to employ Jewish themes explicitly, not merely as subtext, *Fiddler on the Roof* opened in 1964 and went on to become one of the most popular Broadway shows of all time, and moreover, the epitome of American Jewish nostalgia.

Much of the preceding, it should be said, has been amply covered by recent scholarship in American Jewish popular culture, most insightfully perhaps by J. Hoberman and Jeffrey Shandler in their Jewish Museum exhibition and accompanying catalogue, *Entertaining America: Jews, Movies, and Broadcasting.* In large part, Hoberman and Shandler's project is organized around a series of profiles of Jewish stars—an emphasis that prompts further thought about the nature of Jewish fame and celebrity. It raises the following question: What role does celebrity play in the historical relationship between popular culture and Jewish identity? In the early 1960s, I argue, it played a major role. Let us recall that this was an era of heightened celebrity worship in America, reflected by iconic figures such as Elvis Presley, Marilyn Monroe, John F. Kennedy, and Martin Luther King Jr. All had become extraordinarily famous for impressive achievements in their respective fields. But on some deeper level, they were also symbolic exemplars of the profound changes affecting American life in the late '50s and '60s, their larger-than-life personae anticipating many of the cultural, sexual, political, and social revolutions of the time.

As in so many other ways, Jews absorbed this facet of the culture and produced their own new heroes. The arrival of Jews in American popular culture had been brewing for decades, at least since Al Jolson starred in the first movie talkie in 1927 and Bess Myerson was crowned Miss America in 1945. But most famous Jews of the World War II era tended to hide their Jewish identities through name changes, behavior modification, and various other obfuscations. Not until the early 1960s did they attain heights of stardom *and* display an assertive Jewish identity at one and the same time. Extraordinary fame combined with unapologetic Jewishness in a number of these figures, ultimately preparing the way for the subsequent Jewish revival of the later 1960s.

A good starting point is one particularly eventful week during that period. On September 27, 1961, a young baseball pitcher named Sandy Koufax set his first major league strikeout record—just a few years later he would be immortalized as a Jewish hero for refusing to pitch a World Series game during Yom Kippur. Two days later, on September 29, a rising Jewish comedian named Lenny Bruce was arrested for the first time—beginning a downward spiral that would result in his premature death—yet his influence was seminal, long outlasting his own lifetime. And on that same date, the *New York Times* music critic discovered a new talent in town, a twenty-year-old unknown named Bob Dylan—true, his Jewish background remained unknown for a few years longer, but once outed as a Jew named Zimmerman (by *Newsweek* magazine, in November 1963) he came to be seen as the greatest Jewish artist of his generation. Besides Dylan, another young musical phenom also appeared in Greenwich Village around the same time—Barbra Streisand, who auditioned for her first Broadway role in November of that year. Celebrating her Brooklyn Jewishness from the first, she rocketed to stardom nonetheless and found herself playing the White House in just two years time. Very different figures they were, representing a diversity of Jewish possibilities, yet together they form a cohort of very famous Jews in the early 1960s. Each, in his or her own way, introduced a new paradigm of ethnic identification into American Jewish consciousness.

Sandy Koufax, for example, was a nice Jewish boy who happened to be athletically gifted. Well before his celebrated refusal to pitch on the high holidays of 1965, he had become a Jewish icon for his superhuman ability on the mound as well as his gentlemanly demeanor off the field. Though he had been a major leaguer since 1955, it was not until spring training of 1961 that the Brooklyn-born-and-raised Koufax finally found his pitching form—and a new Jewish star appeared on the horizon. Over the course of that historic season (it was the same year as Roger Maris' pursuit of Babe Ruth's home run record), he set a new National League record for strikeouts in a single season with 269, breaking a record that had stood for fifty-eight years (Christy Mathewson's). As he later wrote, "In 1961, a whole new world opened up for me"—a statement that would become emblematic of an entire generation. He thus embodied a new type of American Jew—identifiably and unashamedly Jewish, yet suave, well mannered, and deeply respected at the same time.

Another darkly handsome Jewish boy, Lenny Bruce, developed a less savory reputation. Where Koufax was the archetypal "good Jew," Bruce came to represent just the opposite. Anointed "king of the sick comics" by *Time* magazine in 1959, Lenny attained fame as a comic provocateur and transgressor of social norms. In retrospect, he is considered by many to have been one of the most influential performers in American cultural history and, as a martyr to the cause of freedom of expression, to have been pivotal in inspiring the cultural revolutions of the later 1960s. Less well known is his role in changing the public expression of Jewishness in America. Alone among 1950s standup comedians, Lenny Bruce introduced the subject of being

Jewish into his performances. In his first television appearance (on the *Steve Allen Show* in October 1959), he opened with an unrehearsed quip: "Will Elizabeth Taylor become Bar-Mitzvah-ed?" A few weeks later, appearing on the same show, he held up a Yiddish newspaper and pretended to read its review of his first appearance, "A star is born!" The use of such Jewish references on television would thereby substitute for the obscene language he used onstage—though it was still transgressive, it would pass muster with the censors. By ignoring the unwritten rule not to speak of Jewishness openly, and thus subverting the "too Jewish" taboo, Bruce helped tweak the new Jewish identity of his generation. As Nat Hentoff put it in 1963, "After an encounter with Bruce on one of his more demonic nights . . . you may look at the mirror with gnawing doubt that you indeed know who you are, or rather, what you really feel. About sex. About justice. About Negroes. About being a Jew." In the process, he also unleashed a new wave of brash Jewish comics who, starting in the early 1960s, would begin to inject the complexities and contradictions of ethnic identity into their routines and their personae: Shecky Greene, Buddy Hackett, Jackie Mason, Woody Allen, Joan Rivers, and others. Unquestionably, therefore, Lenny Bruce deserves his place alongside Sandy Koufax in the pantheon of American Jewish icons—Koufax, the "good Jew" who held the line of Jewish difference as Jews' assimilation in America reached its height; and Bruce, the "bad Jew" who, come to think of it, did the same.

On the same day as Bruce's first arrest, a music review appeared in the *New York Times*. Written by critic Robert Shelton, it heralded "a bright new face in folk music." The article was titled "Bob Dylan: A Distinctive Folk-Song Stylist," and it was the first public notice of the man who would become his generation's muse, Irving Berlin and Elvis Presley rolled into one. Among other things, the review noted a comic number he often performed, called "Talking Hava Nagila"—Shelton offhandedly remarks that by performing it, the singer was lampooning himself. That's as close as he or anyone else would come to identifying the twenty-year-old Bob Dylan as a Jew. Like Lenny Bruce, born Leonard Alfred Schneider, Dylan had changed his Jewish name upon entering show business. Yet Dylan, born Robert Zimmerman, had no intention of acknowledging his heritage, keeping his identity hidden until November 1963, when *Newsweek* magazine outed him in an infamous article. Thereafter, he became a Jewish icon despite himself, and, like both Sandy Koufax and Lenny Bruce, modeled a new form of Jewish identity—

one based on a fierce individualism and resistance to being defined by anyone else's norms.

His contemporary, Barbra Streisand, also refused to conform to the expectations of others; in her case, however, she did so with an unabashedly Jewish demeanor. Like Dylan, she also invented fanciful origins at first, claiming to have been born in Burma or in Turkey—yet unlike Dylan's more extreme deception, she then added the more truthful information that she had attended yeshiva in Brooklyn. First attracting notice in Greenwich Village nightclubs in the spring of 1961, by the fall she was appearing regularly on Mike Wallace's television program *PM East*. Then, in November, just as Dylan was recording his first album for Columbia Records, nineteen-year-old Barbra Streisand was cast in her first role on Broadway, playing Miss Marmelstein in *I Can Get It for You Wholesale*. Bob Dylan had attained fame by masking his Jewishness—"Einstein disguised as Robin Hood," according to his own lyrical imagery—whereas Barbra Streisand would claim her celebrity through a series of explicitly Jewish impersonations, from Fanny Brice to Yentl to, most recently, Ben Stiller's Jewish mother in *Meet the Fockers*. Yet what they also share in common with Koufax and Bruce is a refusal to play by the established rules of Jewish American identity—instead, they created their own and helped usher in a new era for all American Jews.

In 1966, Sandy Koufax retired from baseball. Lenny Bruce died tragically of a drug overdose. Bob Dylan had a motorcycle accident and disappeared from public view. Barbra Streisand moved to Hollywood and began to make movies. In the very next year, a Jewish revival began. Coincidence? Well, . . . yes, . . . but still, it is clear that we cannot properly understand the Jewish revival of 1967 without more carefully reviewing and analyzing the several pregnant years before. Revivals do not appear out of the blue, of course. As we learn from our study of American Jewish history, they are cyclical, they are initiated by a vanguard of youthful idealists, and the ground is prepared for them by seismic shifts in the popular culture—as in the case of the early 1960s, by the protean images of our very own American idols, our Jewish stars.

NOTES

Leah Fishbane was a dear friend and a cherished colleague, and like so many others whose lives she touched, I miss her terribly. While Eitan and Leah were living in Los

Angeles, I spent many wonderful Shabbatot at their house, and invariably Leah and I would end up talking about our shared field, American Jewish history. She was full of enthusiasm for her dissertation topic, and was always especially excited upon return from one of her research trips to Philadelphia, where she had discovered a treasure trove of material on the key figures of the late-nineteenth-century American Jewish revival. Such revivalism is, fittingly, the topic of this volume.

1. Jonathan Sarna, *JPS: The Americanization of Jewish Culture, 1888–1988* (Philadelphia: The Jewish Publication Society, 1989), 13.

2. Jonathan Sarna, "The Great American Jewish Awakening," *Midstream* 28 (October 1982); and "The Late Nineteenth-Century American Jewish Awakening," in *Religious Diversity and American Religious History*, ed. Walter H. Conser Jr. and Sumner B. Twiss (Athens: University of Georgia Press, 1997), 1–25.

3. Jonathan Sarna, *American Judaism* (New Haven: Yale University Press, 2004), introduction, xiv.

4. Ibid., xviii.

5. J. Hoberman and Jeffrey Shandler, eds., *Entertaining America: Jews, Movies, and Broadcasting* (New York: The Jewish Museum), 274.

6. Hasia Diner, *We Remember with Reverence and Love: American Jews and the Myth of Silence after the Holocaust, 1945–1962* (New York: New York University Press, 2009).

7. Deborah Dash Moore, "*Exodus*: Real to Reel to Real," in *Entertaining America*, ed. Hoberman and Shandler, 210.

8. Ibid.

9. Quoted in Hoberman and Shandler, eds., *Entertaining America*, 214.

10. Philip Roth, "Some New Jewish Stereotypes," in *Reading Myself and Others* (New York: Farrar, Straus and Giroux, 1975), 138.

11. Albert Vorspan, "A Jew in the White House—a Whimsical Fantasy," *American Judaism* (Purim, 1961), 8.

7 Renewal and Ḥavurah

American Movements, European Roots

The Ḥavurah and Jewish Renewal movements, beginning in the late 1960s, are rightly looked upon as quintessentially American Jewish phenomena. Indeed, from the inception of Havurat Shalom in 1968, this writer and others spoke of the *ḥavurah* as an aspect of the American counterculture, setting our efforts in the context of the communitarian impulses that flourished in the broader youth culture of that era. There is no question that the banal quality of American Jewish life, including a perceived shallowness of the American synagogue, was a major motivating factor in attracting Jews to the self-proclaimed radical alternatives offered within these movements. This was part of a broad reaction against the perceived smugness and self-satisfaction of American postwar bourgeois culture as the baby-boomer generation emerged into postadolescence in the late 1960s. The document that best expressed the ethos of Ḥavurah Judaism, *The Jewish Catalogue*, was as American 1970s a product as one could imagine.

At the same time, however, there was much that was distinctively Jewish, textual, and traditional in the Judaism set forth by these claimants to the countercultural mantle. Havurat Shalom opened its doors with serious text study, including courses taught by Green, Michael Fishbane, and Zalman Schachter, among others. Serious theological conversation, intense singing of Hasidic *niggunim*, and even halakhic debates have been part of the milieu in many of the settings created by both Ḥavurah and Renewal circles in the ensuing decades. The rejected American Jewish style that characterized the postwar era in the community and its institutions was juxtaposed to a more "serious" or "authentic" Judaism learned by these young leaders mostly from European émigré intellectuals, building on developments that had taken place in a now lost and idealized interwar European Jewish community.

From German Jewry came the inspiration of Franz Rosenzweig's Freies Juedisches Lehrhaus, the adult study institute that he founded in Frankfurt in 1920. Appreciation of Rosenzweig had spread significantly in American Jewish intellectual circles following the publication of Nahum N. Glatzer's *Franz Rosenzweig: His Life and Thought* in 1953 and the embrace of his thought by Will Herberg and others. The German term *Lehrhaus* was being used on college campuses by the mid-1960s to refer to a program of Jewish learning that, while not offering college credit, was to be fully as serious as any university instruction. It was, however, to be infused with the Rosenzweigian spirit, which is to say that its aim was personal Jewish quest and not acquisition of academic knowledge. The *Lehrhaus* model of learning may be accurately depicted as the first efflorescence of a postmodern spirit in the American Jewish mind. The link between the founders of the Ḥavurah movement and the Rosenzweig legacy was quite direct; several of the movement's founders had been Glatzer's students at Brandeis University in the years preceding their involvement in creating the movement.

But the legacy of Eastern European Jewry was even stronger. It was clear from the outset that these groups saw themselves as neo-Hasidic, that is to say, carrying certain values of early Hasidism and limited aspects of Hasidic devotional praxis, lifted out of their original context, to Jews who lived far different lives from those of the traditional Hasidic community. While many of these young Jews may indeed be construed as *ḥozrim bi-teshuvah* ("returnees"), Jews more committed to tradition than was their upbringing, they were not on their way toward Orthodox Hasidism, and it would be quite inaccurate to depict them that way. They were Hasidic largely as channeled through the writings and personal influence of Martin Buber and Abraham Joshua Heschel, certainly the most widely read theologians within their circles. To an even greater extent they were inductees into the world of Hasidism as conveyed through the singular personality and teaching of Rabbi Zalman Schachter-Shalomi.[1]

The neo-Hasidism put forth by Schachter and his close friend and colleague Rabbi Shlomo Carlebach was much influenced by their own experiences in Lubavitch in its early Brooklyn years. Though neither Schachter nor Carlebach had been raised as a Lubavitcher,[2] both found their way there during adolescence and had been deeply shaped by the experience. Both had also broken with their mentor, Rabbi Menahem Mendel Schneersohn, a break that was essential to the emergence of the new North American Hasidism they were to create by the mid-1960s.

But neo-Hasidism did not begin in America. The term had been in use in Poland since the turn of the twentieth century. My purpose here is to trace some of that history and thus to show the grounding of American neo-Hasidism in that which had come before it, but had been utterly cut off by the Holocaust. Both Heschel and Schachter, I hope to demonstrate, were active and self-conscious conduits of that legacy.

The idea that Jews living outside the traditional Hasidic world might still have something to learn from Hasidism and the mystical tradition could only have come about after the great battle between Haskalah and Hasidism came to an end at the beginning of the twentieth century. This possibility of rapprochement (heralded as early as Eliezer Zweifel's *Shalom ʿal Yisraʾel* in 1870) happened because modern Jews thought they were witnessing the virtual collapse of Hasidism. By the fourth quarter of the nineteenth century Hasidism was very much in retreat, especially in its original heartland of Western Ukraine and Belorussia (it remained stronger in Galicia and northeastern Hungary). The reasons for this decline of the dominant force in Jewish religious life are complex and do not concern us here, but they include such socioeconomic factors as urbanization, industrialization, and emigration, along with the concomitant rise of Socialist, Zionist, and other secularizing ideologies. In the century's closing decade it became possible for secular historians (S. M. Dubnov in their lead) to take a nonpolemical interest in Hasidism. Shortly afterward, writers, artists, and musicians began to take up the imaginative re-creation of Hasidism that was to exercise such a tremendous hold on the Jewish artistic imagination throughout the twentieth century.

The term neo-Hasidism has been the subject of a fine recent book by Nicham Ross.[3] It was first used regarding literary compositions, especially those of Y. L. Peretz and others in his circle. The term *ha-Ḥasidut ha-ḥadashah* was sometimes used interchangeably with *ha-Ḥasidut ha-sifrutit*. Indeed it was understood both by enthusiasts and critics[4] that Peretz, for one, was not interested in mere nostalgic re-creation of bygone days but wanted to use his old/new Hasidic tales as a platform for a Jewish national revival featuring his own values. This positive appropriation of Hasidism transcended the emerging lines between Hebrew and Yiddish literature (as did Peretz). On the Hebrew side, this is especially associated with Michah Josef Berdiczewsky, S. Y. Agnon, and others, as discussed in full detail by Ross. In Yiddish literature it is represented by such major figures as Sholem Asch, Joseph Opatoshu, Der Nister (Kahanovich), and the Singer brothers.

On the ideological/philosophical side, neo-Hasidism is of course most associated with the works of Martin Buber (1878–1965). Buber began publishing his famous re-creations of Hasidic tales as early as 1906. He wrote in

German, and his works were addressed to a German-reading public, both Jewish and Christian. But at almost the same time, Buber began writing essays that used Hasidism as an expression of his own religious values, some of which authentically derived from early Hasidic writings but were presented with an overlay of the romantic youth-culture mysticism widely popular in the Middle Europe of his day. As Buber's own ideology shifted from mysticism to dialogic thinking in the post–World War I years, he took Hasidism along with him, as it were, reshaping his reading of it to emphasize its interpersonal and communitarian aspects.

But Buber was by no means the only thinker of his generation to have recourse to Hasidism in search of a Jewish religious language that might address a younger generation. Aaron David Gordon (1856–1922), the most important intellectual of the Zionist back-to-the-land movement, was much influenced by his own Hasidic background and the affectionate appropriation of some of the movement's key terminology.[5] Throughout the interwar period, there were various attempts, both in Poland and Eretz Yisrael, to universalize and update some of Hasidism's essential religious insights.[6] The figure most associated with these attempts in Eastern Europe, and one of particular interest to us here, is author-publicist-journalist Hillel Zeitlin (1871–1942).[7]

Coming from a HaBaD family in Belorussia, Zeitlin went through the usual rebellion of Jews in his generation and left the world of religious observance fully behind him.[8] He was a member of the emerging Hebrew literary elite around the turn of the century. Zeitlin attended the fifth Zionist Congress in 1901, at which the Uganda Plan and other ideas for immediate increased emigration from Eastern Europe were discussed. Convinced of this need, Zeitlin wavered between Zionism and Territorialism over the next several decades. A student of contemporary philosophy, Zeitlin was much influenced by Nietzsche, Schopenhauer, and the Russian mystic Lev Shestov. He published books in Hebrew on both Spinoza (1900) and Nietzsche (1905). But by the first decade of the twentieth century, after trying to introduce Western philosophical thought, especially romantic philosophy, into East European Jewish life, he began to seek out an authentic Jewish philosophical language. In doing so, he returned to the philosophical Hasidism of his early years. Unlike any of those mentioned above, Zeitlin took the most unusual step, for his day, of returning to traditional religious observance.

In 1924 Zeitlin began to issue calls for the creation of a movement he named Yavneh. In that year he published a remarkable tract called "The Ark"

(*Di Tevah*, in Yiddish).[9] The pamphlet claims to be a publication of "the re-ligious-ethical circle Yavneh of the Ahavat Re'im Society." It seems likely that both of these nascent "institutions" existed primarily in Zeitlin's mind.[10] This was to be a network of religious seekers and communities who would commit themselves to following a unique list of principles and specific courses of action, outlined in the documents offered in English translation in the appendix to this chapter. These texts constitute the first description of a neo-Hasidic Jewish religious community. The reader is invited to examine these texts before continuing with my discussion of them.

In the introductory essay "What Does Yavneh Want?" Zeitlin (employed throughout this period as a journalist) conducts a sort of interview with him-self. He immediately sets up a juxtaposition between the pristine idealistic Hasidism of the Ba'al Shem Tov's times and the corrupt Hasidism of his own day. (The founder of Hasidism, the Ba'al Shem Tov, is referred to throughout by his acronym, the BeSHT.) It should be noted that despite Zeitlin's return to piety, even to the point of dressing in old-style Hasidic garb, he never was quite trusted by the main Hasidic community of Warsaw, the disciples of R. Abraham Mordecai of nearby Ger (Gora Kalwarya). The antagonism was mutual; Zeitlin saw contemporary Hasidism as deeply flawed by small-mindedness and bickering, by compromise with bourgeois values and world-liness of an unattractive sort. True Hasidism, as Zeitlin describes it, that which Yavneh seeks to revive, is built around the three loves that the BeSHT had claimed were the center of his faith: the love of God, the love of Torah, and the love of Israel. He then goes on to define these in typically romantic-poetic terms.

The Hasidism of the future, however, which is first to be practiced by the proposed Yavneh communities, differs also from that of Hasidism's founder, even regarding some very basic aspects of the Hasidic legacy. Mid-twentieth-century Hasidism is to diverge from two-hundred-year-old precedent in three essential ways. Love of Israel must no longer focus exclusively on shin-ing an inner light on Jews and the Jewish path. "In current times, when a world has been destroyed and a new world is being built, Israel has to be a light both for itself and for all nations," a position then justified by quotations from scripture. Love of Torah is also no longer sufficiently defined in narrow or even exclusively Jewish ways. Now "we must seek the Torah-light also in the greatest works of art and in worldly sciences, which we need to approach with a particular light in our hands." Within the context of Zeitlin's highly pantheistic theology, it would not be far-fetched to seek God in the work of botanists, physicists, artists, or poets. Finally, elements of class struggle, still hardly developed in the BeSHT's day, have to be recognized by the new Hasidism, which is to be much concerned with "the demand for social justice."

Rather remarkably, if we look at the neo-Hasidic Judaism both preached and practiced in North America some eighty years after Zeitlin issued this call, the areas of departure from classical Hasidism are quite the same. He understood the ways in which Hasidic attitudes toward the outside world, both ethnically and intellectually, would have to be reshaped in order to appeal to moderns. While Zeitlin as a traditional worshipper might have had little taste for some of the liturgical innovations of these later circles, he too was author of original prayers composed in the vernacular.[11] Gender egalitarianism was also not yet a central issue for him, though he did publish an early essay on the place of the Jewish woman, again in a highly romantic tone.[12] But the call for a broadening of the Hasidic ethos across once inviolable borders sounds entirely contemporary.

Zeitlin was a well-known and popular writer in interwar Jewish Poland. He contributed columns on aspects of traditional Jewish life for Warsaw's two great secular Yiddish daily newspapers, *Heynt* and *Moment*. He was both prolific and polemical in tone. In the 1930s his writings took on a dark and prophetic tone as he predicted the terrible calamity to come. As a Territorialist, he sometimes entered into sharp conflict with the growing Zionist consensus that emerged as the threat grew greater.

Zeitlin visited Eretz Yisrael in 1924. Following that visit, he asked a few of his followers there, including Yitzhak Landberg (later famed Palmach commander Yitzhak Sadeh) to try to create a Yavneh chapter in Jerusalem. As far as is known, such a group never came to be. But some of the followers of Rabbi Abraham Isaac Kook noticed an affinity between Zeitlin's religious writings and those of their master, and encouraged their publication. After the war a few surviving Polish Jews, especially Simha Bunem Auerbach, continued to write on Zeitlin and see that his works appeared in Israel.[13] In North America he was completely unknown outside Yiddish-reading circles. His books on Bratslav and HaBaD Hasidism, in Yiddish, were published in New York in 1952 and 1957 by his son Aaron Zeitlin, the well-known Hebrew and Yiddish poet.

A surprising area of Zeitlin's influence has to do with translation of the Zohar. Zeitlin was an avid student of the Zohar throughout his adult life. Indeed, the account of his death, reported by ghetto survivor Hillel Zeidman,[14] tells us that Zeitlin went out to the notorious Umschlagplatz, the gathering-place for the journey to Majdanek, wearing *tallit* and *tefillin* and carrying a copy of the Zohar in his hands (I imagine he was thinking of the Tiqquney Zohar's claim, repeated by Rabbi Nahman, that "with this book—the Zohar—Israel will go forth from exile"). Zeitlin had begun to translate the entire Zohar into Hebrew, accompanied by his own partly scholarly, partly neo-Hasidic commentary.[15] The manuscript was lost in the Holocaust, along with Zeitlin himself. Only his translation of the introduction to the Zohar survived, having been printed in London during the war in Simon Rawidowicz's *Metsudah*.[16] But Zeitlin's onetime neighbor (they had once lived in the same building in Warsaw), literary historian Fishel Lachower, was living in Eretz Yisrael. After Zeitlin's death he took up the dream of translating the Zohar into modern Hebrew. He approached Gershom Scholem with this notion, and Scholem linked him up with a young graduate student name Isaiah Tishby. Thus the well-known *Mishnat ha-Zohar* (now available in English as *Wisdom of the Zohar*) came about.[17] The first volume lists Lachower as coeditor with Tishby, though he in fact had died in 1947, well before the volume appeared.

But the connection between Zeitlin and North American neo-Hasidism is of different origins, and is not coincidental.[18] On a visit to Israel in 1959, Zalman Schachter (still a Lubavitcher Hasid but one already open to ever-widening sources of influence) met Natan Hofshi and was introduced by him to Zeitlin's writings, including the call for Yavneh. Schachter had by this time come in contact with Christian monasticism; he often visited Roman Catholic abbeys and convents and was becoming well read in Christian mystical sources. He also recalls having been greatly moved by the discovery of the Dead Sea scrolls, which gave him the opportunity to imagine that some form of monastic living had once been a part of Jewish religious history. All of these, including the influence of Zeitlin, came together in a plan he developed for the creation of a quasi-monastic Jewish community in North America. It was first publicly described in an article in *Judaism*[19] in 1964 titled, "Toward an Order of Bnai Or."

Bnai Or, named for the eschatological community of the righteous described in a Qumran scroll, was to be a full-time communal enterprise for both married and single Jews who wanted to devote themselves wholly to a life of religious devotion. Schachter describes a group whose members would spend eight hours a day in communal prayer, meditation, and study. Another eight hours would be devoted to communally based work in efforts that would both enrich the outside Jewish community and help to sustain the Bnai Or enterprise. These might include, for example, writing (liturgical creativity was to be a special area of concern), teaching, printing/publishing, or artistic and musical endeavors. By the mid-1960s, Schachter had constituted a group of perhaps ten or twelve people (the present writer and his future wife among them) who had expressed serious interest in forming the core of this community, one that never came to be.

In 1967 and 1968, when I (along with several mentors and friends) developed the idea for Havurat Shalom, the Bnai Or concept was certainly in the background. What became the Ḥavurah was somewhat different, primarily because the monastic style that attracted Schachter had less pull for me and I knew it would be a turn-off to the young Jewish seekers we were attracting. Although I am not sure whether I had yet seen Zeitlin's Yavneh-related writings at that time,[20] in some ways Havurat Shalom was closer to their spirit than to the original Bnai Or. The political milieu in which we emerged, the anti–Vietnam War urgency of 1968, made the political and social component more central to us than it had been to Zalman, who in those days was somewhat more otherworldly. While we could have hardly opened our manifesto, as Zeitlin had, with a call to working the land or becoming tradesmen (we were already highly educated and upwardly mobile American Jews, living in the United States of 1968 rather than Poland of 1924), we were indeed attracted to the dream of rural community, and a subgroup of the early Ḥavurah members who met in Somerville, Massachusetts, often talked about moving to western New England to create a communal farm and retreat center, another dream that was never to come to be, though we see shades of it into today's *Teva'* and *Adamah* programs. While Havurat Shalom was quite far from the Orthodoxy of Zeitlin's own religious life, the echoes of his call for religious renewal in the context of a sharp critique of the socioeconomic order were surely well heard in Somerville.

As it happened, Zalman had a sabbatical from his position in Winnipeg during 1968/69, the first year of Havurat Shalom, and he joined us as a Ḥavurah member on a one-year basis, very much enriching the life of that group. Some seven years later, after he moved to Philadelphia (where the Greens also lived by then), Zalman began actively to create what was to become Bnai Or, Pnai Or, and eventually the Aleph/Jewish Renewal movement. The monastic flavor had disappeared, replaced by a much more "Aquarian Age" tempo. Elements of Sufism and Eastern religious practice were rather casually blended with a neo-Hasidic Judaism in a mix that at first demanded very little of traditional Jewish commitment or knowledge and was thus open and attractive to the many seekers who were experimenting with new religious forms in that age. While the casual visitor would have had no encounter with them, Zalman's own translations of pieces by Zeitlin, along with writings of R. Nahman, various HaBaD leaders, *piyyutim*, and *zemirot*, were on the shelves of the original Bnai Or house on Emlen Street, alongside Idris Shah, Timothy Leary, and Baba Ram Dass. A new age had indeed begun.

APPENDIX

What Does Yavneh Want?

Hillel Zeitlin

I. What Does Yavneh Want? (A Dialogue)

What does Yavneh want?

Yavneh wants to bring old Hasidism, that of the BeSHT, back to life and establish it on foundations that are more acceptable in the present time of the "Messiah's footsteps."

Of what does this old BeSHTian Hasidism consist?

Three loves: the love of God, the love of Israel, and the love of Torah.

How did the BeSHT understand the love of God?

Until the BeSHT, even the purest love of God (and we speak here only of the love of God in its purest form. Those who love God because He gives them health, length of days, glory, and wealth, are not being considered here at all) was conceived only like the love of a glorious king or a great sage. Maybe, in the best case, it was like the way one loves a father. But the BeSHT came and taught that one must love with a terrible thirst, a terrible burning, terrible suffering that fills the entire soul and body in such a way that no room for anything else remains.

Was the BeSHT the first to conceive of the love of God this way?

Long before the BeSHT there were those who saw the love of God as entailing suffering as long as the person remains in the body and does not have an actual "outpouring of the soul."

Who were they?

R. Eleazar Rokeach, R. Yehudah he-Ḥasid, and in the time of the BeSHT, R. Ḥayyim Ibn Attar.

And how did such enlightened Jews as R. Bahya Ibn Pakuda, Maimonides, and many others understand the love of God?

They understood "love" as an act of the mind, of consciousness, of knowledge.

And R. Eleazar Rokeach, R. Yehudah he-Ḥasid, R. Ḥayyim Ibn Attar, and the BeSHT think that "love" is not an act of mind, consciousness, or knowledge?

They respect these as well. But they demand that the love of the Most High take in the entire person. It is the highest form of passion, the desire of all desires. It embraces all particular wills, all of a person's senses, the totality of passion, all one's lust for life, all thoughts, all words, all deeds!

Did they come to this all-consuming love just out of their own souls, or were they somehow aided by the ancients?

They saw this love in the words of the poet: "As the hart pants after streams of water, so does my heart pant for You, O God." . . . "My soul thirsts for God, for the living God." . . . "Who else do I have in heaven? I want none but You in the earth." . . . "My flesh and heart wear away, O rock of my heart; God is my portion forever."

If Rokeach, Yehudah he-Ḥasid, the BeSHT, and Ibn Attar saw this in the words of the poet, what did they add to it?

Everyone knows these words of the poet. But they are taken as just that—poetry—unique and special moments of divine inspiration. Along came the Rokeach, R. Yehudah, Ibn Attar, and the BeSHT, and they made it a requirement for every individual in every hour and moment, like the air we breathe.

And what did the BeSHT in particular add to this?

For the Rokeach, R. Yehudah, and Ibn Attar, this all-consuming love was a positive commandment, alongside all the others. But for the BeSHT it is the foundation of everything. He never stops talking about it in all his teachings, stories, and aphorisms.

And how did the BeSHT understand the love of Israel?

He once said to someone: "Believe me, I love the worst Jew in the world much more than you love your favorite child." This is what love of Israel meant to the BeSHT.

And what did the love of Torah mean to him?

If you understand "Torah" only as sharp-minded, expert, deep learning, you can find love of Torah among other great sages and righteous folk, perhaps even more than in the BeSHT. But the BeSHT's love of Torah touches especially upon the light of Torah, the hidden light, attachment to God through the letters of the Torah, the "worlds, souls, and divinity" that exist within every letter. Those letters combine to form words, and out of the joining of these words are formed awesome unifications, bringing near the coming of messiah.

And why do you call all this a "return to the original Hasidism" of the BeSHT? Why don't you simply say: "to Hasidism?"

Because today's Hasidism is very far from the pure Hasidism of the BeSHT.

In what way has today's official Hasidism turned away from the pure Hasidism of the BeSHT?

Simply in the fact that it no longer possesses that love of God, Israel, and Torah.

What do you mean?

Very simple. Today's *hasidim* still *talk* about all these things. But they mix all sorts of incidental things in with them—fanciful interpretations, homilies, intellectual games—until the real point is obscured. Second—and this is really the main thing—for some of today's Hasidim their Hasidism has become a purely external matter. They study without a real taste for it; they pray in the same way. They pursue wealth and glory no less, and sometimes even more, than non-Hasidim. They're always busy praising their own rebbes and castigating all the others, along with their disciples. They've set up rebbes' courts and dynasties and get all involved in the politics of these. They spend a good part of their lives fighting about rabbis, slaughterers, and other religious officials. They consider only themselves to be proper Jews and everyone else to be nothing at all. They make Hasidism consist entirely of external manners, outer dress and outward customs. They regularly mix fanaticism with piety. They pursue the young people over petty and foolish matters, sometimes pushing them away from Jewish religious life with their very hands. . . .

Are you claiming that today's hasidim contain even less true and pure Judaism than the non-hasidim?

God forbid! First, I've only spoken here about a portion of today's *hasidim*, not about all. Certainly there are other sorts of *hasidim* present today as well: those who bear a deep inwardness, a deep attachment, passionate love of God. They have love for all Jews, a love of truth and a longing for peace, a strong, clear understanding of all that is happening around them. Second, even those other *hasidim*, the ones of outwardness and dress, still have lots of good qualities, those that belong to all Jews. Whatever failings a contemporary *hasid* may have, he still bears a certain sense of shame, a fear of God, a brokenness, something of modesty, humility, a leaning toward lovingkindness, goodness, and love. But everyone—the inward *hasidim*, those who concentrate on the externals, and just ordinary

Jews—today needs a new light that will shine into their souls, a Hasidism of the future, rays of messiah's light.

Does Yavneh want to be that "Hasidism of the future," that "ray of messiah's light?"

That Hasidism is not yet here. The rays of messiah's light show themselves hardly at all, only to those most pure of sight. But Yavneh wants to *prepare* for that future. Yavneh seeks, bit by bit, to qualify individuals for it. It wants to create vessels to contain that light, which must come sooner or later.

And in what way is the "Hasidism of the future" to be differentiated, not only from today's external Hasidism, but from that which is inward, and even from the Hasidism of the BeSHT?

Differentiated from inward Hasidism and from that of the BeSHT? Not at all! On the contrary, it will be built entirely on the Hasidism of the BeSHT. But what then? It will go farther, broader and deeper, appropriate to these messianic times.

What will that "going farther," both in breadth and depth, consist of?

In the time of the BeSHT it was enough for Israel to shine a light for itself. In these times, in a time when a world has been destroyed and a new one is being built, Israel has to be a light for itself and for all peoples, as in the verse (Is. 42:6): "I the Lord call you in righteousness and hold fast to your hand, making you as a covenantal people, a light to the nations." And Scripture also says (Is. 49:6): "Is it easy for you to be My servant, to raise up the tribes of Jacob and restore the guarded ones of Israel? I have made you a light unto the nations, so that My salvation reach the ends of the earth." And it also says (Zeph. 3:9): "Then I will turn all the nations toward a clear tongue so that they all might call upon the name of the Lord, to serve Him together."

And in what else?

In the time of the BeSHT we sought the light of Torah only in the Torah itself. Sometimes they also sought it out in ordinary folk-stories, in which they discovered a hidden light. ("Declare His glory among the nations" according to a profound remark of Rabbi Nahman, means that "the glory of God cries forth from all things, even from tales told by the non-Jews). But in the times of this final great purification we need to seek out the Torah-light in all the finest works of art, in all forms of worldly knowledge. We need to approach these with a certain light in our hands, with a certain kind of foresight. "A candle of the Lord is the human soul, searching out all the belly's chambers." It will have to separate, seek out and nullify, casting aside heaps of lies in order to get at the kernel of truth. . . .

And in what else?

In the time of the BeSHT the class conflicts among people were not yet so sharply defined. The demand for social justice had not yet been articulated with full seriousness and honesty. Today we are undergoing horrible evils that are taking place in the world. But these are leading us to a more just and honorable relationship with those who work with sweat on their brows. The "Hasidism of the future" will incorporate all that is healthy, pure, and honorable in Socialism. But it will be with great bitterness that we will cast aside all in Socialism that is petty, egotistical, merchant-like in its materialism, unjust, jealous, or vengeful. It will reject the dark and wild tyranny of the masses and of those adventurers who climb up on the backs of the masses.

In the Hasidism of the future the love of God will shine forth and burn even more brightly than it did in the days of the BeSHT. The "Love of Israel" will be transformed into a great worldwide "Love of Humans." Nevertheless, Israel will always be recognized as the firstborn child of God, the one who has borne, continues to bear, and will continue to bear the godly light. "Love of Torah" will spread forth over all that breathes with sublime wisdom, after the inner light teaches the Jews to distinguish between that within the worldly sciences which is of the divine mind and that which is just self-proclaimed human conviction, error, and lies. "Justice, justice shall you pursue" will be spread through all social relationships. Justice will be demanded not only of the opposing class (as both the capitalists and the proletariat do today), but people will demand justice *of themselves*. Pursuit of justice will be not only a public matter (as it is today), but rather of individual concern. Each person will think not about how to avoid being exploited, but rather about how to avoid exploiting the other.

Perhaps you could outline for me, just briefly, how you see the hasid of the future, that for which the Yavneh member is preparing.

I'll try to do so. The *hasid* of the future will live only from his own physical labor. He will exploit no one in the world, doing not even the slightest harm to anyone. He will partake of God's own holiness, living in uninterrupted communion with the Endless. He will walk through divine fire while praying, will study Torah with an inner godly light, will seek and find everywhere the light of Torah and messianic light. In all his thoughts and deeds he will strive only for true peace and unity. He will be filled with love and compassion for every Jew and non-Jew, for every creature. He will long to raise up the form of the *Shekhinah* in the holy land and to spread her light through all the world. He will be a great seer and a great knower. In his own eyes he will be as nothing at all, having not just an external veneer of modesty but a deep inner recognition, a full consciousness that he is "just a small creature, lowly, dark, standing with but a weak mind before the One who knows perfectly." In that moment he will be a true "chariot" for the divine, a true servant of God, a faithful messenger.

II. Commandments for Every True Member of Yavneh
    (Fourteen Principles)[21]

1. *Support yourself only from your own work!* You must try as hard as you can to support yourself from simple physical work, and not from trade. Trade is based primarily on the deception of customers, and this means lies. And lies completely oppose what the Blessed Holy One, who is Absolute Truth, demands of us ("God, our Sovereign, is truth." And, "the signet of God is truth.").

If you are, brother, a workingman, try to become an expert craftsperson in your field. Don't look forward, as so many do today, to leaving this work so that you can support yourself through easier business. If you are not yet a worker, make the effort to become one. If you have not yet been given the opportunity to join a labor union for religious or moral reasons, try to establish, together with a few of the members of "*Yavneh,*" co-operative workshops and the like.

If you cannot work as a physical worker because of old age or weakness, try at least to choose for yourself a type of livelihood that succeeds with a minimum of commerce in it, and help your friends working with their hands in every way you can.

2. *Keep away from luxuries!* Luxuries throttle the mind and the strength of a person. Luxuries bring on deeds of constant deceit, leading from there to thievery and robbery. Striving for the true Jewish life, and at the same time for a life of luxuries, is like dipping in a purifying pool while holding a defiling abomination in your hand.

Therefore choose a life of modesty, simplicity, keeping yourself far away from all external luxuries. Refrain as much as you can from various habits that cost you money, that do not benefit your body, and harm your soul. My friend, turn your steps away from the theatre, from parties, guard yourself from smoking, from liquor, from expensive clothes, from adorning yourself with rings, and the like. Desire not to adorn your dwelling with costly decorations. It would be better if you would purify and adorn your soul, my dear friend.

3. *Do not exploit anyone!* Were you to support yourself solely by the work of your hands, the length of your days would be surrounded by modesty, calm, and humility, by abstention from indulgence, luxury and pleasure seeking. It will simplify your task to fulfill the great and holy commandment to every pure mortal: do not exploit anyone! Do not "use" anyone, seeking your own benefit without her or his agreement, or even with her or his agreement, if a full exchange of value is not received. Every person is a complete world. From the standpoint of morality and pure religion, every business abuse, in any form whatsoever, is robbery and murder.

A factory boss or supervisor who takes advantage of workers by paying them the lowest wage acceptable on the market, and not the full and proper sum for value received, is exploiting those workers. The merchant who takes unfair advantage in buying or selling exploits the people she or he is dealing with.

Abuses are to be found today also among politicians, journalists, doctors, and the rest of the people involved in the free professions. Every pressing of advantage that is not the result of the complete, considered, free and serious agreement of the person involved, is a sin.

Protect yourself from all this as you protect yourself from fire, my dear brother!

4. *Purify your family life.* The family has always been a stronghold for the Jew. In the face of work, persecution, and daily troubles, the Jew found rest and comfort in his quiet, pleasant, and pure family life. The family has always been the Jew's sanctuary. Even Balaam saw this, and against his will declared: "How good are your dwelling places, O Ya'akov."

Today, to our disaster, the anarchy of the street has broken into the Jewish family. This bulwark, the pure and pleasant Jewish family of Poland, has started to disintegrate since the time of the German conquest [World War I]. Now, this fall is deepening more and more. Further, this decline is abetted by the general moral ruin of the street, the theatre, the movies, the pulp journals, and obscene literature. And a good bit of the so-called better and more serious literature abets this. Knowingly and unknowingly, many of those that declare themselves to be artists contribute to this decline.

Protect your soul from this catastrophe, my dear brother! Strengthen yourself to protect the quiet, the peace, and love in your family!

5. *Sanctify your sex life altogether!* The preservation and sanctification of the covenant, these are the exalted bases of both interior and exterior holiness. Concerning this, we are charged: "Be holy" and "one who sanctifies oneself a little here below, will be greatly sanctified from above." "The sexual organ is the termination of the body, sign of the holy covenant." One who is pure in this matter is holy; one who is impure in this area is defiled. In this one must be guarded not only from actual sin, but also from sinful thoughts. And the proven ways to this are: always to be occupied with work (at best, physical work), and also with the learning of *Torah*, with concentration and depth. "There is no room for sin except in a heart that is void of wisdom," says the Rambam. "*Torah* is good when mated to work; the exertion of both cause sin to be forgotten." Actual work—on no account idleness. Idleness brings on all misfortune.

6. *Guard yourself from forbidden foods!* "You will be defiled by them." Read this as, "You will be *blocked* by them." Forbidden foods defile the body and soul; forbidden foods create vile and impure blood in the human body. If some of today's Jewish youth have a tendency to go toward evil, this is mainly an outcome of not protecting themselves against forbidden foods. Be careful, my sister and brother, of forbidden foods, and thus you will save yourself your impurity, evil and quick temper.

7. *Sanctify your Shabbos!* The Sabbath is not just an ordinary commandment, but the basic foundation. One who weakens the Sabbath, Heaven forbid, desecrates the God of Israel. A person who doesn't sanctify the Sabbath is like one who worships idols. "Keep" and "remember," the single God uttered at once. Unite with the holiness of the Sabbath, and in this way, commune with the Holy Blessed One. The Sabbath, however, must be kept not only on the outside, but also within. This means prayer, learning, a basic stocktaking of the soul, concentration of the mind on holy and pure matters. *Shabbat* upholds the whole Jewish people. The congregation of *Yisrael* and *Shabbat* are truly a pair, and in them resides the Holy Ancient of Days.

8. *Keep your home holy!* Not only the synagogue, the house of learning, the prayer-room, but also every Jewish house is a small-scale sanctuary. When can this be said? When the house abounds with words of *Torah*, prayers, blessings, *Kiddush* and *Havdalah*, and when these are expressed seriously, truthfully, with profound and intent sincerity! When a mother and a father, a

brother and a sister, live in calm and true peace (for in a peaceful place, there is the blessing of the Father of peace); when the children are educated in the spirit of the serious and pure *Torah*; when all the children of the house speak the Jewish tongue and are full of love, honor and recognition for every Jewish thing.

But what is today the structure of a house of an average Jewish merchant? Mostly, it is a place of selling and buying, sometimes a feverish stock market, sometimes a club for a game of cards, and sometimes a hall for parties. The father goes out in search of "pleasures," and the mother she seeks her own. In the house—a constant ill will, constant arguments behind the backs of others, or worse, to their face. The daughters no longer speak Yiddish; the sons are being prepared for empty careers. Even where *Shabbat* is kept in an exterior way, it is without celebration, without soul, without life. They pray, and when they have the opportunity, they fulfill commandments and customs, but everything is mechanical. In a place where there is no light and no fire, no love or devotion—there is no resting place for the almighty God.

Yavnehite! Don't allow your house to become secular and commercial. Let your house be suitable for a Jew—a small Sanctuary of the Lord! Allow the Jewish language to be heard in your house, allow the voice of *Torah*, words of peace, heartfelt prayers, taking part in the immense and tragic mystery of *Yisrael* and silent hopes for redemption.

9. *Live always amid the whole Jewish people and for the whole Jewish people.* Don't be concerned about yourself, but about all of Israel. The pain of all should be your pain; Israel's joy, your joy. Every single Jewish soul is a part of the *Shekhinah*, called *Kenesset Yisra'el* because she is the totality of Jewish souls. The Community of Israel is the lower *Shekhinah*, the Kingdom of Heaven on earth. The suffering of a Jewish soul is distress to the *Shekhinah*, as it were. So how can you, Yavnehite, cause pain to any Jew? Whoever works honestly and wholeheartedly for the redemption of Israel—as he understands it—is working to redeem *Shekhinah*. Blessings to anyone who does something good for the Jewish people—even if his views are far from our own! Blessings to any hand that is stretched out to bring help to Jewry!

Yavnehite! In all your thoughts, all your longings, all your words and deeds, do not have yourself and those close to you in mind, but rather the entire great holy Jewish people. Bring yourself and your loved ones into that whole. The salvation of the whole will be yours as well.

10. *Remove yourself from party politics.* Though you are bound to live as a part of the general community, and work especially for the community, do not join

any particular party, be it ever so close to your heart. As long as the party is occupied with politics, it is bound for the furtherance of that politics to transgress the bounds of justice and communion of all of *Yisrael*. If you are a member of a party, and you find it difficult to leave it, especially if the main purpose of the party is the up-building of the nation—set your heart to scrutinize every act and deed of the party. Your humanity, your Judaism, your hidden treasure, is a thousand-fold more important than even the best and loftiest party.

Whether you are a member of a party or not, you can and ought to participate in the work of any party, to the extent it directs deeds to the building of the whole nation, and to the unification of the nation, and you are bound to remove yourself from it, when it divides Jews, or when, to achieve its purpose, it uses means that are contrary to the Jewish spirit, which is that of love, justice, and holiness.

11. *Remember and never forget the three loves!* The Yavnehite is bound to seek religious perfection: avoidance of sin, and the fulfillment of commandments in real acts. But, one is especially bound to awareness of the three loves: the love of God, the love of *Yisrael*, and the love of Torah.

12. *Subdue pride!* Pride—this is the most profound and strongest idol. Pride—this is "the strange god in a human's body." Pride has deeply rooted itself in us, and in order to uproot it, concerted effort over decades is necessary. We must combat it all the days of our life. As long as it rests in us, it hides God, it hides others, and it hides the world outside ourselves. We cannot reach the light of truth as long as pride rests in us. "Pay attention to this cursed one—and bury it!"

13. *Sanctify speech!* Speech is the expression of the soul. Guard the covenant of the tongue; the holiness of the tongue. Not one word of evil speech! Not one round of gossip! No idle words at all; and it goes without saying, not to defile your tongue with filth. Do not think that there is no damage from speech. What difference does it make? A vulgar joke? Whom does it hurt? No, dear brother! A word has the power to build and destroy worlds. It is your duty, Yavnehite, to be a builder, a creator, repairing lives that have been destroyed. Therefore, let your words be holy.

14. *Sanctify your inner life!* Let not a day in life pass, without taking stock of your soul. Every day, learn or hear *Mussar*. Books like *The Duties of the Heart, The Path of the Upright, The Way of the Righteous, Tanya, Likkutey Eitzot* should always be your companions.

Even if you are busy, and cannot afford more time, separate yourself for five to ten minutes every day, in your chosen corner, for a short and precise tally of your soul. And at this same time, let there be a short silent prayer in your heart:

"Sovereign of the world, set me on the right path, on the path of light."

Note: Any reader who has firmly decided to start living in accord with the fourteen principles outlined above, even if gradually, in steps, may turn in this regard either orally or in writing to Hillel Zeitlin, Szliska 60, Warsaw.

NOTES

1. Neo-Hasidism remained the dominant ideology of what came to be called the Jewish Renewal movement, carried out by such institutional bearers as Bnai Or (later: Pnai Or) Religious Fellowship, Aleph, OHALAH, and many varied local Renewal groups, all of which were created by Schachter or under his direct influence. For the Ḥavurah movement, the remarks on its neo-Hasidic content refer primarily to Havurat Shalom in Boston. The broader movement (especially as carried on by the National Ḥavurah Institute) became most fully committed to an egalitarian and participatory style of Jewish expression, welcoming all sorts of ideological influences if presented within those parameters.

2. Schachter is from a Belz Hasidic family that migrated to Vienna in the 1920s and had become somewhat assimilated to Austrian Jewish life, educating their eldest son at the modern Orthodox Chajes-Gymnasium rather than within the Hasidic domain. Carlebach was the scion of a well-known German Orthodox rabbinic family. His father, Naftali Carlebach, had been rabbi in the resort town of Baden-Baden before the war.

3. Nicham Ross, *A Love/Hate Relationship with Tradition: Neo-Hasidic Writing at the Beginning of the Twentieth Century* (Beersheva: Ben Gurion University Press, 2010) (Hebrew).

4. Among the fiercest of these was Shai Ish Horowitz (1861–1922), who referred to neo-Hasidism as *tenu'at ha-bimbum*. See Stanley Nash, *In Search of Hebraism: Shai Hurwitz and His Polemics in the Hebrew Press* (Leiden: E. J. Brill, 1980).

5. See Avraham Shapira, *The Kabbalistic and Hasidic Sources of A. D. Gordon's Thought* (Hebrew title: *Or ha-Hayyim be-"Yom Ketanot"*) (Tel Aviv: Am Oved, 1996).

6. Two significant examples of this trend are Menahem Eckstein's *Tena'ey ha-Nefesh le-Hassagat ha-Ḥasidut* (Vienna, 1921); translated as *Visions of a Compassionate World: Guided Imagery for Spiritual Growth and Social Transformation* (New York: Urim, 2009), and the writings of Kalonymos Kalman of Piasecna.

7. The most important studies of Zeitlin in Hebrew are the biography by Shraga Bar-Sela,' *Between the Storm and the Quiet: The Life and Works of Hillel Zeitlin* (Tel Aviv: Hakibbutz Hameuchad, 1999), and several articles by Yonatan Meir. My volume, *Hasidism for a New Era: the Religious Writings of Hillel Zeitlin*, is to appear in the Classics of Western Spirituality series published by Paulist Press.

8. Zeitlin's brief autobiographical memoir titled *Kitsur Toldotai*, written in 1928, will appear in translation at the head of the introduction to my forthcoming volume (see n. 7 above).

9. Most of the Yiddish text (with the exception of some poetic—and highly messianic—sections) was translated into Hebrew by Natan Hofshi and published in Hebrew in 1962 (n.p.).

10. In a letter written to a Jerusalem disciple in 1925, Zeitlin mentions the existence of a Warsaw group. We have no external confirmation of this group, its size, or its longevity. See Z. Harkavy, "Perurim," in *Sefer Zeitlin* (Jerusalem, 1945), 127–48.

11. *Gezangen tsum Eyn Sof* (Warsaw, 1931). Most of the prayers included here were first published in Hebrew in *Ha-Tekufah* 12 (1921): 370–92. The prayers, translated by Joel Rosenberg, will be included in my forthcoming volume (see n. 7 above).

12. "Di Froi bey Yudn," *Yugent-Velt* 1 (1908). Hebrew translation "Ha-Ishah etsel ha-Yehudim" in Zeitlin's *Alef Bet shel Yahadut* (Jerusalem: Mossad ha-Rav Kook, 1983), 123–28.

13. A bibliography of Zeitlin's writings as well as discussions and reviews of his work by A. R. Malachi appeared in *Ha-Tekufah* (1948): 848–76. Auerbach's memoir of Zeitlin, *Toledot Neshamah Aḥat*, was published in Israel (n.p., Shem va-Yefet) in 1953.

14. Published in the New York *Morgn-Zhurnal*, v. 46, nos. 13,650 and 13,676 (29 Av and 29 Elul, 5706/1946).

15. See the thorough study of Yonatan Meir, "Zeitlin's *Zohar*: The History of a Translation and Commentary Project," *Kabbalah* 10 (2004): 119–57 (Hebrew). This project was entirely different from that of Zeitlin's fellow Warsaw Jew R. Yehudah Leib Ashlag, whose translation and commentary, *Ha-Sulam*, follows his own Lurianic reading of the Zohar. On Zeitlin and Ashlag see Y. Meir, "Wrestling with the Esoteric: Hillel Zeitlin, Yehudah Ashlag, and Kabbalah in the Land of Israel" in H. Pedaya and E. Meir, eds., *Judaism, Topics, Fragments, Faces, Identities: Jubilee Volume in Honor of Rivka* (Beer-Sheva: Ben Gurion University Press, 2007), 585–648 (Hebrew).

16. Vol. 1 (1943), 40–82. See also three letters by Zeitlin to Rawidowicz about his Zohar translation, two published to introduce the translation and the third in *Metsudah* 3–4 (1945): 339–41. The translation and commentary were reprinted after the war in Zeitlin's *Be-Pardes ha-Hasidut ve-ha-Kabbalah* (Tel Aviv: Yavneh, 1960).

17. This history is more fully treated in Meir, "Zeitlin's *Zohar*," cited above (n. 15).

18. Elsewhere (Arthur Green, "Three Warsaw Mystics," in *Qolot Rabbim: The Rivka Schatz-Uffenheimer Memorial Volume*, ed. R. Elior and J. Dan [Jerusalem, 1996], v. 2) I have discussed Zeitlin's influence on Heschel, the other major conduit of his approach to Judaism.

19. *Judaism* 13 (1964): 185–97.

20. I read Zeitlin's *"Yesodot ha-Hasidut"* as early as 1961, probably led to it by Schachter. I also read parts of Zeitlin's book on Rabbi Nahman sometime in those years.

21. Revision of a translation first made by Rabbi Zalman Schachter-Shalomi.

Afterword

Jonathan Sarna's introduction to this volume, like Leah Levitz Fishbane's unfinished dissertation, begins with Sarna's reference to a "group of earnest young Jews" who met one night in 1879 and "bound themselves together in a solemn covenant 'for God and Judaism.'" It is striking, as one reads through the essays collected here, just how often that pattern has repeated itself in the modern history of Jews and Judaism, and how crucial every one of the elements named by Sarna has been to the success of these attempts at "renaissance and revival." In every case there was a *group*. The individuals gathered together were *young*. The endeavor and those who undertook it were *earnest*. And the members of the group were determined to be *Jews* in a way not currently supported by their community or the larger society, in part because their innovation involved a reconception of Jewish *faith*. They saw in themselves the very elements of covenant, renewal, solemnity, and Judaism that they strove to revive. This gave them confidence that their effort was worthy of great striving—and that they were worthy of undertaking it.

Community was the essential means and end to all the projects recounted in this collection. It has been so to many other Jewish innovations over the past two centuries. Think of the Lehrhaus in Frankfurt, Limmud gatherings in North America and Western Europe, Zionist youth groups in Central Europe and America, Zionist settlements in the Land of Israel, Zeitlin's plan for "Yavneh," Boston's Havurat Shalom and other *havurot* of the 1960s and '70s, or, finally, of the dozens of independent minyanim that have sprung up in the past few years in the United States and Canada. Without community (group, covenant, mutual responsibility, shared effort, peer pressure, the pleasure of shared activity), one lacks the "plausibility structure" needed to strike out against the overpowering force of what is and sustain the conviction that things should and could be otherwise. Community magnifies individual agency exponentially. The mathematical language of "power" testifies to the fact that ten is often far more than a mere multiplier of one, despite and because of the conflicts inevitably engendered by group dynamics. The histories recounted in this volume chronicle a set of remarkable achievements that testify individually and collectively to the power of community.

This is fundamental stuff in religion and the study of religion, of course, laid out a century ago by Emile Durkheim in his classic work, *Elementary Forms of the Religious Life*. Communal activity provides the individuals involved in it with incontrovertible evidence of a greater self and the promise that that self can routinely and predictably be theirs. Young Jews in Philadelphia and New York in the late nineteenth century, as in major cities from Boston to Los Angeles in the late twentieth century, resonated to and acted on that promise. They created intentional Jewish communities and the institutions needed to support and perpetuate those communities. This is the point at which we encounter a development that bears out a key lesson of Max Weber's *Sociology of Religion*. Institutions harden over time. "Routinization" sucks the life out of projects and communities alike. Both give way to organizations. Revival quickly gets old, as we would say in recent slang; slang too gets old, and marks one in the eyes of the young as no longer qualified to lead revival. They must do it for themselves. The cycle then repeats.

Arthur Kiron contributes an important piece to the understanding of this dynamic by linking "renaissance" to "a specific kind of appeal to the past and a specific set of activities—teaching, reading, translating, printing, publishing, preaching, and otherwise publicly communicating classic works of Judaism and Jewish thought." This feature of course figures in many a religious, cultural, or national renaissance, but it has arguably been of special import in modern movements of *Jewish* renaissance. Except for Zionist projects in Palestine and Israel, they have all taken place in relation to what George Steiner called Jewry's "portable homeland," the text. Jews have a long history of reading themselves into sacred texts and of finding themselves, their situation, and their deepest anxieties in the books they have pored over. They have probably pored over the books all the more assiduously because that result was predictable and authorized.

The Torah, we might say, invites Jews to step into its pages by means of engaged reading. The very fact that "Torah" denotes not only Five Books of Moses but untold thousands of books by thousands of students of Moses— and the lives that many millions of Jews have led in keeping with Moses' teaching—provides all the authority and incentive young Jews have needed, generation after generation, to undertake new readings, translations, and communities. The study of Jewish *history* in the modern period has served a similar function in a similar way. It has linked the Jews who read historical studies such as this one to ancestors who lived different sorts of Jewish lives in diverse landscapes and civilizations, but whose story a modern Jew can credibly claim to be part of and continue.

Historians debate whether such purported continuities are factual or fictitious. Either way, they convert contemporary life into *revival* and learning into *renaissance*. Reading is the opposite of passive when undertaken in this spirit for this end. Translating from Hebrew or Aramaic to English or French involved no less interpretation than teaching the sacred text in the original. Both activities "publicly communicate" more than words or information. The editors of the *Jewish Encyclopedia*, reports Shuly Rubin Schwartz, "both reflected the state of Jewish knowledge and shaped it" on every page. This is how Jews have read, translated, and communicated text for a long time, all the more when they have placed reading in the context of ritual and ritual in the midst of learning, and when ritual and learning both have served the quest for connection to God and the revival of faith.

The efforts at cultural, religious, or communal revival often fail, of course. Its proponents can misjudge conditions or themselves. Economic or political circumstances might not be propitious. The motives of those involved are not usually as ethically pure or demanding as Hillel Zeitlin's plan for Yavneh—and communal designs so pure and demanding are sometimes the last thing wanted by the individuals whose allegiance they seek. (The growth of Havurat Shalom was assisted by its ability to grant deferments from the military draft at the height of the War in Vietnam.) Arthur Green's fascinating account of the connection linking Zeitlin's "Commandments," Zalman Schachter-Shalomi's urge to renewal, and the American Ḥavurah movement is yet another case study in the history of unintended and unforeseen consequences. Causes far removed in time or space from Jewish communities in twentieth-century America have borne effects that for many readers of this volume, myself included, have proved a great blessing.

This is from first to last a very personal book. It remembers in multiple ways the person and writing of a young scholar who, applying energy and brilliance to efforts at new life for American Jewry, had her own life and scholarship cut short. I met Leah Levitz Fishbane only briefly and yet am brought close to her through this volume, for I am in many ways the direct beneficiary of the initiatives she described or intended to describe. I am a Philadelphia Jew, the son of a proud member of Hadassah, a former student at Gratz College who was shaped decisively there and elsewhere by graduates of The Jewish Theological Seminary, a reader from childhood of books issued by the Jewish Publication Society, and now a successor to Cyrus Adler as chancellor of that seminary. Many readers, I imagine, have experienced a similar set of connections to Leah Levitz Fishbane's story of American Jewish revival. May we carry her memory forward by carrying that story forward in ever-new learning, innovation, revival, and community.

Contributors

Arnold Eisen is the seventh chancellor of The Jewish Theological Seminary of America and the author of *Taking Hold of Torah: Jewish Commitment and Community in America* (1996), *Rethinking Modern Judaism: Ritual, Commandment, Community* (1998), and other studies in American Judaism.

Eitan P. Fishbane is assistant professor of Jewish thought at The Jewish Theological Seminary. He is the author of *As Light before Dawn: The Inner World of a Medieval Kabbalist* (2009) and *The Sabbath Soul: Mystical Reflections on the Transformative Power of Holy Time* (2011).

Leah Levitz Fishbane z"l was a PhD candidate in the Department of Near Eastern and Judaic Studies at Brandeis University, where she studied American Jewish history and modern Judaism under the guidance of Jonathan Sarna. Based on research conducted in New York and Philadelphia archives, her writing explores the creativity and leadership of a group of young men and women who went on to found some of the great institutions of Jewish culture in late-nineteenth-century America. She died tragically, from a previously undiagnosed brain tumor, in March 2007.

Arthur Green serves as rector of the Rabbinical School and Irving Brudnick Professor of Jewish Philosophy and Religion at Hebrew College in Newton, Massachusetts. He was the founding spirit behind Havurat Shalom and has been a leading figure in the Havurah movement since 1968. A student of the Jewish mystical tradition, he writes both as a historian and theologian.

David E. Kaufman teaches at Hofstra University, where he holds the Robert and Florence Kaufman (n.r.) Endowed Chair in Jewish Studies. Previously, he was associate professor of American Jewish History at the Hebrew Union College in Los Angeles. He is the author of *Shul with a Pool: The "Synagogue-Center" in American Jewish History* (UPNE, 1999) and a forthcoming book that focuses on the intersection of American celebrity and Jewish identity in the early 1960s.

Arthur Kiron is the Schottenstein-Jesselson Curator of Judaica Collections at the University of Pennsylvania Library and adjunct assistant professor of history in Penn's History Department. He is the director of the American Genizah Project, an international initiative based at Penn, which seeks to locate, scan, catalog, and provide dynamic on-line access to American Jewish historical documents.

Paul Mendes-Flohr, professor emeritus at the Hebrew University of Jerusalem, is currently on the faculty of the Divinity School, The University of Chicago, where he teaches modern Jewish thought. He is the author, most recently, of *Progress and its Discontents: The Struggle of Jewish Intellectuals with Modernity* (2010), in Hebrew.

Jonathan D. Sarna is the Joseph H. & Belle R. Braun Professor of American Jewish History at Brandeis University, chief historian of the National Museum of American Jewish History in Philadelphia, and author or editor of more than thirty books on American Jewish history and life. His *American Judaism: A History* won six awards including the 2004 Everett Jewish Book of the Year Award from the Jewish Book Council.

Shuly Rubin Schwartz is the Irving Lehrman Research Associate Professor of American Jewish History and Walter and Sarah Schlesinger Dean of Graduate and Undergraduate Studies at The Jewish Theological Seminary. Dr. Schwartz's most recent book, *The Rabbi's Wife: The Rebbetzin in American Jewish Life* (2007), won the National Jewish Book Award in the area of modern Jewish thought.

Index

"Association Day," 61; call for national union of, 18–19; entertainment programs, 93; founding of, 47–50; membership categories, 34n7, 67n9; in Philadelphia, 17, 92–94; and revival of Hanukkah, 14–15; and synagogues, 61; and UAHC, 55

Young Men's Hebrew Literary Association (Philadelphia), 88

Young Men's Literary Association of Philadelphia, 65n3

Young Men's [Literary] Society (Philadelphia), 88

youth, Jewish, 32; and YMHA, 93
youth movements, American Jewish, 10
YouTube, 112

Zeidman, Hillel, 150–51
Zeitlin, Aaron, 150
Zeitlin, Hillel, 148–51, 167; *What Does Yavneh Want?*, 153–63 (appendix)
Zionism, 136, 148, 166
Zionist Congress, fifth, 148
Zohar, 150–51
Zunz, Leopold, 129
Zweifel, Eliezer, 147